An Insider's Guide to Robert Anton Wilson

An Insider's Guide to Robert Anton Wilson

by

Eric Wagner

Introduced by

Robert Anton Wilson

NEW FALCON PUBLICATIONS
TEMPE, ARIZONA, U.S.A.

International Standard Book Number: 1-56184-165-X
Library of Congress Catalog Card Number: 2003104248

First Edition 2004

The paper used in this publication meets the minimum requirements of the American National Standard for Permanence of Paper for Printed Library Materials Z39.48-1984

Address all inquiries to:
NEW FALCON PUBLICATIONS
1739 East Broadway Road #1-277
Tempe, AZ 85282 U.S.A.

(or)

320 East Charleston Blvd. #204-286
Las Vegas, NV 89104 U.S.A.

website: http://www.newfalcon.com
email: info@newfalcon.com

DEDICATION

to my Debra

Oink the Magus now decides
every day to improvise
form delights, ignore all fools
weaving spells round all the rules
He ignites
you every night
shoulders soft &
filled with light
joy ascends and passions rise
weary ends and dreams advise
I love you & heal your heart
We unite & woes depart

Love,

Eric

A Book About

Anna Livia Plurabella,
Ludwig van Beethoven,
Discordia,
Godzilla,
Robert Heinlein,
Vulcan, Zukofsky,
"The Chimes at Midnight",
Tantra,
William Butler Yeats,
Kabbalah,
Timothy Leary,
Wolfgang Amadeus Mozart,
Nanokabbalah,
E-prime,
Space,
Pranayama,
Tsarism,
Quantum Mechanics,
Ishmael Reed,
Percy Shelley,
You,
Taoism,
Universe,

and all the other wonderful people, places and things in
Robert Anton Wilson's wide, weird world, etc.

TABLE OF CONTENTS

INDUCTION

Appreciation, hearkening is the only true criticism.
— James Joyce, "Ibsen's New Drama"
Joyce Critical Writings, pg. 67

You damned sadist—you want to make your readers think!
— e.e. cummings on Ezra Pound

I first wrote to Bob Wilson in 1986 C.E. We have corresponded ever since, by snail mail and then by e-mail. He has always proved most helpful, informative and kind. We first met in Dallas in 1987 C.E., where I also got to meet Rev. Ivan Stang of the Church of the SubGenius at a seminar Bob gave on *Finnegans Wake*. Some friends and I (including the mysterious Frank Dracman) brought him to Arizona in 1988 C.E. to give a talk and a seminar. When planning a trip to Ireland in 1989 C.E., my cousin CJ and I had lunch with Bob, and Bob made a Joycean map of Dublin for me, and gave me copious advice for a fun-filled trip, both during lunch and in a rich batch of letters. Around that time I published 33 issues of a poetry/basketball newsletter called *noon blue apples*. Bob provided lots of encouragement and commentary and a couple of contributions.

In 1999 C.E. my fiancée, Debbie, and Wilson scholar Mike Johnson both suggested I write a book on Wilson. I told Bob about the idea, and he enthusiastically agreed. (Remember, "enthusiasm" used to suggest the possibility of mental unbalance. Thomas Jefferson called Adam Weishaupt an "enthusiastic philanthropist." See Aleister Crowley's "Energized Enthusiasm.")

When Barbara Leaming approached Orson Welles about writing a biography which would tell the truth about him, Orson explained the impossibility of that task. He suggested that instead she should write a book about trying to discover the truth about Orson Welles. This book will explore how I have tried to understand Robert Anton Wilson's books over the last twenty-two years.

PREFACE

by Mordecai Malignatus,
High priest, Head temple, Order of the Illuminati
"On the site of the beautiful future San Andreas canyon"

What can I say about this wonderful book? Written by one of my favorite exegetes and dealing with my all-time favorite writer, it held me spellbound from the first letter of the first word to the period after the last. What can I possibly add to such a treasury?

Well, in the "mirror of memory," or the junkyard of real memory and fantasy that we usually mistake for a mirror, I know a few things about Wilson and his works that even the canny Eric Wagner has not unearthed. After all, I have known RAW for almost 73 years now and Eric has only known him for less than twenty...

No Governor

In the mirror of memory...

Juang Jou says, "There is no governor anywhere." RAW discovered this aphorism *circa* 1966 and immediately saw in it both [1] the simplest and clearest expression of Daoist atheology and [2] a bridge from Daoism to his own emerging system of socio-cybernetics—i.e., anarchism. After all, the only way a social system, or ANY system, can evolve without a central governor somewhere must involve a decentralized governor everywhere, or continuous "smooth" feedback between and within all sub-systems.

RAW therefore quoted this mantra frequently, usually to-gether with his exegesis on it. One result: Robert J. Shea, later the co-author of the *Illuminatus!* trilogy, began an irregular liber-

tarian journal called *No Governor*. Another result: another libertarian, Kerry Thornley, put his own spin on this and printed
thousands of cards saying:

THERE IS NO ENEMY
ANYWHERE

Thornley, at that time, devoted most of his energies to pro-
moting the Church of Laughing Buddha Jesus, and genuinely
believed what that card said.

When RAW and RJS got around to writing *Illuminatus!*,
RAW included both Thornley's card and its Hegelian antithe-
sis—

THERE IS NO FRIEND
ANYWHERE

and mischievously attributed them both to Hagbard Celine,
an apparently fictitious individual.

Thornley, meanwhile, gave up on the Church of LBJ—I
hope you noticed those initials?—and, as a result of some Bad
Acid, decided RAW, RJS and most of his former friends "were"
all C.I.A. agents involved in a complex and baroque conspiracy
to frame him for the JFK assassination. Eventually, he seems to
have believed there is no friend anywhere.

You can learn more about Kerry—and how his life and ideas
influenced RAW—in *The Prankster and the Conspiracy: How
Kerry Thornley Met Oswald and Inspired the Counterculture,* by
Adam Gorightly, ParaView Press, New York, 2003.

Indeed do many things come to pass.

Eternal Flower Power

One of the unsolved mysteries of *Illuminatus!* involves the
stamp that Simon Moon found on the toilet paper in the men's
room at the Biograph Theatre:

OFFICIAL
BAVARIAN ILLUMINATI
"EWIGE BLUMENKRAFT"

Since this has five words and hence fits the Law of Fives[1], it looks like an authentic Illuminati production—but why would the omnilethal Illuminati get involved in the toilet paper business, and brazenly advertise the fact?

Simon, you may remember, decided the next day that he must have hallucinated the whole experience, or, as he expressed it, "the fucking dope really fucked up my fucking brain."

This conclusion has not satisfied many Chicago area readers who had also found the Illuminati stamp on toilet paper, not only at the Biograph but at many other cinemas, some fine Chinese and Italian restaurants and especially at I.W.W. headquarters on North Halstead. Some of them may still wonder about this, occasionally.

Actually, this mystery did get explained, in the original, unpublished text of *Illuminatus!* but some executives at Dell fought others for five long years about whether the book could or could not succeed commercially, and they finally reached a compromise: Dell would publish the monstro-novel but only if RAW and RJS cut 500 pages out of the damned thing. Most of RAW's elaborate Cabalistic symbolism got lost along the way, and the solution to the Toilet Paper Puzzle got thrown away along with it. RAW and RJS had simply decided that if Dell bought literature by the pound, the mutilations should appropriately occur at random intervals.

In the original [unmutilated] text, the stamp clearly belonged to me. You see, sometime in the late 1960s—after all these years, who can remember exactly when?—I saw an ad for an outfit called Walter Drake and Sons, who would make any rubber stamp you wanted, containing up to three lines, for only $1 each. I ordered about three dozen, all containing messages calculated to produce that "sense of wonder" from which Einstein said all creative thought begins. I used these stamps promiscuously— on personal mail, billboards, *everywhere*—including on toilet

---

[1] "I find the Law of Fives more and more manifest the harder I look." — Kerry Thornley.

paper in men's rooms, especially at the holy Biograph where St. John the Martyr got gunned down by Hoover's thugs.

Malaclypse the Younger borrowed these stamps once and used a different one on almost every page of the *Principia Discordia.*

My favorite of all these stamps by the way said simply:

SEE MENTAL HEALTH RECORDS

I used this on all unsolicited mail that came with a postpaid return envelope, especially ads for credit cards I didn't want and inquiries from government agencies, Ads for penis enlargement devices got the same stamp but I forwarded them to Christian Crusade in Tulsa OK.

I hope all this pious endeavor did create a sense of wonder in some of the recipients.

All Critterkind

Eric's exegesis on this coinage seems accurate but incomplete. RAW coined "congressentity" because "congressperson" seemed *politically* incorrect to him due to its unconscious but arrogant human chauvinism. His Adorable Wife Arlen corrected it to *congresscritters*, and he immediately recognized that as an improvement.

While not shy about the literary merit of his prose, RAW always considered Arlen the better poet. After all, *critter* or *entity*—which word would Pound or Williams or Ginsberg prefer? Which sounds more like natural speech?

Which sounds fancy and pretentious?

Arlen won without formal debate. RAW now regularly uses clergycritter, postalcritter, critterkind, critterhole [in place of the ungainly personhole], critterroach, waitcritter, housecritter, etc.

When this semantic reform becomes generally accepted, we can all enjoy the talking heads on TV debating when the fetus attains critterhood.

The Final Secret

Adam Gorightly in *The Prankster and the Conspiracy* claims that all recent Illuminati research [post-1960s] has become confused and chaotic because of a hoax conspiracy, also called the Illuminati, founded by Kerry Thornley—the Discordian Pope accused of involvement in the JFK assassination by New Orleans D.A. Jim Garrison.

According to Gorightly, this neo-Illuminati aims only to bedevil and mock the efforts of sincere conspiracy researchers, and he even accuses the subject of this monograph [R.A.W.] of involvement in this Fiendish Plot!

RAW of course, refuses to dignify this absurd charge with a denial, which nobody would believe anyway. Besides, as Rev. Ivan Stang of the Church of the Sub-Genius says in *Maybe Logic*, "Well, if I was a member of the Illuminati, I wouldn't say so, would I?"

Neither would I.

— Mord Mal, Deep Underground,
Somewhere in the Occupied U.S.A.

INTRODUCTION

by Robert Anton Wilson

You just read it!

"We operate on many levels here!"
— Robert Anton Wilson, The Bunker Below Mord,
Deeper Underground

Overture

Of Ostriches, Etc.

by Robert Anton Wilson

THEY'LL TAKE MY MEDICINE AWAY WHEN THEY
PRY MY COLD DEAD FINGERS FROM THE PILL
BOTTLE!!!!

After refusing many pleas to run for governor, I have reconsidered and now enter the race as an unofficial write-in candidate. After all, why shd I remain the ONLY nut in California who ain't running?

My party, the Guns and Dope Party, invites extremists of both right and left to unite behind the shared goals of

1. Get those pointy-headed Washington bureaucrats off our backs and off our fronts too!

2. Guns for everybody who wants them; no guns for those who don't want them

3. Drugs for everybody who wants them; no drugs for those who don't want them

4. Freedom of choice, free love, free speech, free Internet and free beer

5. California secession— Keep the anti-gun and anti-dope fanatics on the Eastern side of the Rockies

6. Lotsa wild parties every night by gun-toting dopers

7. Animal protection—Support your right to keep and arm bears

More position papers will follow; we know at least 69 good positions.

— Robert Anton Wilson, Guns and Dope Party

To the States or any one of them, or any city of the States:
RESIST MUCH, OBEY LITTLE,
Once unquestioning obedience, once fully enslaved,
Once fully enslaved, no nation, state, city of this Earth, ever afterward
    resumes its liberty.
                        — Walt Whitman

Americans now live in fear of the rest of the world and the rest of the world lives in fear of America.
                        — Harry Browne

GUNS AND DOPE PARTY: DON'T TREAD ON ME

EVERY MAN AND EVERY WOMAN IS A TSAR

A NATION WITH ONLY ONE TSAR = TYRANNY

Official motto: "Like what you like, enjoy what you enjoy, and don't take crap from anybody."

Major goal of first term: California secession. [Oregon, Washington State and British Columbia invited to join Freetopia...]

First order of business on assuming office: Fire 33% of the legislature [names selected at random] and replace them with full-grown adult ostriches, whose mysterious and awesome dignity will elevate the suidean barbarity long established there.

Tsar cards granting full autonomy available from rawlist@maybelogic.com

"I'M NOT A NUT"

"THEY'LL TAKE AWAY MY MEDICINE WHEN THEY PRY MY COLD DEAD FINGERS FROM THE PILL BOTTLE!"

— J.R. "Bob" Wilson, Guns and Dope Party

Both the pro-gun people and the dopers [medical, religious and/or recreational] feel like minorities, and the TSOG agrees with this estimate of their weakness. Our contention holds that in California both groups woikin' together make a MAJORITY. Ergo, they have much to gain and nowt to lose in combining forces. Each side only has to realize this and agree "We'll tolerate their hobbies if they'll tolerate ours" and we can even beat Schwarzenegger.

— GADP [Guns and Dope Party]

Anna Livia Get Your Gun:
23 Questions for California's Next Governor

by Robert Anton Wilson & Eric Wagner

1. In your novel *Illuminatus!* Hagbard Celine hands out cards that say "There is no governor anywhere." What do you think he would think of your campaign?

He approves of making every man and every woman a Tsar and says Crowley really meant that but had dyslexia. After all, "no governor anywhere" means every critter takes charge of their own life.

2. What is the sound of one chad hanging?

FNORD!

3. Timothy Leary ran for governor of California in 1970 C.E. Does your campaign resonate with his?

I hope not; They put him in jail because They feared he might win. I feel sure They won't feel that frightened of a nut like me. They won't know wot hit Them until They count the ballots!!

4. Your clear, common sense answers remind me of John Anderson's campaign for President in 1980 C.E. I felt that his clear, honest answers made him unelectable. Do you think your campaign would fair better if you BS'd more?

B.S., like sugar, goes down smoothly but eventually leads to gagging and acid reflux. We think the people of California have had a diabetic dose of B.S. and badly need a purgative. Our platform means VICTORY OVER BULLSHIT

5. As governor, you will have responsibility for the education of the population of California. What ideas do you have for helping that population prepare for the challenges of the coming century?

The Guns and Dope Party believes that education begins with doubt and questioning. Ergo, without spending money on new and expensive textbooks, using only the current curriculum, we shall grade students by their ability, using search engines, to find the largest number of websites contradicting whatever "facts" or opinions appear in each week's lessons. For instance, a student can confront the section on Columbus with such matters as assertions that the Americas got "discovered" by various bronze people from Asia, by black people from Africa, and/or by earlier Europeans [St. Brendan, Lief Erikson etc.]; or by challenging the popular image by dissenters identifying Columbus as a pirate, a Jew, two different men [one of whom never left Europe], a Gay, a Gay Jewish pirate, etc., etc. When the students reach appropriate age, we will apply the same zetetic approach to physics, rocket science, medicine etc. Students accustomed to the hunt for truth through labyrinths of uncertainty—cured of the delusion that truth exists in one source and you only have to memorize it—will unleash an Intelligence Explosion.

6. Great answer! I will use that assignment next month. You have suggested previously that voting often seems in retrospect a mistake. Why should critters vote for you, and why won't they regret it in 23 years?

Voting has only seemed a mistake to me when, in a state of temporary insanity, I voted for one of the major parties. I have never regretted my write-in votes for Wile E. Coyote, Count Dracula or Daffy Duck. People, ostriches and critters in general should vote for me only if they support my platform. Why vote for a platform you don't support? The Libertarian Party, of course, represents similar positions to mine, but have you read any of their literature? They sound like medieval monks argoofying over Nacheral Lore or law school students debating what they call "hypotheticals." Reading that stuff feels like having your head stuffed with pillows and styrofoam. We say, Phooey on your nacheral lore and your hyperdermics and your other metaphysics; we just want to KEEP OUR GUNS AND OUR MEDICINE and get rid of any pointy-headed bureaucrats who try to take them away from us. Period. That says it all. Vote for me and Olga if you agree. Otherwise, vote for one of the other scoundrels—whoever represents the kind of fascism that best suits you.

7. Timothy Leary wrote:

> We now understand that spaceship Earth is a delicate, complex web of energy processes that must be understood and harmonized if we are to survive. Politics has become too important to be left to politicians who cannot and will not comprehend the situation. Our rulers in the future must be people with scientific training and with brains wired to handle relativistic complexity. We would not let the controls of a 747 fall into the hands of a congressman.
> — Leary, *The Politics of Self-Determination,* pg. 96

What do you think of this quote, and how does it apply to your campaign?

Once again Dr. Leary expresses an attitude so close to mine that I feel as if we came out of the same egg. I would only add that in the T.S.A.—the Tsarist States of America—the situation seems particularly anachronistic. Their politicians almost all come from law schools, which seem to me as archaic and pre-scientific as theological seminaries. In fact, I regard law as a branch of theology played with deuces, eights and one-eyed jacks wild.

In general, the pragmatist looks at the *present* and asks what might work, and the radical looks at the *future* and asks what might work even bette*r,* but the lawyer and theologian looks at the *past* to see what some abstract logician conjectured in the dark ages. This explains why I think California should secede from the T.S.A. Lawyer-Politicians should not monkey with the plumbing in an ordinary toilet, much less fly airplanes or decide what scientific research to allow or forbid.

8. Would you attempt to eliminate all taxes as governor?

No, I'd follow Lysander Spooner's voluntary tax plan combined with the lightspeed of Internet. Every citizen would receive a semi-annual Republic budget, telling what the Republic of California wanted to do for them or to them, and each would send in their share of the fee for whatever projects seemed sensible and useful to them. Nobody would pay a penny for anything that seemed pointless, useless, invasive, tyrannical or even annoying to them. If nobody paid for a project, it would get dumped for lack of funding. As Spooner wrote earlier:

> Constitutions are utterly worthless to restrain the tyranny of governments, unless it be understood that the people will by force compel the government to remain within constitutional limits. Practically speaking, no government knows any limits to its power except the endurance of the people Voluntary taxation expresses the endurance of the people directly and immediately, "before the horse gets out of the stable."

9. Whom, if anyone, do you think the Republic should incarcerate?

Let's step back one pace: why incarcerate at all? The only sane function of incarceration seems to me segregation—to use walls and guards to protect us from the dangerously violent. [A] Incarceration, in cages, dungeons etc. or whatever compromise between the rational function of segregation and the irrational revenge-sadism reflexes; or [B] implantation of tracking/warning devices or [C] exile—these seem the best methods known at present, but none works perfectly. I think we should free all the nonviolent noncriminals and use a little of the 70% of our penal budget thus saved—maybe 7%—to fund scientific research on better methods of defanging the predators. Another 60% should go to a trust to compensate the victims. The remaining 3% can go for healthy and tasty food for the misfortunate ostriches who have to associate with the suidea until the latter get replaced by higher critters.

10. Emotional plague and muscular armoring seems to me like a major health issue in California. How would address this problem as governor?

The Guns and Dope Party intends equal liberty for all. The free market and the free marketplace of ideas and systems, including Orgonomic physicians, homeopaths, nutritionists, herbalists, voodoo and hoodoo and vedic medicine, etc. all competing in a free marketplace. If any allopaths can survive in such a free system, good luck to them!

11. When you become governor, Hollywood will likely jump on the bandwagon and make movies based on your books. What actors and actresses do you see playing some of the characters from your immortal works?

Al Pacino as Hagbard Celine, Michelle Pfeiffer as Eris, Robert Duvall as Aleister Crowley, Johnny Depp as Sigismundo Celine, Winona Rider as Maria, Nick Cage as James Joyce, Jon Cipher as Wilhelm Reich.

12. Do you plan to move to Sacramento when elected?

Hell, no. I've visited there and the climate seems worse than the Avocado Jungle of Death, where the cannibal women live, south of Bakersfield. Everything I need to do, I can do from my home via Internet.

13. Some call the 21st century C.E. the "Asian Century." You have said that interaction between east and west might prove the major theme of this century. California has a large population of Asian ancestry. What would you do as governor to foster multicultural understanding?

Our restaurants have already become multi-cultural, so I'd work for a law compelling people to learn something about each culture before getting a seat to eat the food of that culture. Persian history & culture for Persian food, French for French food, Chinese for Chinese, etc. Those who fail the entrance exam not only don't get seated but get assigned two weeks hard labor in the clean-up crew for the ostriches.

I know this will provoke knee-jerk rejections by some Libertarians but remember it only binds those who pay voluntary taxes to enact & enforce such a compact. I'd gladly pay my share of the bill, because at my age life becomes a race between the desire to learn more and the tick=tick=tock mentioned by Cole

Porter. Even lazy as I seem, I think the desire for another Thai meal would force me to squeeze lessons on Thai poetry and history into my schedule. [Thanks to Ez and Fenollosa, I've aced Chinese and Japanese and under my tax reform (voluntarism) can feast tax-free on their cuisine.]

14. Terrence McKenna saw wild stuff happening between now and December 21, 2012 C.E. How do you think Californians can best prepare themselves to live long and prosper in the crazy days ahead?

They should all buy [b,u,y, BUY, not rent] the video or DVD of *Southern Star*, a comedy starring Orson Welles as a Gay bandito and Olga, an ostrich, as a diamond thief. At certain points, if you've taken your pain medicine for the day, Olga speaks directly to the audience—to YOU—and her words always contain both pragmatic and mystic wisdom. For instance, once I asked her how to contribute most to the coming unity of all critterkind, instilling respect for "all life however small" as it says in the Upanishads, and she suggested appointing ostriches as 1/3 of the legislature. Of course, some left-wing aardvarks have complained about this [they call it "bipedal chauvinism"] but I trust Olga. Most humans haven't gotten to the level of realizing the personhood of other races yet, you know. Bipedalism represents a great leap forward toward universal critterkind, and you have to take these things one step at a time. The six-legged majority still inspire fear and loathing in backward societies.

If Olga doesn't talk to you, you need more pain medicine, and frankly I don't understand how you've survived three years of George W. Bush without it. Maybe you should try the Bible or the Koran or Chinese fortune cookies.

15. In your wonderful book *Everything Is Under Control* you talk about the Collier brothers' theory about the likelihood of computer fraud in elections. What would you do as governor to prevent fraudulent elections?

I don't understand how my own computer does some of its bizarre tricks, and you expect me to answer this? I'd turn it over to my tech department. Besides, I have a 99% suspicion, amounting almost to a 100% certitude, that nonfraudulent elections, like unicorns and Tin Woodsmen and Mad Hatters, exist in the divine world of imagination and not in the human world of power politics. Madison said we need eternal vigilance to protect any liberties we think we have, and I agree heartily. Expect crooked elections and set up more and more traps to catch the scoundrels who rig them; the traps, again, I leave to the techies.

16. If you had a coat of arms, what would you like it to include?

The three ostriches in Tsarist regalia, rampant with motto: *Et in Arcadia Struthio camelus.*

17. Timothy Leary called the generation following the Baby Boomers, born after 1965 C.E., the "Whiz Kids." What name would you give the generation entering high school today, born after, say 1985 C.E.? What do you see as their morphogenetic role in the cosmic scheme?

They should function as bullshit fighters. They all need the built-in cast-iron shockproof bullshit detectors suggested by Mr. Hemingway. In my youth, after a political speech, we would chant "Grab your shovels and run for the hills/It's oozing over the window sills." Now the political speeches have a higher BS quotient than ever, and many of them disguise themselves as newscasts, and it looks like it has reached the third floor. Grab your shovels, kids.

18. You've talked with me before about the importance of understanding *The Cantos* of Ezra Pound. What advice would you give young people approaching The Cantos for the first time?

The first time, read as fast as you can, without worrying about obscurities and details. Then, when you have some sense, however dim, of the structure of the whole, what Ez affirms and celebrates, what he denounces, where he changes his mind and reverses himself, etc., read it slowly, sippingly, the way great poetry deserves, as often as it draws you back. It remains the most revolutionary and innovative poem of the last century, so don't even try to swallow it in one gulp.

19. Would you please discuss the phrase "hilaritas et amor?"

I use that as signature in my email. It comes from the *paradiso* section of the *Cantos* of Ezra Pound. "Hilaritas," despite its etymological link to the English "hilarity," does not mean merely a sense of humor, although it includes that; it more basically means cheerfulness, or "good nature." Pound lifted it from a neo-pagan 15th Century philosopher, Gemito Plethon. To Pound we have no knowledge of any post-mortem *paradiso,* but we can imagine—and maybe even create—a *paradiso terrestre,* an earthly paradise, which incorporates all we can learn from the best people and best epochs of history. That centers on *hilaritas* and *amor;* I assume fans of Dean Martin and Grand Opera will easily translate the second term as "love." The three agonies of Pound's terrestrial Hell, incidentally, he lists as pride, wrath and possessiveness. And his purgatory Cantos seem dominated by Ching Ming, two ideograms from Kung fu Tsu signifying unrelenting struggle to clarify the language—"the lyf so short, the art so long to lerne."

20. What sort of monetary system would you like your new country to have?

We would repudiate the monopoly of the Federal Reserve banks and refuse to accept any more of their counterfeit money. We would replace them with free enterprise banking—including anarchist "People's Banks" which would charge no interest at all—and any other rival alternatives that proved acceptable to customers. We assume that, however many kinds of coin and currency came into circulation, the people in each county or township would learn which they could trust and which they should shun "as the devil flees holy water." This follows naturally from our axiomatic position that people know how to handle guns and dope intelligently without a Tsarist tyranny deciding for them. For further details on free market banking, see lysanderspooner.org.

21. Whose pictures would you like on the money? Just ostriches?

Well, I love Irish currency, which has Maev, the queen of the fairies, on the one-pound note, and such luminaries as Swift, Scotus Erigena and Yeats on higher denominations.

Following that system of values, I would want my own bank notes to have Marilyn Monroe on the $1, followed by Ezra Pound, Bucky Fuller and Emperor Norton.

22. Why should people read my book?

It will add three inches to their brain in just one week.

23. How do you think the U.S. government would respond to an attempt by California to secede from the U.S.A.?

I assume they'll put me to death by lethal injection, in the spirit of compassionate conservatism, although they'd probably really like to hang me. With my age and health, and all the necessary legal appeals in death penalty cases, that won't shorten my life expectancy much, and meanwhile I'll get free room and food and even free medical care—hell, I might outlive my life expectancy on the outside, just on the free meds alone. Other GADP organizers will probably get off with short jail terms, but still I admire their courage. If you haven't reached my age, those Tsarist bastards can really scare you.

INFOMERCIAL

An athletic man with white hair walks forward smiling. The wall behind him has a very large illustration of the back of a one dollar bill with two changes: It says "In Goddess We Trust" instead of "In God We Trust," and the Pyramid in the left hand circle has the word "fnord" written across it in blue. Two pillars reach from the ground to ceiling in the foreground. The one on the left has the letter B on it, the one on the left has the letter J. Ike and Tina Turner's version of "Rolling on the River" begins softly in the background.

Hi, Tim Leary here from beyond the grave [big smile] to talk with you about Robert Anton Wilson. Novelist, playwright, stand-up philosopher, Robert Anton Wilson's time has come, and You have the chance to get in on the ground floor. Send no money, just lie down on the floor and relax. In the early 1970's, Robert Shea and Robert Anton Wilson wrote a wonderful novel called *Illuminatus!* They'd realized how the fears of the left and right had come full circle and overlapped, and that seems like a good place to begin our story.

Back on May 1, 1776, an ex-Jesuit named Adam Weishaupt founded a secret society called the Bavarian Illuminati. It only admitted 33rd degree Freemasons, so it became a secret society inside of another secret society, the Freemasons, founded by an ex-member of a group widely suspected of conspiratorial activity, the Jesuits. The Bavarian government banned the Illuminati a few years later, but for over two hundred years some have suspected that the group survived and continues to play a secret role in world power-struggles.

Robert Shea and Robert Anton Wilson decided to write *Illuminatus!* to explore the ideas of those who suspected the

Illuminati of continuing to exist. Interestingly, those who have investigated the world of the Illuminati over the past two centuries have come to startlingly different conclusions. Some have determined the nature of the Illuminati as anarchist, some as communist, some as fascist. Others see Weishaupt as a new age prophet or as evil incarnate. These multiple mutually exclusive models fascinated Wilson. He saw them as paralleling the multiple models of contemporary physics, as well as the multiple viewpoints of the modern and/or post-modern art works of James Joyce, Orson Welles, Ezra Pound and others. Robert Anton Wilson went on to write a number of highly entertaining books illuminating the possibilities of this multiple model approach. (Robert Shea went on to write some terrific books as well.)

Born on Long Island in 1932 C.E. to John Joseph and Elizabeth Wilson, Robert Anton Wilson had an Irish-Catholic upbringing like his great predecessor James Joyce. Over the years he would play many roles, including novelist, poet, playwright, lecturer, stand-up comic, Futurist, psychologist and Damned Old Crank (what he calls himself currently), etc.

Robert survived a childhood bout of polio, cured by the Sister Kenny Method and/or his mother's prayers to the Blessed Virgin Mary. The American Medical Association condemned the Sister Kenny Method at the time. The fact that it seemed to have cured Robert helped lead him to a lifetime skepticism concerning official science and medicine. Years later that childhood illness would keep him out of the draft at the time of the Korean War. He didn't have great difficulty walking after his cure until years later in the 21st century.

Like Joyce, Robert attended a Catholic elementary school, but, genetically prepared for the role of evolutionary bard-philosopher with a gift of gab, Robert convinced his parents to send him to a public school which focused on math and the sciences. (He intended to avoid the beatings he had heard awaited him at the 1940's Catholic high school, but his choice also helped develop his mind mathematically and scientifically more than Joyce had, as suited Robert's later role as a scientific prophet of the Roaring Twentieth Century. Little did Robert know then that he would spend much of his life writing about

Space Migration, Intelligence Increase and Life Extension: S.M.I².L.E.)

As a child Robert loved the movies, especially those with a fantastic quality, like *The Wizard of Oz*, *King Kong*, *I Married a Witch*, *Frankenstein*, etc. As he grew older he began to read voraciously. He read a great deal of highly regarded contemporary literature, with the idea that he might find it useful to read the writers of his own time. This led him to read Hemingway, Steinbeck and Faulkner, etc. He also developed a passion for science fiction writers like Robert Anson Heinlein, Theodore Sturgeon and Olaf Stapledon, etc.

Robert had always wanted to live out the life-script of a writer, but his family discouraged him, warning him of economic peril. This led him to try a variety of "safer" paths before succumbing to his morphogenetically forecasted life-role. He worked as an engineering aid and an ambulance attendant while getting his degree in mathematics, and when he discovered he didn't seem suited for the roles of engineer, mathematician or teacher, he got a series of jobs as an editor, culminating with a job as an Associate Editor at *Playboy* from 1965–71 C.E. Work as an editor seemed closer to his life-dream of writing than other jobs had. He kept writing, though, publishing many articles beginning in the late 1950's C.E., on an enormous variety of topics, many of which this book will explore. While working at *Playboy,* Robert met fellow editor Bob Shea and the fun really began, as they got the idea of writing a vast novel about conspiracies, a rock festival and a yellow submarine that would become *Illuminatus!*.

In 1958 he met and married his brilliant and lovely life companion, Arlen Riley Wilson (born July 16, 1925 C.E.), who would provide him the love, inspiration and courage to survive the roller coaster ride ahead. Her love and intelligence helped Robert navigate the difficult economic, political, literary, and erotic course of his career as a writer/intelligence agent.

The complete manuscript of *Illuminatus!* contained so much evolutionary material it had to wait five years to find a publisher willing to send it out into the wider world, finally appearing in 1975 C.E. In the meantime, Robert Anton Wilson took the plunge and became a full time free lance intellectual, quitting his job at *Playboy* in 1971 C.E. and quickly falling, alas, into poverty. His savings lasted a year, and then he and his family spent two years on welfare before his writing began to earn him a living wage.

On October 3, 1976 C.E., a man beat Arlen and Robert's teenage daughter Luna to death. This tremendous loss, probably the greatest tragedy of their lives, rocked Arlen and Robert's reality to the core. In healing over the next few years Robert manifested books which showed a whole new level of wisdom: *Cosmic Trigger I* (1977 C.E.), *Schrödinger's Cat* (1980–81 C.E.), *The Illuminati Papers* (1980 C.E.), *Masks of the Illuminati* (1981 C.E.), *Right Where You Are Sitting Now* (1983 C.E.), *The Earth Will Shake* (1983 C.E.) and the seminal *Prometheus Rising* (1983 C.E.). (That last, magnificent work originated with his doctoral thesis at the "alternative" Paideia University). In these works Robert shared his pain with the world, as well a vision of higher intelligence for all of humanity, with many practical techniques to help each of his readers increase their own compassion, sense of humor and intelligences on all levels of their mind-body systems. Years before Ted Sturgeon had written that shared pain lessens and shared joy increases. Robert displays that process over and over again in these books.

From 1982 to 1988 C.E. Robert and Arlen lived in Ireland in protest over the election of Ronald Reagan as President, as well as to explore their fascination with their Irish ancestries. All the while Robert wrote books filled with bardic wisdom, helping to shape the minds of his contemporaries and preparing sombunall of the best minds of the twentieth-first century to learn how to build the worlds of their CHOICE. Robert's Irish home base proved an ideal location for him to continue his *Historical Illuminatus* series begun with *The Earth Will Shake*, completing *The Widow's Son* (1985 C.E.) and *Nature's God* (1991 C.E.). While living in Ireland, Robert took advantage of a local library's complete set of Jonathan Swift, reading Dean Swift's complete writings, which helped give Robert's *New Inquisition* (1986 C.E.) and *Natural Law or Don't Put a Rubber on Your Willy* (1987 C.E.) some real Swiftian bite.

Robert and Arlen then returned to California, this time landing in L.A., giving Robert a few years to explore the realities of the movie making world. In this period Robert deeply explored his love of film, as well as the McLuhanesque way cinema had shaped somebunall of his ideas and experiences. (Even *Illumina-tus!* years earlier had had a plot structure based on D.W. Grif-fith's *Intolerance.*) His non-fiction work *Quantum Psychology* (1990 C.E.), *Cosmic Trigger II* (1991 C.E.), *Chaos and Beyond* (1994 C.E.) and *Cosmic Trigger III* (1995 C.E.), show this re-newed focus on film and especially the influence on Wilson of the work of Orson Welles, as do Wilson's two hilarious screen-plays, *Reality Is What You Can Get Away With* (1992 C.E.) and *The Walls Came Tumbling Down* (1997 C.E.).

In the mid-1990's C.E. Arlen and Robert tired of the metropolitan environment and moved to Capitola, California, near Santa Cruz. Interestingly, another great American novelist, Robert Anson Heinlein, made his final home in the Santa Cruz environs. At this time Wilson became fascinated by the possi-bilities of Internet, and he created his chrestomanthy of conspir-acies with web research collaborator Mimi Hill, *Everything Is Under Control* (1998 C.E.), using many web resources.

Alas, the following year Arlen passed away on May 22. The pain of this loss aged Robert, but slowly he has come to learn the truth of what Confucius said, "How is it far, if you can think of it?" Robert had read those words in Kung and in Ezra Pound, and he had quoted them himself many times as well. Of course, loneliness has its own reality as well.

In recent years, Robert's post-polio sequilae has put him in a wheelchair some of the time, as discussed in his wise and hilari-ous *TSOG: The Thing That Ate the Constitution* (2002 C.E.). That book also contains a preview of his work in progress, *Tale of the Tribe*, which looks like it will examine how Internet will help to bring about the end of civilization as we know it, or at least manifest a process something like Bucky Fuller's idea of desovernization (see Wilson's entry on desovernization in *Every-thing Is Under Control* and Bucky's *Grunch of Giants* for more on this concept.) At 72 Robert continues growing more intelli-gent and funnier by the day.

(For more information on Wilson's life, please check out the three *Cosmic Trigger* volumes and the Wilson biography by Mike Johnson at www.rawilsonfans.com.)

I call this piece an Infomercial because I want to sell you something. I want to sell you intelligence, humor, compassion and vision, etc. I want to sell you the visions of Robert Anton Wilson. I want to sell you the tools to build your wildest and sanest desires, the writings of Robert Anton Wilson, and this book, which provides a skeleton key to that non-simultaneously perceived n-dimensional labyrinth of words.

Note: References to *Schrödinger's Cat* and to *Illuminatus!* refer to the one-volume editions. References to *The Trick Top Hat*, *The Homing Pigeons* and *The Universe Next Door* refer to individual volumes of *Schrödinger's Cat* as originally published, which contains lots of stuff cut from the revised one volume edition.

All references to *Cosmic Trigger I: Final Secret of the Illuminati* refer to the New Falcon Publications edition. All references to *Prometheus Rising* refer to the Second Revised Edition of 1997 C.E.

BOOKS BY
ROBERT ANTON WILSON

Book of the Breast (The) (1974 C.E., revised as *Ishtar Rising: Why the Goddess Went to Hell and What to Expect Now That She's Returning* 1989 C.E.). It has seven sections, which correspond with the seven chakras. Wilson designed this book as a history of the role of the breast in history as well as an introduction to Taoism. The book examines how society has viewed the female breast at various times in history, and he traces how other societal values correspond with attitudes towards the breast.

Chaos and Beyond: The Best of Trajectories (1994 C.E.). Wilson tried to pack as much information as possible in this collection of the best material from Wilson's periodical *Trajectories*. Wilson writes about brain machines, the Fully Informed Jury Amendment, E-Prime and many other fun topics. He includes commentaries upon his commentaries with his usual good humor and insight.

Cosmic Trigger I: The Final Secret of the Illuminati (1977 C.E.). Once upon a time, a very fine time it seemed, Robert Anton Wilson indulged in a variety of experiments in induced brain chain, ranging from the magickal experiments of Aleister Crowley to the reimprinting experiments of Timothy Leary, etc. *Cosmic Trigger I* tells of these many experiments and how they affected Bob and his loving family. This book remains a favorite of many Wilson fans. Tim Leary wrote a forward, and Bob wrote a new preface for the 1986 edition.

Cosmic Trigger II: Down to Earth (1991 C.E.). Wilson has called this a Buddhist book which presents different sides of his personality. This book combines essays about various stages in

Wilson's life with essays on a wide variety of topics, especially movies. In this book one can really see the influence of Bob's move back to the United States from Ireland. While living in L.A. he began to write much more about the influence of film on his life and his thought.

Cosmic Trigger III: My Life After Death (1995 C.E.). In the style of *Cosmic Trigger II*, this book contains a mix of personal reminiscences with essay on a variety of topics. This book contains a wide range of writings, from Wilson's response to rumors of his own death, to his response to the death of his dear friend and collaborator, Robert Shea. I particularly like his essay on alternative calendars and his writings about Orson Welles.

Coincidance (1988 C.E.). This wonderful collection of essays provides Wilson's richest collection of writings on James Joyce. It also contains witty and wonderful essays on "Religion for the Hell of It," Allan Ginsberg, quantum physics, Marilyn Monroe, etc. Wilson had deeply explored Timothy Leary's eight circuit/ system/dimension model of the mind in many of his earlier books, but in this book he focuses in instead on the model of consciousness Joyce designed for *Finnegans Wake*. *Coincidance* provides a great entry point for the Joyce neophyte, as well as a wealth of information for the Joyce connoisseur.

Earth Will Shake (The) (1983 C.E.). This novel, the first of Wilson's *Historical Illuminati Chronicles,* tells the story of young Sigismundo Celine in Naples, Italy, beginning in 1761. He becomes embroiled in various occult conspiracies such as the Freemasons, the Illuminati, the Rosicrucians, etc. The descendants of the characters of this novel and its sequels will inhabit Wilson's other novels. This includes two of my favorite Wilson characters, Abraham Orfali, a Jewish healer, and Sigismundo's uncle Pietro.

Email to the Universe (2005 C.E.).This suite of essays draws on Wilson's work over the past 45 years. It contains a powerful piece on the harassment of Madalyn Murray due to her attempt to remove prayer from the public schools and other essays on a panoply of topics ranging from Joyce and Daoism to Aleister Crowley and beyond. This book reminds me of a baroque set of variations, where the dozens of separate pieces cohere to reveal the intricate beauty both of Wilson's mind and the magickal world in which we live.

Everything Is Under Control (1998 C.E.). This book gives an alphabetical series of brief essays on "Conspiracies, Cults and Cover-Ups." It provides an invaluable resource on topics as varied as Orson Welles, Shakespeare and Sex Magick. Wilson did not intend this book for sequential reading. Rather, he wanted the reader to follow the links from one essay to the next, jumping around from one conspiracy to the next. For instance, the entry on paint forger Elmyr, about whom Orson Welles made the film *F for Fake,* has links to Clifford Irving, Orson Welles, Howard Hughes, Nicholas Bourbaki, *Buckaroo Banzai*, Castro as Super-Mole, Jean Cocteau, *Gemstone File* and Noon Blue Apples. Each of those entries has links to other entries, so on and so forth.

Game of Life (The) with Timothy Leary (1979 C.E.). Another volume written mostly by Leary with a little help from his friend Dr. Bob. The book includes a list of the pages Bob wrote. In an essay written after Dr. Leary's death, Bob referred to this book as perhaps his favorite of Leary's books. This volume continues Leary's "Future History Series."

Illuminati Papers (The) (1980 C.E.). A wonderful collection of essays, on topics ranging from Ezra Pound to Beethoven to James Joyce and beyond. It also contains the essay "Ten Good Reasons to Get Out of Bed in the Morning," which I have found continually inspiring over the last two-plus decades.

Illuminatus! with Robert Shea (1975 C.E.) Originally released as three paperbacks: *The Eye in the Pyramid, The Golden Apple* and *Leviathan*. Later released in various one-volume editions with no changes to the text.

Many of the appendices do not appear in the book as published. In the struggles to get the book published, the authors had to cut about 500 pages from the text, including the missing appendices. Wilson no longer has a copy of the missing pages. That means that this novel only exists in a fragmented form, similar to Ezra Pound's uncompleted Cantos.

The novel is composed of ten trips, based on the sephiroth of the tree of life and twenty-two appendices based on the paths of the tree of life.

In addition to the kabbalistic form, the authors divided the book into five books, following the law of fives and the five fold Illuminati division of the cycles of civilizations: chaos, discord, confusion, bureaucracy, and aftermath, or in German *Verwirrung, Zweitracht, Unordnung, Beamtenherrschaft* and *Grummet*. The first three trips form Book One, chaos or *Verwirrung*. The kabbalistic crossing of the Abyss takes us from Book One to Book Two, which begins with the fourth trip, Chesed, the first sephiroth below the Abyss.

Masks of the Illuminati (1981 C.E.). This novel tells about a rich young student of magick and the kabbalah who meets Aleister Crowley, Ezra Pound, James Joyce, Albert Einstein, William Butler Yeats, Lenin and Carl Jung. Written as a wild mystery novel, Wilson demonstrates the parallels between Einstein's Theory of Relativity, the relativity of the multiple viewpoints in the writings of Joyce, and the multiple levels of meaning in the kabbalistic writings of Crowley. See **Appendix Ayin** for a discussion of the influence of James Joyce on Wilson's writing of this book.

Maybe Logic: The Lives and Ideas of Robert Anton Wilson (2003 C.E.). A 2-DVD set directed by Lance Bauscher which gives a good overview of Robert Anton Wilson's philosophy. The film itself integrates interviews with Dr. Wilson with portions of talks he has given over the years. The second disc contains more excepts from talks on *Finnegans Wake* and the eight circuit/dimension/system model of the nervous system, etc. It also includes some nifty brain-change exercises from Dr. Bob and a bunch of interviews with famous folk about Dr. Wilson, including Ivan Stang of the Church of the SubGenius and novelist Tom Robbins. Director Lance Bauscher also runs the Maybe Logic Academy, which provides online courses with Robert Anton Wilson at www.maybelogic.org. Readers of this book will likely enjoy the Maybe Logic courses.

Natural Law or Don't Put a Rubber on Your Willy (1987 C.E.). This delightful little book deals with the differences between scientific "laws," always subject to experimental verification and "natural laws" which some consider absolutely true despite their resistance to experimental verification. Wilson wrote this book in an acerbic, witty style much influenced by Jonathan Swift.

Nature's God (1991 C.E.). This third novel of the *Historical Illuminati Chronicles* tells of the continuing adventures of Sigismundo Celine, James Moon, and Maria and Sir John Babcock in America, England and France. George Washington shows up and Sigismundo has an encounter with a Native American shaman. A very thought-provoking and amusing novel.

Neuropolitics with Timothy Leary and George A. Koopman (1978 C.E., revised as *Neuropolitique* by Leary in 1988 C.E.). Principally a Leary text, Bob co-wrote a number of pieces which deal with brainwashing, re-imprinting and the eight-circuit model of the brain. This volume forms part of Leary's "Future History Series."

New Inquisition: Irrational Rationalism & the Citadel of Science (The) (1986 C.E.). This book examines how people calling themselves skeptics can act without much skepticism of their own models when confronting ideas they consider "unscientific." Specifically, it deals with the Committee for Scientific Investigation of Claims of the Paranormal (CSICOP) and their reticence to employ scientific method when examining threatening ideas. Wilson divided this book into eight sections corresponding with the eight system/circuit model and discussed many other ideas along the way. He focuses particularly on the processes we go through as we perceive the world around us.

Playboy's Book of Forbidden Words (1972 C.E.). Bob calls his first published book "a discursive dictionary of obscenity and invective" (*Coincidance,* pg. 31). The editor heavily rewrote the book, and Bob commented, "I dread the day when scholars rediscover it and begin blaming me for all that is wrong with it" (*ibid.,* pg. 32). Bob reconstructed a portion of the book for "The Motherfucker Mystique" section of *Coincidance.* He has suggested he may rewrite the whole book.

Prometheus Rising. A wonderful book, full of exercises for improved brain functioning.

I have spent a great deal of time with these exercises over the last nineteen years. I found the exercise on seeing the Thinker and the Prover hilarious sometimes, especially once when some Nichiren Buddhists tried to convince me to subscribe to their newspaper. Getting a new computer always seems to go along with an improvement in brain- and life-functioning (chapter 2). :) Taking kung fu seems very cool to me, although I find myself progressing slowly. Playing with babies often seems delightful and enlightening.

Hagbard Celine associates Prometheus with the snake in the Garden of Eden. Percy Shelley associated Milton's Satan with Prometheus in the preface to his *Prometheus Unbound.* Aeschylus wrote *Prometheus Bound* and *Prometheus Unbound,* but the latter play didn't survive, so Shelley wrote his own version. See the entry on **G.**

I remember going to *Who Framed Roger Rabbit* when it first came out to fulfill the second system exercise. I still wonder whether the Roger and Jessica in *Gravity's Rainbow* inspired the Roger and Jessica in the Disney film. (I later saw a billboard with a missing letter: *Who Framed Roger Rabbi.*)

Quantum Psychology. A wonderful book designed for use in a group. I have worked all the way through this book with two groups and I highly recommend it.

Chapter One contains a parable building on Franz Kafka's door of the Law. It sounds like cocaine addiction, with the man selling all he owns to bribe the guard of the door. It also reminds me of Bucky Fuller's notion that we serve as the sense organs of Universe. We each have our door of the Law, through which we perceive and act and ameliorate (or not) Universe. As to why the man couldn't pass through the door, it reminds me of Hugh Kenner's discussion of "The Waste Land." He said various models (other than his) fit various portions of the poem, so that if you squint you can think you understood it. I feel that way about this chapter. Wilson used to give a talk wherein he said of *Finnegans Wake* that any model of it would eventually prove inadequate. (Nietzsche said the same thing about Universe.) Perhaps it means we have to "rush the guard" to pass through the door, *carpe diem,* etc. Note: if "each person finds a personal and unique meaning" to this meta-parable, that would fit with the idea of each person having their own door to the Law.

Reality Is What You Can Get Away With: An Illustrated Screenplay (1992 C.E.). This entertaining screenplay gives a tour through the wacky world of Robert Anton Wilson. Man, I wish someone would make this movie! The screenplay tells the adventures of Ignatz and his wife as they travel through the various channels of a seriously weird television, encountering Dan Quayle, various monsters, Jane Russell, Humphrey Bogart, etc. J.R. "Bob" Dobbs and Beethoven's Ninth make appearances as well. Don't miss it!

Right Where You Are Sitting Now (1983 C.E.). A collection of essays, plus a short story. It includes discussions of the cut-up writing style of Williams S. Burroughs, an interview with Buckminster Fuller, a discussion of the interactions between the Amazing Randi and various researchers, and various analyses of trajectories affecting our present and our future.

Schrödinger's Cat Trilogy (The) (1979–1981 C.E.), originally released as three wonderful paperbacks: *The Universe Next Door* (1979 C.E.), *The Trick Top Hat* (1981 C.E.) and *The Homing Pigeons* (1981 C.E.). They then reappeared as a single volume, with slight revisions and substantial cuts in 1988. I like both versions, although I favor the original, longer version.

One may view each character in *Schrödinger's Cat* as both a wave and/or a particle. For instance, look at Beethoven's role in the novel. Ludwig's works play a major role in Wilson's writing, especially *Schrödinger's Cat*. Wilson seems deeply fascinated by Beethoven's later works, especially the Ninth Symphony and the "Hammerklavier" sonata. (For a detailed discussion of the "Hammerklavier," see Charles Rosen's *The Classical Style*.) Beethoven keeps popping up in the novel like a particle, but the sustained idea of the "Hammerklavier" as a great, yet incomprehensible artwork runs through the whole book. Wilson seems to model the "Hammerklavier" as the proto-postmodern work.

Sex and Drugs: A Journey Beyond Limits (1973 C.E., revised as ***Sex, Drugs and Magick*** 2000 C.E.). Early Wilson nonfiction work, originally published by Playboy Press. He later revised it as *Sex, Drugs and Magick*. It has seven chapters, along with a variety of interludes and prefaces and such. The book moves from:

1. Overview, to
2. Horned Gods & Horny Potions, to
3. The Smoke of the Assassins (hashish). to
4. The Mexican Weed (marijuana), to
5. Powders White & Deadly, to
6. Tibetan Space-Time-Warp Star-Nova Trips, and finally to
7. 2000: An Inner Space Odyssey.

The "horny potions" corresponds with the idea of the relationship between the second chakra and sexuality. The connection between the third system (the intellect) and hashish comes up in *The Widow's Son*, wherein the narrative voice suggests the need for immersion in the works of British philosopher and historian David Hume to make sense of the hashish experience. The text of *Sex and Drugs* deals with the traditional association between marijuana and sexuality (the fourth system). Note: In Leary's system, the second system deals with emotions and territoriality, while traditional Hinduism associates the second chakra with sexuality. I think the conservatism of much Hindu mysticism links emotionality with sexuality.

The higher systems/chakras also seems to correspond with the chapters, as least vaguely, in this book. In *Prometheus Rising*, Wilson mentions that the more powerful psychedelics tend to activate the sixth and seventh systems, once again confirming this analysis of the chapters of *Sex and Drugs*.

Sex Magicians (The) (1973 C.E.). I have never read this early, out-of-print erotic novel. However Wilson has commented that he reused the best parts in *The Schrödinger's Cat Trilogy*. This novel also introduced the character of Markoff Chaney, who reappears in *Illuminatus!* and *The Schrödinger's Cat Trilogy*, causing much mischief.

TSOG: The Thing That Ate the Constitution (2002 C.E.). This book covers a wide variety of topics, from a paradisical image of

Amsterdam to a discussion of the Tsarist Occupation Government (TSOG) and why the United States has a Tsar even though the Constitution makes no mention of such an office. This book concludes with a tantalizing look at the upcoming *The Tale of the Tribe*, a book Wilson has worked on over the past few years, looking at the power of Internet to transform society, drawing on the influence of Ezra Pound and James Joyce on Malcolm McLuhan and others.

Walls Came Tumbling Down (The) (1997 C.E.). This entertaining screenplay tells the tale of a conservative scientist who begins to have odd experiences, encountering a variety of altered states of consciousness. The screenplay looks at how these experiences affect his marriage, his career, and everything else in his life. The story echoes experiences from Bob's own life, as well as those of Philip K. Dick and others. I think this would make a great film.

Widow's Son (The) (1985 C.E.). The second volume of the *Historical Illuminati Chronicles*. Wilson has repeatedly called this his favorite of his books. It continues the story of Sigismundo Celine and the various characters from *The Earth Will Shake*, and introduces new characters like Irish rebel James Moon. Historical material from *Holy Blood, Holy Grail* and other sources fills the books, and the footnotes almost take over the novels. Wilson developed the footnote device from that employed by Flann O'Brien in *The Third Policeman* and Vladimir Nabokov in *Pale Fire*.

Wilhelm Reich in Hell (1987 C.E.). This stage play, or "punk rock opera" as Wilson calls it, deals with Wilhelm Reich on trial in the afterlife. Reich died in prison after years of controversial scientific work. Wilson draws parallels with others imprisoned for their ideas, such as Timothy Leary and Ezra Pound. One can also see parallels between this play and *The Devil and Daniel Webster*, one of Bob's favorite films in his youth. This book also includes a lengthy introduction by Bob dealing with Reich and related subjects.

LEXICON

Act on perfect love. What Miss Portinari tells the Dealy Lama that she and Hagbard Celine have failed to do. (*Illuminatus!*, pg. 726) Its initials, A.p.l., fit in with the ALP/111 theme of *Finnegans Wake*. (In the Kabbalah, the letters A+L+P add up to 111. Joyce uses this in *Finnegans Wake* which deals with the goddess *A*nna *L*ivia *P*lurabella. Wilson uses devices learned from the Kabbalah and Joyce in all of his books.)

Afghanistan. According to ILLUMINATI PROJECT: MEMO #2, citing Akron Daraul's *A History of Secret Societies*, "...in the 16th century, in Afghanistan, the Illuminated Ones (Roshinaya) picked up the original tactics of the Order of Assassins." (*Illuminatus!*, pg. 15)

According to the BBC, Afghan opium production has increased 1400% since the removal of the Taliban. (news.bbc.co.uk/1/hi/world/south_asia/2282617.stm. 9/26/2002)

Alucard, John. One of the lawyers for the Burro of Indian Affairs in *Illuminatus!* (Robert Morning Sky suggested this name for the B.I.A.) Lon Chaney Jr.'s character in *Son of Dracula* took the name Alucard (Dracula spelled kabbalistically backward).

Anna Livia Plurabella. The goddess of *Finnegans Wake* by James Joyce. Also the river Liffey in Dublin, the wife of H.C.E. (Humphrey Chimpden Earwicker, perhaps the dreamer of *Finnegans Wake*), etc. Joyce often implies her presence through the initials A.L.P. or the number 111. (In Hebrew the letters A (1) + L (30) + P (80) add to 111.)

Arbeit macht frei. German for "Work will set you free." These words appeared over the gates to Nazi concentration camps. Joe Malik refers to this. (*Illuminatus!*, pg. 620)

Archangels. Rapha-El, Gabri-El, Micha-El and Auri-El are mentioned repeatedly in *The Earth Will Shake*. The healer Abraham Orfali helps Sigismundo visualize them to aid him in his personal development.

Artaud. Antonin (1896–1948). A pioneer surrealist whose play *There Is No More Firmament* deals with the star Sirius (*Cosmic Trigger I*, pgs. 226–227).

Assassins. Secret society led by the Old Man of the Mountain, Hassan I Sabbah. Our words for hashish and assassin come from his name (at least according to some). He taught that "nothing is true and everything is permissible." One of the Illuminati Memos in *Illuminatus!* traces the Illuminati back to the Assassins.

Atoh Malkoth, ve-Geburah, ve-Gedullah, le-olahm. "For Thine is the kingdom, the power, and the glory, forever." In *The Earth Will Shake* Abraham Orfali says on page 125, "I say it before each healing, because it is not I, Abraham Orfali, who heals people; it is God working through me." Students of the kabbalah will recognize the names of the tenth sephiroth, Malkuth, the kingdom, and the fifth sephiroth, Geburah, usually translated as strength and here translated as the power.

Babadalgharaghtakamminarronnkonnbronntonnerronntuon nthunntrovarrhounawnskawntoohoohoordenenthurnukPerk odhuskurunbarggruauyagokgorlayorgromgremmitghundhu rthrumathunaradidillifaititillibumullunukkununklikkaklakk aklaskaklopatzklatschabattacreppycrottygraddaghsemmihsa mmihnouithappluddyappladdypkonpkotBladyughfoulmoeck lenburgwhurawhorascortastrumpapornanennykocksapastip patappatupperstrippuckputtanachThingcrooklyexineverypas turesixdixlikencehimaroundhersthemaggerbykinkinkankan withdownmindlookingatedLukkedoerendunandurraskewdyl ooshoofermoyportertooryzooysphalnabortansporthaokansak roidverjkapakkapuk.Bothallchoractorschumminaroundgans umuminarumdrumstrumtruminahumptadumpwaultopoofoo

looderamaunsturnup!pappappapparrassannuaragheallachn
atullaghmonganmacmacmacwhackfalltherdebblenonthedub
blandaddydoodlehusstenhasstencaffincoffintussemtossemda
mandamnacosaghcusaghhobixhatouxpeswchbechoscashlcarc
arcaractUllhodturdenweirmudgaardgringnirurdrmolnirfenr
irlukkilokkibaugimandodrrerinsurtkrinmgernrackinarockar
! The ten thunderwords (nine with 100 letters and the last on with
101 letters) from *Finnegans Wake* put together to make a 1001
letter metathunderword. Each thunderword represents a thun-
derclap during the storm while the dreamer, HCE, sleeps. 1001
seems an important number relating to *The Arabian Nights*, Sir
Richard Francis Burton, etc. Numeration plays a great role in
both *Finnegans Wake* and in Wilson's work. Emerson said each
word contains a fossil poem. Well, to Joyce and Wilson, numbers also seem to contain fossil poems.

Wilson draws on a variety of traditions in explicating the
poetic role of numbers in our minds. He uses the frequent sets of
twelves and sevens in world mythology, following the ideas of
Jung about how these patterns repeat from culture to culture.
Wilson also draws heavily from the kabbalistic tradition of number analysis, following in the footsteps of Aleister Crowley.

Sir Richard Francis Burton also wrote a book called *From
Liverpool to Fernando Po*, as well as translating *The Arabian
Nights*. *Illuminatus!* features the island of Fernando Po (respelled
Poo) and a yellow submarine inspired by four lads from Liver-
pool.

Bach, Johann Sebastian (1685–1750). George Dorn thinks of
Stella, "Bach could hint the delight of those purple-tinted lips in
that black face." (*Illuminatus!*, pg. 493) In *The Earth Will Shake*
Sigismundo Celine meets Johann Christian Bach, one of Johann
Sebastian's sons, who introduces Celine to J.S. Bach's music.
Celine gets depressed because J.S. had years earlier done what
Celine dreamt of doing musically. Celine particularly likes "The
Goldberg Variations."

In *Prometheus Rising* Wilson says of J.S. Bach that he "may
have written the sexiest music in history." (*Prometheus Rising*,
pg. 135) Wilson makes this observation in a discussion of the
Princess of Wands tarot card, which he associates with fire of
fire, "sexuality at its most powerful." Most tarot analysts, includ-

ing Aleister Crowley, associate the Princesses with earth and the Knights (in Crowley's Thoth deck) or the Kings (in the Waite and most other decks) with the element of fire. Wilson comments that people of the fire/fire personality type usually act quite promiscuously, but "sometimes they pour all their erotic energy into one mate and raise huge families, parenting being a strong part of the fourth circuit, e.g., J.S. Bach, who may have written the sexiest music in history, had twenty children" (*Prometheus Rising*, pg. 135).

Three dimensional space "easily expands into multidimensional sensory space such as the esthetically sensitive can enter by closing their eyes when listening to Bach or Vivaldi..." (*Ishtar Rising*, pg. 169)

Bateson, Gregory (1904–1980). Author of *Mind and Nature*. Wilson recommends this book in the chapter on the fourth dimension/system/circuit in *Prometheus Rising*.

Beckett, Samuel (1909–1989). Wilson refers to him as a "great fellow novelist" of Joyce's on page 5 of *Coincidance*. Hugh Kenner's book on Irish literature *A Colder Eye* has a chapter on Beckett called "The Terminator," as in the Terminator of modernism. I always have this vision of Arnold Schwarzenegger as Beckett.

Kenner also discusses "Irish facts" in this book. "Irish facts" often contradict each other, if not themselves. Wilson frequently cites Kenner's notion of Irish facts. Kenner and Marshall McLuhan knew each other in college and visited Ezra Pound together. Both Kenner and McLuhan have influenced Wilson.

Kenner sees many "Irish facts" in Richard Ellmann's "standard" biography of Joyce. In various books Kenner points out where elements of the novel *Portrait of the Artist as a Young Man* describing the "fictitious" Irish writer Stephen Dedalus show up as biographical details in Ellmann's "non-fiction" book about the "real" Irish writer James A. Joyce. Similar boundary crossing pervades Wilson's books, especially in his discussions of *F for Fake* and Elmyr in *Cosmic Trigger III*. In that book he even mentions me on page 97 as a "poet" rather than as a pseudonym for the author of the very egregious tome you hold in your hands at this moment.

For more about Samuel Beckett, you might enjoy Richard Ellmann's *Four Dubliners*, about Oscar Wilde, Yeats, Joyce and Beckett, which has many amusing stories.

Beethoven, Ludwig van (1770–1827). Wilson makes more references to Beethoven's music than to any other music in his books. In *Illuminatus!* a character talks about the late quartets. Beethoven's late music permeates *Schrödinger's Cat*: the "Hammerklavier" gets mentioned over and over again, "Dr. Raus Elysium" in that novel comes from a pun on the Ode to Joy ("Tochter als Elysium"), "Muss es sein?" comes from the quartet Opus 135, a character calls the Ninth "unsuccessful tantric sex," etc.

Wilson uses Beethoven's Ninth Symphony, along with other music, as soundtrack in both of his screenplays. He has an article on Beethoven in *The Illuminati Papers*. *Prometheus Rising* mentions the Ninth and the "Hammerklavier." For Wilson, Beethoven's heroic struggle against deafness parallels humanity's struggle against barbarity, as well as the struggle for gentleness against cruelty, intelligence against stupidity, etc. See also *Muss es sein?*

Bell's Theorem. A controversial creation of physicist John S. Bell. Many physicists (including Einstein) disliked the uncertainty of quantum mechanics. They didn't like the fact that many equations yielded at least two answers, as opposed to the single answers typical of nineteenth century physics. Some physicists posited the existence of a hidden variable at work beneath the quantum level which would resolve the uncertainties of quantum mechanics. Bell proved (or least many physicists think he proved) that any hidden variable below the quantum level would have a grossly non-local character. This means that the hidden variable would act instantaneously across space and time, seemingly violating relativity, which prohibits instantaneous action.

Bell's Theorem has fascinated Wilson since the 70's. It provides the form for *The Trick Top Hat*, and shows up in most of his books.

Bermuda Triangle.

FT FT FT FT FT	FT FT FT FT FT
FT	FT
FT	FT
FT FT FT FT	FT
FT	FT
FT	FT
FT	FT
FT	FT

"The case that really made the Bermuda Triangle a permanent part of folklore was the disappearance of Flight 19—five Navy bombers on a routine training mission, which disappeared entirely after sending back an incoherent message that repeated the letters FT and then faded away." (*Everything is Under Control*, pg. 67) You might also check out "Bermuda Love Triangle" on the Negro Problem's CD, "Welcome Black."

Binyon, Lawrence (1869–1943). Translator of Dante's *Comedia*. *The Portable Dante* contains his terrific complete translation of the *Comedia*, plus Dante Gabriel Rossetti's beautiful translation of *La Vita Nuova*, both of which Pound recommended. Binyon said "slowness is beauty," which the Dealy Llama quotes. (*Illuminatus!*, pg. 687)

Blake, William (1757–1827). An English poet at the time of the French Revolution. His line about "the doors of perception" inspired Aldous Huxley's book of that name (about psychedelic mushrooms), which in turn provided a name to the rock band The Doors. He also inspired the name of the scientist Blake Williams in *Schrödinger's Cat*.

Blue light. In *Illuminatus!*, Mary Lou Servix sees a "big blue halo" around Simon Moon while practicing sex magick. Ezra Pound writes in Canto CXIII:

And in every woman, somewhere in the snarl is a tenderness,
A blue light under stars.
— *The Cantos*, pg. 789–790

and in the Notes for Canto CXVII:

For the blue flash and the moments
    benedetta
                     — *The Cantos*, pg. 801

The Notes for that Canto ends:

To be men not destroyers.
                     — *The Cantos*, pg. 802

Pound scholar Carroll Terrell says Pound wanted the Cantos to end with that line. In *Illuminatus!* Mary Lou Servix continues, "But that light... My God, I will never forget that light." (*Illuminatus!*, pg. 45)

Bohm, David (1917–1992). An influential quantum physicist. Wilson often mentions his book *Wholeness and the Implicate Order*. (Some conspiracy theorists think that when Richard Nixon wanted to refer to the Kennedy assassination, he would use the code phrase "The Whole Bay of Pigs Thing." Perhaps I will write a book about quantum mechanics and Watergate called *The Whole Bay of Pigs Things and the Implicate Order*.)

Bohr, Niels (1885–1962). Yet another great quantum physicist. He had the Taoist yin and yang symbol on his coat of arms. His contributions to physics rival Einstein's and Newton's. He created the Bohr model of the atom, which quantum mechanics largely superceded. He coined the term "complementarity", which means that the wave and particle theories complement each other and both have valuable uses, even though they seem to contradict each other. He also came up with the Copenhagen Interpretation of Quantum Mechanics, which suggests that human science describes the mathematical systems we have created to describe the physical world rather than describing the world itself. Wilson wrote that *Prometheus Rising* "owes everything" to Niels Bohr.

Book of the Law (The). The central text of Aleister Crowley's life, composed and/or received by him and his wife in Cairo in 1904 C.E. It contains such lines as "Do what Thou wilt shall be the whole of the Law" and "Every Man and Woman is a Star." In the Preface to this book, Mordecai the Foul changes this to "Every Man and Woman is a Tsar."

Burton, Sir Richard (1821–1890). African explorer, translator of the *Kama Sutra* and author of *From Liverpool to Fernando Po*. Aleister Crowley considered him a major influence, Sayed Idries Shah considered him a Sufi, and science fiction writer Philip Jose Farmer made him a major character in his Riverworld novels. The wonderful film and novel *Mountains of the Moon* tell the story his search for the headwaters of the Nile. Burton also greatly influenced Joyce's *Finnegans Wake*. He has influenced Wilson through Crowley and Joyce.

Burroughs, William S. (1914–1997). Novelist, author of *Naked Lunch*, *The Soft Machine*, *The Job*, *The Western Lands*, etc. He introduced Wilson to his fascination with the number 23. Burroughs adapted Brion Gysin's cut-up method to fiction. Burrough's greatly influenced Wilson. Burroughs once called *Finnegans Wake* experimental writing gone too far.

I first came in contact with William Burroughs through Philip Jose Farmer. Farmer's book *Riverworld and Other Stories* contains a story called "The Jungle Rot Kid on the Nod." Farmer described this story as his idea of what would have happened if William S. Burroughs had written the Tarzan stories instead of Edgar Rice Burroughs.

Calendars. In the 1990's C.E., in anticipation of the millennium in the Gregorian calendar, Bob began to use a wide variety of calendars, including the Jewish, Muslim, Chinese, Discordian, Thelemic, etc. (He had used alternative calendars before this, but in the 1990's he radically expanded this practice.) He used these to encourage people not to confuse the map with the territory, not to confuse our terrestrial calendars with some absolute structure of Scenario Universe (as Bucky Fuller might say).

Cannabis. A rapper. Also an illegal drug first given to Bob during a performance by the Modern Jazz Quartet in the men's room of the Village Vanguard in Greenwich Village in the fifties.

Carlin, George (1937–). Comedian, whom Bob calls the World's Greatest Philosopher on his webpage, rawilson.com. Bob refers to George Carlin in *Quantum Psychology*. Carlin used Wilson's *Playboy's Book of Forbidden Words* to aid him in structuring a routine on alternative names for sex acts. I remember hearing a great radio ad for a George Carlin concert where Carlin talked about how humor can stimulate healing chemicals in your brain.

Celine, Hagbard. A major character in *Illuminatus!*, captain of the yellow submarine *Leif Erickson*. Wilson has also published articles under this name.

Celine, Sigismundo. The main viewpoint character of the *Historical Illuminatus Chronicles*. Born in Naples, Italy, he travels to Paris, London, North Africa, America, etc.

Chandler, Raymond (1888–1959). Author of mystery novels featuring the detective Philip Marlow. One of Wilson's favorite authors. Wilson wrote an article on Chandler in *The Illuminati Papers*. Wilson said he found living in Los Angeles "like living in a Raymond Chandler theme-park," just as he found Dublin like living in a James Joyce theme-park.

Chaney, Markoff. A character in both *Illuminatus!* and *Schrödinger's Cat*. His unpredictability helps to undo the Illuminati in the former, and he has many sexual and literary adventures in the latter.

Chief, Rhoda. She appears in both *Illuminatus!*, as the lead singer for the Heads of Easter Island who spikes the Kool-Aid with LSD at the Ingolstadt Festival, and *Schrödinger's Cat*, as an experimental subject at Orgasm Research.

Chimes at Midnight (The). A film directed by Orson Welles based on Shakespeare's *Henry IV, Parts One and Two*, with bits from *Merry Wives of Windsor*, I think, focusing on the character of Falstaff, played by Welles. The phrase refers to the metaphor of the day paralleling a human life, with birth in the morning and death at night. The chimes at midnight suggest the end of the day, or the end of the struggle. Hagbard quotes it in the Tenth Trip of *Illuminatus!* to Joe Malik (*Illuminatus!*, pg. 587), and Sir

John Babcock discusses it with James Joyce in *Masks of the Illuminati*. Joyce contemplates the fact that midnight would seem later in the pre-electric agricultural economy of Falstaff's time.

Chips, Fission. Agent 00005 in *Illuminatus!*, a satire of James Bond's 007.

Church of the SubGenius (The). Praise "Bob!" This religion out of Dallas, TX, worships a former aluminum siding sales-critter named J.R. "Bob" Dobbs, who had a close encounter with either aliens or L. Ron Hubbard. The DVD, *Maybe Logic,* contains an interview with Rev. Ivan Stang of the Church of the SubGenius discussing Robert Anton Wilson.

Complementarity. See **Bohr, Niels**.

Conspiracies. Don't really exist. Relax. Pay your taxes. Nothing you can do about death and taxes.

Or con-spire means to breath together (like res-piration). Those who act together look like affinity groups from the inside and conspiracies from the outside. Conspiracies play a role in most Wilson books, especially his novels and *Everything Is Under Control.*

Constitutional Propaganda. In Pitkin County, CO, a potential juror got charged with contempt for handing out information about jury nullification. The charges eventually got dropped. In various articles Wilson has shown great enthusiasm for the notion of jury nullification, which he sees as an opportunity for individual citizens to take action against a state in which they have practically no voice. Wilson notes that jury nullification has a tradition going back to the Magna Carta, and that nullifications of alcohol-related trials helped to overturn prohibition. (A Grateful Dead bumper sticker says, "I got called for Jerry Duty.") See **Jury Nullification.**

Creeley, Robert (1926–). A wonderful American poet, much influenced by Ezra Pound and William Carlos Williams. He taught at Black Mountain College with the poet Charles Olson, who had spent a lot of time with Ezra Pound at St. Elizabeth's Mental Hospital. Olson had developed what he called "Projective Verse," based largely on his development of Pound's ideas.

Creeley traveled west and became friends with many of the San Francisco poets like Allen Ginsberg, Gary Snyder, and Michael McClure, who wanted to talk to him about Projective Verse, Pound and Olson. Creeley greatly influenced Ginsberg who greatly influenced Wilson.

Critter. Well, Bob commented some years ago that he used the word "Congressman" to refer to a member or Congress," but that seemed to imply male chauvinism, so he began to say "Congressperson" instead. However, the more he thought about it, he realized that "Congressperson" implied human chauvinism, so he switched to "Congress-entity." These days Bob refers to members of Congress as Congress-critters—when he doesn't refer to them as scoundrels and thieves.

Crowley, Aleister (1875–1947). The man, the myth, the legend. Crowley grew up in a house where his mother limited his reading to "Christian" material, so he read the Bible very attentively, fascinated by the long names and identifying himself with the Great Beast of the Apocalypse. Go figure. He went on to join the Hermetic Order of the Golden Dawn, siding with Macgregor Mathers when the Golden Dawn splintered. He eventually feuded with Mathers as well.

In 1904 Crowley received and/or composed *The Book of the Law* with his wife. At first, he wrote, the *Book*'s message horrified him, but eventually he devoted the rest of his life to spreading its message. Along the way Crowley wrote lots of books which eventually played a major role in Robert Anton Wilson's life.

Bob had lunch with his friend Alan Watts one day in 1970 C.E., and Alan recommended Israel Regardie's *The Eye in the Triangle* which dealt with Crowley's life and work. This proved a pivotal point in Bob's life. He went on to devour all of Crowley's books and perform many of the magickal exercises contained therein. Wilson included Crowley as a major character in *Masks of the Illuminati*, and Crowley has influenced most of Wilson's subsequent writing. Bob values how Crowley applied the scientific method to altered states of consciousness. As Crowley wrote:

We place no reliance on virgin or pigeon,
Our method is Science, our goal is Religion.

Wilson also likes how Crowley loaded many levels of meaning into each sentence—much as James Joyce did—but using different tools. Crowley developed a very personal conception of the Kabbalah which he used to pile layer upon layer of meaning into his writing. Wilson studied these methods deeply, combining them with methods learned from Joyce, Burroughs and elsewhere, and adding his own spin to them. See **Appendix Samekh** for a detailed examination of Wilson and Shea's Kabbalistic methodology in *Illuminatus!*

CSICON. The Committee for Surrealistic Investigation of Claims of the Normal. Bob discusses this [fictional] group at length at rawilson.com and in *TSOG*. Some crickets complain CSICON doesn't seem to act in a very surrealistic fashion, redressing etiquette and refuse too. Publican tarts of sigh and titric studio who. are. yousion they dike. See **CSICOP**.

CSICOP. The Committee for Scientific Investigation of Claims of the Paranormal. Bob discusses this [non-fictional] group at length in *The New Inquisition*. Some critics complain CSICON doesn't seem to act in a very scientific fashion, suppressing evidence and refusing to publish reports of scientific studies whose conclusions they dislike. See **CSICON**.

Cut-up. A device created by William S. Burroughs and Brion Gysin consisting of taking a page of text, tearing it into four parts, rearranging the parts, and extracting any new combinations of words which seem interesting. For example: Wilson frequently mentions J-interrelated web of coinciding opposites. Ho fiction, spontaneously occurring, interrelating synchronothing about James Joyce, Einstein's conversation in the style of the IthaGolden Dawn Kabbalah, Burroughs' cut-up tech humor. Just as Leopold Bloom's thoughtsossoms into the full blown Wakean-style Boylan and Molly Bloom in the Leopold Bloousness in the drug scene at the end, Joyce dwells on (probably false) infokes and acronyms. As Hugh Kenner commented: Ough the worlds of *Finnegans Wake* gone farther, divining, no, Heisenberg and Gödel, his years frequently focused on Joyce.

Numbers play a po number 23 which haunt this and all of his nove influence over postmodern novelist Robert Crowley. His novel *Masks of the Illuminati* contains a fossil poem, and Joyce allowed the Wilson's novels. Similarly Wilson uses 23 as a leit-mote in the Joyce corpus, and structural devices mentions Conan Doyle, anticipating Joyce's Wilson's comparison of Joyce and Sherlock*iminati* in 1982. Any time at all, any time at all all you gotta do is call & I'll be there. I'll be there to make you feel glad if you're feeling sorry and sad. Don't you be sad, just call me tonight. Hello Debbie. :) Call me tonight & I'll come to you. At the time I knew next to Joyce in a parallel universe become Pope Sed.

Wilson masks into the world of James Joyce. Of course, Aleister has spiked the champagne. About *Ulysses*, "A mentor is advisable: The reader first encounters Einstein an the key books of the space-time age."

"Stately Wilson has mentored me and many others thru Buck Mulligan while Joyce once again plays *Ulysses*, *The Cantos* and beyond." Stately, plump Albert Einstein came from the lenses of various psychological theories, from paleyellow tray on which two mugs of beer slocating Stephen Dedalus in space-time Masks. "!" silence, exile and cunncidences. Samuel Beckett saw the "presence of the absent Wilson Cake." Bruno saw reality as a skyscraper, in which every part is jug truths of history.

Some people find cut-ups annoying. Wilson has used them in all of his novels, especially for drug and/or dream sequences. See also **Nine Basic Winner-Loser Scripts.**

Dalliance. "The most pleasant word for sex in the present English vocabulary..." (*Ishtar Rising*, pg. 167)

Dashwood, Dr. Frank. A sex researcher in *Schrödinger's Cat*. Various characters in the third part of that novel, *The Homing Pigeons*, perceive him as George Dorn, which tends to annoy him.

Dealy Lama. A very, very, very old man who lives beneath the Dealy Plaza (site of the John F. Kennedy assassination) in Dallas, TX, in *Illuminatus!* He acts as a spiritual advisor to Hagbard Celine, Miss Portinari and Fission Chips, etc.

Dick, Philip K (1928–1982). The novelist whose work inspired *Blade Runner, Total Recall* and *Minority Report,* etc. In the early seventies he had a series of very odd experiences which seem to parallel Bob's Sirius experiences, Tim Leary's Starseed experiences, and the McKenna brothers' zany mushroom adventures, etc. Philip Dick's last four novels and voluminous (and largely unpublished) "non-fiction" deal with these odd experiences.

Phil read *Cosmic Trigger* and met Bob once at a science fiction convention. Phil's books have profoundly affected Bob's writing, especially *The Walls Came Tumbling Down.*

Digital McLuhan. A book by Paul Levinson which Bob includes on his recommended reading list at rawilson.com. This book looks at Marshall McLuhan's books and ideas about communications through the lens of the Internet age. It ends with the line "Read McLuhan, read books and essays about his work, reread this book, and decide for yourself." A nice ending, reminiscent of the Buddha's dying words, "Doubt and find your own light," as well as the ending of Ezra Pound's obituary of T.S. Eliot, "READ HIM." I might steal such a line as a conclusion to this book.

Discordianism. A religion which worships Discordia, the Roman goddess of chaos, discord, confusion, bureaucracy, and international relations, known to the Greeks as Eris. Kerry Thornley and Greg Hill founded this religion in 1958 C.E., and Bob Wilson enthusiastically embraced it when he and Thornley became friends in 1967 C.E. Wilson took the Discordian name Mordecai the Foul, and his Discordian writings appear in the *Principia Discordia,* the holy book of Discordianism, for which he also wrote an introduction. Robert Shea and Robert Anton Wilson dedicated *Illuminatus!* to Hill and Thornley.

As some Christian sects make all members ministers, the Discordians make all members Popes, subject to no authority on earth, at least from their perspective. Both the *Principia Discordia* and *Illuminatus!* contain copies of the Discordian Pope card, which identifies the bearer as a "Genuine and Authorized Pope." They invite readers to reproduce these Pope cards freely. Wilson also performs pontifications at his public appearances, making all members of the audience Discordian Popes.

Dorn, George. Perhaps the main viewpoint character in *Illuminatus!* He works for Joe Malik as a reporter for *Confrontation* magazine and gets sent to Bad Ass, TX, to research a recent assassination. He gets put in jail for possession of marijuana and then the fun begins. He ends up traveling to Atlantis and Ingolstadt with Hagbard Celine, and he may become Dr. Frank Dashwood in *The Homing Pigeons.*

"Down, down, down." This phrase occurs over and over again in *The Earth Will Shake.* It also appears in Dylan Thomas' poem "Ballad of the Long-Legged Bait."

> Down, down, down, under the ground,
> Under the floating villages,
> Turns the moon-chained and water-wound
> Metropolis of fishes

Wilson used this passage at a seminar in Phoenix in March, 1988 C.E., in an exercise similar to those in *The New Inquisition* and other books, where he defines various statements as true, false, meaningless, a game rule, etc. He defined this passage as "poetry." He said Thomas did something similar in poetry to what Joyce did in *Finnegans Wake.*

Aside: For a good discussion of Dylan Thomas, see the poet Donald Hall's *Their Ancient Glittering Eyes Are Gay* (a revised version of his *Remembering Poets*). Hall knew the poets Dylan Thomas, T.S. Eliot, Ezra Pound, Robert Frost, Ivor Winters and Marianne Moore personally. In this book he shares his memories of them as well as discussing their writing, reputations and interactions. I loved this book. (*Remembering Poets* contained shorter versions of the discussions of Thomas, Eliot, Pound and Frost. He expanded those and added sections of Winters and Moore for *Their Ancient Glittering Eyes Are Gay.*)

Wilson uses the triple pattern "down, down, down" in other ways in *The Earth Will Shake*: "harpsichord, harpsichord, harpsichord," etc. In *Prometheus Rising* chapter one he has an old lady say, "It's turtles-turtles-turtles, *all the way!*" (pg. 25). He echoes this in Chapter 18 with, "It's circuits-circuits-circuits all the way." (pg. 267)

Wilson told me in conversation that he didn't intend to use this pattern from the Thomas poem. He patterned much of *The Earth Will Shake* on Dante's *Inferno*, to which he intended the "down, down, down" references to refer.

Bobby Zimmerman changed his last name to Dylan in honor of Dylan Thomas.

Dracman, Frank. Combination of Frankenstein, Dracula and the Wolfman. Pseudonym of Joycean Conrad Holt, a central figure among RAW's Arizona fans. The classic Universal films of *Frankenstein, Dracula* and *The Wolfman* greatly influenced Wilson.

Dragnet. TV show about detective Joe Friday. "It was last Friday. Joe told me he had a lead that interested him..." (*Illuminatus!*, pg. 21, speaking of Joe Malik.) Phil Dick made much of this sort of coincidence in his psychic detective work. You might also enjoy reading about Ishmael Reed's psychic detective Papa LaBas in *Mumbo Jumbo* and *The Last Days of Louisiana Red*. As Thomas Pynchon said in *Gravity's Rainbow*, "Check out Ishmael Reed. He knows more about it than you'll ever find here" (pg. 588).

Drake, Robert Putney. A major character in *Illuminatus!* Born to a wealthy New England banking family, he strives to transform himself in a variety of ways, from psychotherapy to self-mutilation to yoga and magick, etc. Eventually he strives to become involved with the Illuminati and succeeds, becoming the head of all organized crime in the U.S.

E-Prime. English without the verb "to be." Count Alfred Korzybski suggested the "is" of identity (as in "I am a student") tends to distort perception. The "is" of identity suggests mathematical equivalence ("2 + 2 is 4"). One can improve the situation by adding "etc." ("I am a student, etc.," since I also play the role of teacher, son, brother, etc.)

David Bourland, Jr., a student of Korzybski's, suggested dropping the verb "to be" entirely, creating E-prime. ("I sometimes play the role of a student." Wilson has written a great deal in E-prime, including *Quantum Psychology* and *Cosmic Trigger III*.

Eco, Umberto (1932–). Italian novelist and literary theorist. Many have compared his *Foucault's Pendulum* with *Illuminatus!* I really enjoyed his *The Name of the Rose*. (I do not recommend the movie, however, which I think perverted many of the points of the text.) In *The Postscript* to *The Name of the Rose* Eco wrote that the title of a text serves to hide the meaning of the text, and he defines a novel as a machine for generating interpretations. Great stuff.

Egyptian mouth-breeders. Type of fish who die in the explosion at *Confrontation* magazine at the beginning of *Illuminatus!* Ironically, Wilson and Shea later suggest that Isis resurrects the slain Osiris by oral sex.

Eight circuit model of the brain. Dr. Timothy Leary suggested that the human nervous system has eight circuits. Each of these circuits can become imprinted at various phases of a human being's life, allowing for rapid transformation of the mind/body metasystem. Leary saw the first circuit becoming activated at birth. That circuit deals with biosurvival issues like food and physical sensation, the issues which occupy an infant's mind. Carl Sagan calls this part of the brain the reptile brain, since reptiles haven't evolved any other circuit.

Next, the child activates the second circuit when it attempts to master gravity. The toddler learning to walk activates the emotional/territorial system/circuits. (Wilson has taken to calling these sub-systems of the human nervous meta-system "systems" instead of "circuits." See **Appendix Shin.**) Carl Sagan calls this the mammal brain. It concerns itself with ego-role within the tribe or family.

Next, the child learns to speak and activates the third system/circuit. The brain rapidly develops language ability and learns to manipulate symbols. At adolescence the fourth circuit/systems becomes activated with puberty and the socio-sexual transformation of the teenager.

Leary suggested that these circuits/systems reside in the left hemisphere of the brain, and that most people only activate these first four circuits/systems during their lifetimes. However, he suggested that the right hemisphere of the brain contains four parallel systems/circuits, which various shamanic and yogic practices can activate.

Leary called the fifth circuit the cyber-somatic. It deals with the rediscovery of the body, the sense of body delight felt by practitioners of yoga. The sixth circuit, the cyber-electric, allows for reprogramming the nervous system. The cyber-genetic seventh circuit (or morphogenetic as Wilson calls it—see **Appendix Shin**) allows access to the DNA archives. The Cyber-Nano-Tech eighth circuit allows awareness and manipulation of the quantum mechanical level.

Robert Anton Wilson embraced Leary's eight system/circuit model and he explicates it in many of his books, especially *Prometheus Rising*, which contains many exercises to aid in mastering the individual systems/circuits. For various forms of the eight system/circuit model, see **Appendix Shin**.

Eliot, T. (Thomas) S. (Sterns) (1888–1965). American poet who later took English citizenship, so you will find his work in anthologies of English literature and of American literature (as you will that of W.H. Auden, born in the UK who migrated to the USA). Wilson quote Eliot's great last set of poems, *The Four Quartets*, twice in *The Universe Next Door*. Frank Dashwood encounters roses with "the look of roses that are looked at" in a dream, and Mary Margaret Wildeblood quotes from "the gospel of her youth" "humility is endless." Wildeblood, a "New York Intellectual" in 1983 C.E., would naturally have encountered Eliot as the "gospel of her youth:" Eliot exerted a huge influence on literary life in the English speaking world. George Dorn quotes "humility is endless" repeatedly. (*Illuminatus!*, pgs. 402, 407) (Eliot patterned *The Four Quartets* on Beethoven's late string quartets, to some extent.) Much less contentious than his friend Ezra Pound, he became the dean of English poets and English critics during his lifetime. I highly recommend Stephen Spender's book *T.S. Eliot*. (Spender, like Auden, migrated westward from the UK to the USA.)

Readers of Robert Anton Wilson will find an understanding of Eliot very useful in helping to understand Eliot's friends and contemporaries James Joyce and Uncle Ezra. Eliot wrote some interesting things about Joyce and he dedicated "The Waste Land" to "il miglior fabro, Ezra Pound." This dedication comes from a reference to troubadour Arnaut Daniel in Dante's *Purgatorio*. It means "the better craftsman."

Ezra wrote a moving obituary for Eliot, included in his *Selected Prose*. It ends, "READ HIM."

Elvis needs boats. An explanation for the Bermuda Triangle mystery offered by songwriter Mojo Nixon in his song "Elvis Is Everywhere." Bob might rewrite the title in E-prime as "Elvis Seems Everywhere." Or, he might relate it to the Atlantean pyramid beneath the Bermuda triangle in *Illuminatus!*

Emmanuel. An angel whose name means the presence of God. Abraham Orfali calls on him on page 125 of *The Earth Will Shake*.

Erickson, Milton H. (1901–1980). Innovative hypnotherapist who influenced both Richard Bandler, inventor of Neurolinguistic Programming, and Ernest Rossi, author of *The Psychobiology of Mind Body Healing*. Both Bandler and Rossi have greatly influenced Wilson.

Erigina, John Scotus (c. 810–c. 877). A medieval mystic philosopher who wrote, *"Qui sunt, omnia sunt."* ("All things that are, are lights.") A major influence on Ezra Pound, and through him on Dr. Wilson. He also inspired the name of Bob Shea's *All Things Are Lights*.

Eris. Greek goddess of chaos and confusion. Roman form Discordia. Worshipped by the Paratheometamystichood of Eris Esoteric (P.O.E.E.). She rolled the golden apple into a wedding feast leading to the Trojan War, according to legend. The worship of Eris plays a central role in *Illuminatus!*

Everett-Wheeler-Graham model. See **Wheeler, John A.**

Ewige Blumenkraft! "Hail flower power" in German. ("Say it with flowerpots.") (*Leave it to Psmith*, P.G. Wodehouse.) A supposed motto of the Bavarian Illuminati. This becomes "Earwicker, Bloom and Craft" to George Dorn's ear (*Illuminatus!*, pg. 74). Earwicker refers to Humphrey Chimpden Earwicker, the dreamer of *Finnegans Wake*, Bloom refers to Molly and Leopold Bloom in Joyce's *Ulysses*, as well as to blooming flowers, and craft refers both to freemasonry and witchcraft.

After winning on *Jeopardy* on December 1, 1999 C.E., (1 Zeus, 79 p.s.U.) I came in second on December 2 (Zeus 2), missing the Final Jeopardy answer about which city the Romans founded and whose name comes from the Latin for "to blossom." My mind raced to Bloom, hence Bloomsbury, a part of London. Although the Romans did found London, I knew I didn't have the correct question. Alas, I didn't think of Florence. However, coming in second I won the computer on which I write this book. Ewige Bloomencraft!

Faulkner, William (1897–1962). Nobel prize winning novelist. Sheriff Cartwright of Mad Dog, Texas, "seemed immensely pleased with his own oratorical style, like one of Faulkner's characters. (*Illuminatus!*, pg. 31)

Wilson wrote a positive review of Joel Williamson's *William Faulkner and Southern History* in *Trajectories* #16/17, pg. 30, in which Wilson wrote, "In the 21st Century, I suspect, Faulkner will seem even more important than he did in his own time, or in ours, because racism remains the one great unsolved problem of humanity and no writer of genius has ever looked into that unpleasant subject as closely and painfully as Faulkner did, or expressed not just the social injustice but the human shame of it with so much compassionate insight into both the racists and their victims." I think perhaps Ishmael Reed and John A. Williams, who both seem to me writers of genius, have looked into racism even more closely than Faulkner. I say read all three and reach your own conclusions.

The reading list at rawilson.com includes Faulkner's *Go Down, Moses*, which Wilson calls "perhaps his funniest, certainly his saddest and probably his most eloquent book." (*Trajectories* #16/17, pg. 30)

The poet Donald Hall tells of "The time they cleaned out his [Faulkner's] office after he had left Warner Brothers, and in his desk found only an empty bottle and a sheet of yellow foolscap on which he had written, five hundred times, 'Boy meets girl'" (*The Oxford Book of American Literary Anecdotes*, pg. 266).

FDA. U.S. Food and Drug Administration. *Everything Is Under Control* discusses their attempts to suppress alternative health companies.

Fernando Po. Island off the coast of Equatorial Guinea in Africa. It plays a role in *Illuminatus!*, which calls it Fernando Poo, the last outcropping of the lost continent of Atlantis. Sir Richard Burton wrote a book called *From Liverpool to Fernando Po*, but it doesn't have any yellow submarines in it.

Finn, Huck. At the end of Mark Twain's novel, *Huckleberry Finn,* Huck decides to "light out for the territory ahead of the rest," to prevent Aunt Sally from "sivilizing" him. Tim Leary considered this his favorite book, and he always saw himself "lighting out for the territory." Wilson called his tribute to Tim after Tim's death "Lighting Out for the Territory" (*Trajectories* #16/17, pg. 3).

Also Huck plays a major role in *Finnegans Wake* (Finnagain). The Mississippi (Mrs. Liffey) parallels the river Liffey in Ireland. Also Twain's wife Livy parallels HCE's wife Anna Livia, as well as the Roman Livia, a.k.a. Augusta. (Through an error, Joyce had the feminine middle name Augusta instead of Augustus.) Also *Finnegans Wake* includes Marcus Lyons, who corresponds with Mark the Evangelist and the lion in the vision of Ezekiel, and King Mark from the Tristan legend, both of whom correspond with "Mark the Twy."

Finnegans Wake. Novel by James Joyce. Joyce wrote it after having completed *Ulysses*. In *Finnegans Wake* Joyce combines many words and fragments of words to provide multiple layers of meaning. In Lewis Carroll's *Through the Looking Glass and What She Found There* Humpty Dumpty calls the elision of words "portmanteau" words. Martin Gardner in *The Annotated Alice* observes that *Finnegans Wake* contains these words by the thousands. For example, page 143 in the riddle chapter of the *Wake* contains the phrase "camelot prince of dinmurk." This phrase appears in the context of explaining the experience of dreaming, showing how different literary and mythical figures can blend in the dream world. Here Joyce parallels the Arthurian legends of Camelot with Shakespeare's *Hamlet*. One can see parallels between the infidelity between Guinivere and Lancelot and the possible infidelity between Gertrude and her dead husband's brother, or with the King Mark, Tristan and Isolde triangle. The "portmanteau" expression "dinmurk" suggests dim and murky, for the nighttime dream world of the *Wake*, as well as the synesthesia of din and murky, sound and sight. The din suggests the sound of thunder that terrifies the dreamer in the *Wake*, as well as philosopher Giambattista Vico's theory of thunder as the origin of religion. Similarly, in Wilson's *The Homing Pigeons* a passage from a dream of a scientist researching sexuality contains the line "Gothin haven, annette colp us!" (*The Homing Pigeons*, pg. 15) This combines "God in heaven" with the adult film actress Annette Haven, as well as suggesting Anna Livia Plurabella, the goddess of *Finnegans Wake* and the French *cul*. Wilson's *The Universe Next Door* has a character repeating the mantra "Om mane padme hum," which mutates into "O how money makes me hum" and then to "Oh mommie take me home." (*Universe Next Door*, pp. 202–203)

In *Prometheus Rising* Wilson mentions participating in a *Finnegans Wake* study group. When I read that in 1985 C.E., it inspired me to start a *Finnegans Wake* study group in Tempe, AZ. At the time I couldn't make head nor tail out of the book. Aided by wonderful Arizona Joyceans like Steve Williams and Frank Dracman, we gathered together on Thursdays for the next twelve and a half years to understand and misunderstand this book.

Flegenheimer, Arthur (a.k.a. Dutch Schultz) (1902–1935). A mobster who when shot many times did not die right away, but rather spoke some remarkable words to a police stenographer. This inspired William S. Burroughs' *Last Words of Dutch Schultz* and played a major role in *Illuminatus!*

Fleming, Ian (1908–1964). Author of *Chitty Chitty, Bang Bang* and the James Bond books. Born May 28 (the same as me). Wilson and Shea satirize Bond as Agent 00005 in *Illuminatus!*

One can see the film *The Rock* as a deconstruction of the Bond reality-tunnel, even bringing in the Kennedy assassination and aliens in Roswell. See **Assassins.**

Fnord. In the novel *Illuminatus!* the word "fnord" causes great anxiety to most Americans when they read it. They learn in the early years of elementary school not to consciously see the word, to suppress seeing it, but they still feel the anxiety. News stories tend to contain many fnords, while advertisements contain none, encouraging Americans to spend and spend to relieve their anxieties. "Seeing the fnords" serves as a major breakthrough for characters in the novel attempting to gain control of their own nervous systems.

Frawley, William (1887–1966). Actor who played Fred Mertz on "I Love Lucy." (Wilson has written about the Church of Fred Mertz Bodhisattva.) Fraley also played an advisor to the judge in *The Miracle on 34th Street*. In this movie a handsome man with a pipe (Santa's lawyer) realizes the importance of sales and publicity. This film reveals the secret origin of the Church of the Sub-Genius. Wilson hinted at this when he taught the seminar "Modernism and Sales, or will the real Leopold Bloom please stand up?" at Miskatonic University. (An accountant named Leo Bloom appeared in Mel Brooks's masterpiece *The Producers.*)

In *The Miracle on 34th St.*, the proto-Bob Dobbs tries to get the court to recognize a man as the real Santa Claus. This playing with the notion of "real" versus fake shows up over and over again in Wilson's work. Wilson examines this most closely in his discussion of Orson Welles' film *F for Fake*.

Frankenstein, Johann Dippel von. A character in the *Historical Illuminatus Chronicles*. Victor von Frankenstein in Mary Shelley's novel attended the University of Ingolstadt. Wilson once told me that her husband Percy encouraged her to include that detail because of his interest in Adam Weishaupt, founder of the Bavarian Illuminati, who taught canon law there.

Freud, Sigmund (1856–1939). Father of modern psychology. He saw the human personality developing through oral, anal, latency and phallic periods, which Wilson associates with the first four systems/circuits of Leary's eight system/circuit model (*Prometheus Rising,* pg. 126).

Fuller, R. Buckminster (1895–1983). Architect, mathematician, poet, economist, etc. A pivotal influence on Wilson. Bucky, as he liked people to call him, felt we could "advantage all without disadvantaging any." Wilson interviewed Bucky in *Right Where*

You Are Sitting Now, and Bucky has influenced all of Bob's books. Wilson included Bucky's *Critical Path* on the rawilson.com reading list.

FUCK-UP. Hagbard Celine's computer in *Illuminatus!*

G. The letter G appears inside a compass on the outside of Masonic temples. Bob theorizes about the Masonic G in his *Historical Illuminati Chronicles.* Perhaps it stands for Godzilla, leader of the dinosaurs who rule the hollow earth. Note that Raymond Burr starred in the first Godzilla film, and he later starred in the TV show *Perry MASON.* Perry of course relates to Parsival, the pure fool, and to both Percy Blakeney, the Scarlet Pimpernel, and Percy Shelley, who wrote in *Prometheus Unbound*:

> To suffer woes which Hope thinks infinite;
> To forgive wrongs darker than death or night;
> To defy Power, which seems omnipotent;
> To love, and bear; to hope till Hope creates
> From its own wreck the thing it contemplates;
> Neither to change, nor falter, nor repent;
> This, like thy glory, Titan, is to be
> Good, great and joyous, beautiful and free;
> This is alone Life, Joy, Empire, and Victory.

I look forward to the film *Godzilla vs. Leviathan.*

George, Henry (1839–1897). An economist who influenced Wilson. George suggested that the government own all the land and act as the only landlord.

Gesell, Silvio (1862–1930). A radical economist who suggested a currency which declined in value over time to discourage the hoarding of money. He greatly influence both Ezra Pound and Robert Anton Wilson. Wilson included his *The Natural Economic Order* on the rawilson.com reading list.

Gibson, William (1948–). Author of a bunch of great novels (*Neuromancer,* et al.), often considered "the father of cyberpunk." Timothy Leary loved Gibson's work and interviewed him in *Chaos and Cyberculture*. Gibson has influenced Wilson through Leary.

Ginsberg, Allen (1926–1997). A poet, one of the original "beats," along with William S. Burroughs, Jack Kerouac and Neal Cassidy. Wilson wrote an article about Ginsberg in *Coincidance*, and Ginsberg makes a cameo at the 1968 C.E. Democratic Convention in *Illuminatus!*

I love the story about Allen visiting Ezra Pound in Italy in 1969 C.E. Ezra, age 83, had rarely spoken for the previous seven years, and he sat in silence as Allen played *Sgt. Pepper's Lonely Hearts Club Band*, Bob Dylan and Donovan, etc., for him. Pound remained silent, and Allen asked Ezra mistress Olga Rudge whether he liked the music. She replied, "If he didn't like it, he'd leave." Wilson tells about talking about this meeting with Ginsberg and Burroughs on page 25 of *TSOG*.

Gnosticism. A religion, or group of religions, based on "knowledge" of God (from the Greek "gnosis": knowledge). Scholars disagree about the dates of its origin; some, like Gershom Scholem, seeing it originating before Jesus, others see it beginning as late as 100 C.E. Scholem thought the Kabbalah arose from a revival of Jewish Gnostism in Medieval Provence and Spain. Some of the Illuminati Memos in *Illuminatus!* trace the Illuminati back to gnosticism.

Golding, Arthur (c. 1536–c. 1605). Elizabethan translator of the Latin poet Ovid's *Metamorphosis*. Ezra Pound called Golding's *Metamorphosis* the most beautiful book in English. Shakespeare refers to Ovid more than to any other poet, often using Golding's translation. Shakespeare knew "little Latin and less Greek" according to his friend Ben Jonson. Wilson included Ovid in his list of "Brain Books" in "Trajectories."

Golding, William Gerald (1911–1993). Author of *Lord of the Flies*. He suggested the name Gaia to his neighbor, James Lovelock, to describe the interlocking systems of life (and matter) on our planet. Leary associated Lovelock and Margulis' Gaia Theory with the neurogenetic circuit/ system, which Wilson calls the morphogenetic system/circuit in *Quantum Psychology*.

Goodman, Rebecca. Named after *Rebecca of Sunnybrook Farm*. A character in *Illuminatus!*, a former drug addict and anthropology student married to the much older police-critter, Saul Goodman.

Goodman, Saul. A character in *Illuminatus!*, a police-critter married to the much younger Rebecca. His investigation of the *Confrontation* magazine explosion with Barney Muldoon leads to radical changes in his life, as well as giving him the opportunity to save the world from the Illuminati. Well, *an* Illuminati. Really. If you haven't read *Illuminatus!* yet, I highly recommend it. It might change your life. It sure changed mine.

Graves, Robert Ranke (1895–1985) . Author of *The White Goddess*, *I, Claudius*, *The Black Goddess*, etc. *The White Goddess* had a huge impact on Wilson. In turning Marilyn Monroe into Eris in *Illuminatus!*, Hagbard Celine has her read horse-doctor's doses of Graves. (I think Wilson and Shea meant Marilyn Monroe—perhaps they meant another famous actress.) Graves also wrote the introduction to Idries Shah's *The Sufis*. Hugh Kenner has written slighting comments about Graves' novels, but I highly recommend *I, Claudius* and *Claudius the God*, as well as the BBC version available on VHS and DVD.

The introduction to Graves' *Love Poems* has an interesting discussion of the difference between poets and others. Graves writes that most people in our modern world have lost an intimate connection with the physical world. They come closest during adolescence when they first fall in love, and the connection between the physical, emotional, intellectual, sexual, etc., worlds come together. Most people put "childish things" behind them, as St. Paul wrote, and grow out of that phase of ecstatic fumbling and oneness. Poets never grow out of that. I realized that at the Ezra Pound centennial at the University of Maine, Orono, in 1985 C.E. 59-year-old poets Allen Ginsberg and Robert Creeley looked uncomfortable sitting still on the podium, out of place in dress clothing. They talked inappropriately about politics and personal subjects during scholarly discussions. In short, they hadn't put aside childish things. However, the Ph.D.'s from around the world, many of them twenty years younger than the poets, seemed much more "adult," at home in their professional attire, sitting still and paying attention where appropriate, never breaching decorum.

(Note: Graves, like Pound and Eliot, emphasized the importance of learning Latin for aspiring poets.)

Grok. The Martian word for "drink," "love," "hate," etc., in Robert Heinlein's *Stranger in a Strange Land*. Hagbard Celine uses it repeatedly on page 399 of *Illuminatus!* I first encountered this word in the bumper sticker "I GROK SPOCK."

Harris, Thomas (1940–). 1) Author of *Black Sunday*, *Red Dragon*, *Silence of the Lambs* and *Hannibal*. Wilson has expressed great enthusiasm for the last three books, all of which deal with Hannibal Lecter.

2) A General Thomas M. Harris (1817–1906) wrote *Rome's Responsibility for the Assassination of Abraham Lincoln* according to pg. 165 of *Illuminatus!*.

Heinlein, Robert Anson (1907–1988). Bob Wilson once told me he considered Heinlein the first science fiction author to include sociology in his work. Heinlein wrote such novels as *The Moon Is a Harsh Mistress*, *Stranger in a Strange Land* and *Starship Troopers*, etc. He also wrote a number of short stories and novels which formed a future history. These tales of space migration and life extension influenced both Wilson and Timothy Leary.

Heisenberg, Werner (1901–1976). A quantum physicist, famous for his "Uncertainty Principle," which proved that the more we know about the velocity of a particle, the less we know about its position, and vice versa. This uncertainty seemed to some traditional physicists totally foreign to the nineteenth century idea of science. Wilson discusses some of Heisenberg's theories in *Cosmic Trigger I*.

Herbert, Nick (1937–). A physicist and member—along with Wilson, Jack Sarfatti, Saul-Paul Sirac and Fred Alan Woolf, etc.—of the Physics-Consciousness Research Group in Berkeley in the 1970's C.E. He has written a number of non-technical books on quantum mechanics, including *Quantum Reality*, which Wilson has mentioned and recommended.

Hesse, Herman (1877–1962). A German poet and novelist who greatly influenced Timothy Leary and the 1960's in general. The band Steppenwolf took their name from one of Hesse's novels. Leary wrote essays on Hesse in early works like *The Politics of Ecstasy* and one of his last books, *Chaos and Cyberculture*. (Wilson includes *Chaos and Cyberculture* in his list of recommended reading at rawilson.com.) Leary particularly liked the image of the Glass Bead game from Hesse's *Magister Ludi*, which appears over and over again in Leary's writing. Hesse's Glass Bead Game seems like a very complex game-meditation-artform, which Leary found a powerful model for our changing lives in the 20th and 21st centuries.

Higgins, George Vincent (1939–1999). One of Bob's favorite writers, author of *The Friends of Eddie Coyle*, *The Friends of Richard Nixon*, and a terrific book on the Boston Red Sox, etc. Many of his books have a Boston locale and give a great picture of the politics of the city.

Hoffman, Albert (1906–). A Swiss chemist who accidentally discovered LSD in 1943 C.E. Wilson frequently mentions Hoffman and his most famous discovery.

Hubbard, Barbara Marx (1929–). A futurist whom Bob discusses in *Right Where You Are Sitting Now*. Commenting on her bubbly enthusiasm, anthropologist Margaret Mead once told her, "Barbara, you've got to stop talking that way. People will *stop worrying*." (Wilson *Right Where You Are Sitting Now*, pg. 37)

Hyatt, Christopher S. (1943–). An author who writes about transforming the human nervous system. Bob has written the introduction for a number of Dr. Hyatt's books, and particularly recommended *Undoing Yourself With Energizing Meditation* in *Prometheus Rising*.

Illuminati. Perhaps an organization of the imagination. Most reference books say that Adam Weishaupt founded the Bavarian Illuminati on May 1, 1776. *Illuminatus!*, in a series of memos, gives a number of alternative histories which trace the Illuminati much further back in history. Some folks think the Illuminati still exist. (See also the **Infomercial** chapter.)

Info-Space. The idea that information corresponds with unpredictability has greatly influenced Wilson. This accounts for his own writing style, as well as for his passion for the unpredictable, information-rich writings of Ezra Pound, James Joyce, Aleister Crowley, Timothy Leary, etc., as well as the music of Beethoven, Mahler and Bach, etc. One can view any text as an information space, from the delightful simplicity of Dr. Seuss' *Green Eggs and Ham*, to the labyrinthine intricacies of Joyce's *Finnegans Wake*. One can view the life work of a poet as an info-space, and one can view the internet as an every growing and mutating meta-info-space.

The highly intertextual nature of Wilson's writing reveals the links between info-spaces, and also how we each construct our own info-spaces within our heads. We each have our own version of this book and every other text we have encountered and endured, and all of these constructed info-spaces blend in the meta-info-spaces of each of our individual minds. Whenever we encounter a new text, its info-space merges, at least briefly, with the meta-info-space of our mind-body in a sort of poetic yoga. New ideas sometimes blossom from these unions.

Ingolstadt. The town in Bavaria where Adam Weishaupt founded the Illuminati. I visited Ingolstadt on July 23–24, 1985 C.E. and noted an eye in the triangle on the side of an apartment building, rosy crosses from the eighteenth century in a graveyard, and an eye of Horus in a poster for an exhibit on Egyptian medicine at the medical museum. Ingolstadt and Weishaupt frequently show up in Wilson's fiction.

Ireland. Island to the west of England, birthplace of James Joyce, W.B. Yeats, James Stephens, Jonathan Swift, Oscar Wilde, Samuel Beckett, etc. Arlen and Bob Wilson moved to Dublin, Ireland, in 1982 C.E. after the election of Ronald Reagan in the U.S. Both Arlen and Bob wanted to learn more about their Irish heritages, and Wilson included a ton of Irish material in his books composed there, especially *The Widow's Son*.

Ishtar. The Babylonian goddess of love. Carl Jung would associate her with fellow goddesses Isis, Aphrodite, Astarte, Venus and Erzulie, etc. Wilson tells a parable about Ishtar on page 19 of *Cosmic Trigger I*. Wilson renamed his *Book of the Breast* as

Ishtar Rising. Some people consider the movie *Ishtar* the worst movie ever made. The film deals with two lousy songwriters manipulated by the C.I.A. in North Africa. One of their songs, "Dangerous Business," contains the lines:

Telling the truth can be dangerous business.
Honest and popular don't go hand in hand.
It's hard to admit that you play the accordion
if you're a singer in a rock and roll band.

Isis. Egyptian goddess who married her brother Osiris. They had a son, Horus. After Set murdered Osiris, dismembered his body and scattered the pieces, Isis gathered all the scattered pieces and performed "the Black Rite" (*Cosmic Trigger I,* pg. 221) to bring him back to life. Robert Temple in *The Sirius Connection* demonstrated that the image of Isis with a star above her and one beneath serves as a symbol of the double star system of Sirius (*ibid.,* pg. 187).

Jackson, Peter. An editor at *Confrontation* magazine in *Illuminatus!*

Jarry, Alfred (1873–1907). A presurrealist French writer. His concept of "pata-physics" influenced Wilson's "pata-psychology" in works like *The Widow's Son.*

Johnson, Samuel (1709–1784). Author of the first dictionary in English. Interestingly, he wrote about the importance of the writer's having a high writing location to look out at the city for perspective. Wilson wrote about looking out of his window at the city of Berkeley for perspective. Johnson lived in a narrow, four-story house in London (now a Samuel Johnson museum) very similar to Dante's narrow four-story home in Florence (now a Dante museum). Perhaps one or more of Bob's residences will become a museum in the future

Joyce, James (1882–1941). A major influence of Wilson, author of *Finnegans Wake*, *Ulysses*, *A Portrait of the Artist as a Young Man*, *Dubliners*, etc. Many people, including myself, find Joyce very challenging at first. To reduce this challenge a bit, I recommend reading Wilson's *Masks of the Illuminati* and Joyce's children's book *The Cat and the Devil* (taken from a letter to his grandson).

In *Prometheus Rising* Wilson mentions participating in a *Finnegans Wake* study group. At the time I read that (1985 C.E.), I had had little success in reading the *Wake*. Frank Dracman and I then formed the Finnegans Wake Decoding Society, and I have found myself enjoying the *Wake* more and more ever since. Many others Finned with us over the years, and painter/musician Steve Williams formed an essential addition in 1989 C.E. We renamed the group Finnegans Isle on the day of the Energetic Harmonic Convergence (August 16, 1987 C.E., the tenth anniversary of Elvis' death), when I realized the isomorphism between the seven castaways on "Gilligan's Isle" and the seven dancing girls in *Finnegans Wake*, which also correspond with the seven days of the week, the seven planets in Medieval astrology and Snow White's seven dwarves. Of course the initials of the Energetic Harmonic Convergence reminded me of the H.C.E.'s that recur throughout *Finnegans Wake*.

Jung, Carl (1875–1961). Famous psychiatrist and psychologist, and a major influence on Wilson. His concepts of the archetype, the collective unconscious and synchronicity frequently show up in Wilson's writings. Jung posited that the unconscious does not just include personal material pertaining to guilt and repression as Freud suggested. Jung found that some material showed up in many people's dreams and seemed to come from a collective unconscious, a level beneath the personal unconscious explored by Freud. Jung found this collective unconscious inhabited by archetypes—recurring images which showed up with slight variations in a wide variety of times and places. One might consider the Great Goddess one such archetype, which appears in various forms as Anna Livia Plurabella in *Finnegans Wake*, the virgin Mary, Isis, Aphrodite, Ishtar, Astarte, etc.

Jury Nullification. The idea, which goes back to the Magna Carta, that the jury has the right, duty and obligation to judge the law as well as the facts of the case. If the juror considers the law unjust, they have the right to acquit, according to this tradition. Wilson discusses this in *Chaos and Beyond* and in the "Fully

Informed Jury Amendment" entry in *Everything is Under Control.* See also **Constitutional Propaganda.**

Kabbalah. The scholar Gershom Scholem defines kabbalah as "the traditional and most commonly used term for the esoteric teachings of Judaism and for Jewish mysticism, especially the forms which it assumed in the Middle Ages from the 12th century onward" (Scholem pg. 3). These teachings greatly influenced European occultism, including the Golden Dawn and its members such as Aleister Crowley, William Butler Yeats and Israel Regardie. Crowley and Regardie's writings on the kabbalah greatly influenced Robert Anton Wilson. See **Appendix Samekh** for a kabbalistic analysis of Wilson and Shea's novel *Illuminatus!*

Kenner, Hugh (1923–). A major critic of the modernist period. His books on Pound and Joyce have greatly influenced Wilson. He and Marshall McLuhan visited Pound in St. Elizabeth's Hospital for the Criminally Insane. Wilson frequently mentions Kenner's books on Pound and Joyce.

Kierkegaard, Søren (1813–1855). A Christian existential philosopher whom Wilson discusses in *Quantum Psychology.* He may or may not have influenced Nietzsche.

King, Francis (?–). A historian of the occult, who has written about Aleister Crowley, tantra, the Golden Dawn, etc. Wilson refers respectfully to King's writings.

Knights Templar. A medieval order of warrior monks. The Pope disbanded the order in 1307 (except in Spain and Portugal) and executed the leader Jacques de Molay. Many conspiracy theorists trace more recent secret societies back to the Knights Templar. Wilson refers to them in many of his books. A few years ago I saw a car with a bunch of Masonic bumperstickers including one which said "De Molay Is O.K."

Korzybski, Alfred (1879–1950). Author of *Science and Sanity* and founder of General Semantics. Korzybski asked himself the question, "What differentiates humanity from the other animals?" He came up with the answer that humanity communicates over generations, which he called time-binding in his *Manhood* *of Humanity* in 1919. He went on to create General Semantics with his *Science and Sanity* in 1933, a major influence on Wilson. Korzybski saw how the mathematical language of science closely resembles the structure of the physical world, and he created General Semantics to help people use language in ways which more closely resembled the methods of the mathematical sciences. He hoped this would lead them to happier and healthier lives. Korzybski's work influenced Buckminster Fuller, Robert Heinlein, William S. Burroughs, Israel Regardie, Richard Bandler (creator of NLP) and others. Korzybski has influenced all of Wilson's books, particularly *Quantum Psychology*.

Kubrick, Stanley (1928–1999). Film director. Wilson has a piece about Kubrick's *Barry Lyndon* in *The Illuminati Papers*. The expression "purity of essence/peace on earth" from *Dr. Strangelove* plays a role in *The Universe Next Door*. I teeter back and forth between naming Kubrick or Welles my favorite director. In my more Wilsonian moods I favor Orson; today I favor Stanley.

Landlords. A recurring leitmotif in Wilson's works. Sigismundo Celine recalls a story "everyone had heard about the landlord who was particularly cruel, monstrous even for Sicily." (*The Earth Will Shake*, pg. 200) *Quantum Psychology* asks why TV has so many shows about cops and so few about landlords, and how our perceived reality would change if TV had as many shows about landlords as it now does about cops. (*12 Adam St*? *Hill Street Vacancy Blues*? *NYC21 Blues*? *MacMillan and Wife Escrow*?) *The Homing Pigeons* includes the Stephenites, who accept any consensual sexual behavior, but consider owning slum property a very serious sin.

Latimer, Jonathan (1906–1983). Author of hardboiled screwball comedies along the lines of Dashiell Hammett's *The Thin Man*. Detective Bob Crane appears in five of Latimer's novels, always solving the crime despite generally seeming drunk or hung over. Wilson mentions Latimer in *The Homing Pigeons*.

Law and Order. Wilson's all time favorite TV show; also one side of the core duality of Discordianism.

Leiber, Fritz (1910–1992). A writer of horror, fantasy and science fiction, and a correspondent of H.P. Lovecraft's. Wilson readers might enjoy his *Our Lady of Darkness*, a magnificent tale of San Francisco and the occult power of books. The book mixes Wilsonesque love of Lovecraft and a fascination with secret societies.

Leif Erickson. A Viking explorer; also the name of Hagbard Celine's yellow submarine in *Illuminatus!*

Leviathan. A gigantic one celled organism in *Illuminatus!* It falls in love with the super-computer FUCK-UP. Ain't love grand?

Lewis, Sinclair (1885–1951). Author of *It Can't Happen Here*. George Dorn keeps his pot in a hollowed out copy of this book. (*Illuminatus!*, pg. 30)

Logic. "The study of the principals of reasoning," according to my *American Heritage Dictionary*. Standard Aristotelian logic has only two values: true/false also designated yes/no or 1/0. Wilson has written a great deal about alternative logical systems which allow for more values, like the three-valued yes-no-maybe system and Korzybski's infinite-valued system, which yields probabilistic values from 100% (absolute certainty) to 0% (absolute impossibility). Wilson suggest that most real life situations call for neither absolute certainty nor absolute impossibility.

For instance, maybe you'll love all of this book, maybe you won't. I wouldn't bet on either extreme, but would rather guess that you will enjoy less than 100% of it. Wilson likens Aristotelian two-valued logic to seeing in black and white, and Korzybskian infinite-valued logic to seeing in color.

Lovecraft, H.P. (1890–1937) Novelist and a character in *Illuminatus!* For more about him check out Dan Clore's Necronomicon Webpage. Lovecraft's supernatural horror greatly influenced Wilson, as well as Stephen King, Fritz Leiber and others.

L.s.d. Pounds, shillings, pence: the British monetary system. This tends to confuse some modern readers of Joyce. When a character in a Joyce novel says they only care about L.s.d., they mean money not d-lysergic acid diethylamide, the hallucinogen discovered by Albert Hoffman in 1943 C.E.

LSD. A hallucinogen, d-lysergic acid diethylamide. Wilson has written extensively about this drug and its effects.

Luttwak, Edward (1942–). Author of *Coup d'Etat: A Practical Handbook*, which Captain Ernesto Tequila y Mota used to guide him in his take-over of the island of Fernando Poo in *Illuminatus!* (pg. 18).

Machen, Arthur (1863–1947). A horror writer who influenced both H.P. Lovecraft and Wilson. Wilson makes use of Machen's book *The Great God Pan* in *Masks of the Illuminati.*

Machiavelli, Niccolò (1469-1527). Italian historian and philosopher, author of *The Prince*, etc. Machiavelli suggested that people in government sometimes act in their own self interest rather than looking out for the best interests of society as a whole. Wilson included the essay "Ecology, Malthus and Machiavelli" in his collection *Right Where You Are Sitting Now.*

Magick. Aleister Crowley defines "magick" as "the Science and Art of causing Change to occur in conformity with Will" (Crowley, *Magick in Theory and Practice* pg. XII). Crowley added the "k" to the spelling to differentiate "magick" from stage magic. Aleister Crowley greatly influenced Robert Anton Wilson's writing, and Wilson even made Crowley a major character in *Masks of the Illuminati.*

Malaclypse the Elder. A holy man of sorts from *Illuminatus!* He achieved transcendental illumination (which includes immortality) from the energy released from a mass murder he observed in ancient Greece. He went on to teach the disciples Bingo after the Crucifixion.

Malatesta, Sigismondo (1417–1468). A controversial Renaissance figure, called, variously, a tyrant, a heretic and a patron of the arts, etc. Ezra Pound devoted Cantos VIII–XI to Sigismondo. Sigismondo preferred the company of philosophers and artists to that of aristocrats. He frequently got in trouble with the Pope (who eventually canonized him to hell), and he would work as a general for the Papal States try to resolve those conflicts. Even while leading a military campaign, his letters find him concerned with the construction of a temple to St. Francis. Some contemporaries, however, considered this temple more pagan than Christian. He hired some of the greatest artists of the day, including Piero Della Francesca and the sculptor Duccio, to work on the Tempio. Sigismondo even brought the ashes of the neo-pagan philosopher Gemesthon Plethon from Greece to put into the Tempio.

In the *Historical Illuminati* books, Wilson has the character Sigismundo Celine descended from Sigismondo Malatesta, and Wilson has his Sigismundo visit the Tempio of his ancestor. For some cool photos of the Tempio Malatesta, check out english.uiuc.edu/maps/poets/m_r/pound/tempio.htm.

Malik, Joe. One of the main characters in *Illuminatus!* Simon Moon and others lead him from a disappointment with conventional liberalism into the worlds of chaos, black masses and the dawning of the Age of Bavaria.

Joe also shows up in various guises (and various genders) in *Schrödinger's Cat.*

Mama Sutra. A tarot reader in *Illuminatus!*

Manicheans. Followers of the syncretic, dualistic religious philosophy taught by the Persian prophet Manes, combining elements of Zoroastrian, Christian, and Gnostic thought and opposed by the imperial Roman government, Neo-Platonist philosophers, and orthodox Christians. The philosophy divides the world between good and evil principles or regards matter as intrinsically evil and mind as intrinsically good. Ezra Pound, a major influence on Wilson, wrote that he did not consider Scotus Erigena a Manichean, despite Erigena's condemnation as such after his death.

Mao Tu Tsi. A character in *Illuminatus!* who aids in the illumination of Joe Malik.

***Marat/Sade** (Persecution and Assassinations of Jean-Paul Marat as Performed by the Inmates of the Asylum at Charenton Under the Direction of the Marquis de Sade, The)* 1966. The play (and film) influenced Wilson. See "Thirteen Choruses for the Divine Marquis" in *Coincidance*. It also influenced *Wilhelm Reich in Hell*.

Marijuana (aka Cannabis). Just say no, thank you. Bob has written extensively about this illegal drug, especially in *Sex, Drugs and Magick*.

Mavis. A character in *Illuminatus!* who seems an aspect of the goddess Eris, or of the movie star whom Hagbard helped brainwash into becoming Eris or into thinking she had become Eris. Mavis and Stella seem two mirror aspects of Eris, much as Joyce divides Isis into "Is" and "Si" ("Yes!") aspects in *Finnegans Wake*, and Alice exists both in our world and *Through the Looking Glass*. See also **Stella**.

MC-5. A Detroit based rock band that recorded "Kick Out the Jams," a song mentioned many times in *Illuminatus!* Wilson mentions meeting a member of the band in *TSOG*.

Mermaid. One form of the Babylonian goddess Ishtar, whom Wilson discusses in *Ishtar Rising* and *Cosmic Trigger I*.

Metanoia. At a talk in L.A. in 1988 C.E. Bob defined metanoia as the opposite of paranoia; i.e., one can define metanoia as the model that Universe conspires to help you. One might see Snoopy/Joe Cool (cousin to Finn McCool) as saying "Get Metanoia!" when he says, "Get Met!" A message from the Dog Star in the ads for Metropolitan Life, the insurance company whose four M symbol resembles the four E diagram from *Finnegans Wake*.

Bucky Fuller traces a lot of trouble with our economic system back to Renaissance insurance for sea trips in his book, *Grunch of Giants*. The risks associated with Renaissance ocean commerce provide the background for Shakespeare's *Merchant of Venice*. I love the analysis of that play in Leslie Fiedler's *The Stranger in Shakespeare*.

Miskatonic Messalina. What Clark Kent calls Doris Horus. (*Illuminatus!*, pg. 606) Lovecraft invented Miskatonic University in his horror stories, and Wilson and Shea use it as a local in *Illuminatus!* Messalina, wife of the Roman Emperor Claudius, slept with many, many men, even having a competition with the head of the Roman prostitute's guild to see who could have sex with the most men in a night. Messalina won. See Robert Graves' *Claudius the God*, sequel to *I, Claudius*. The BBC miniseries includes elements of both novels, including the story of Messalina and Claudius.

Modern Jazz Quartet. Ensemble composed of John Lewis, piano, Milt Jackson, vibraharp, Percy Heath, bass and Connie Kay, drums. (Originally Kenny Clarke played drums for them.) Wilson first smoked marijuana in the bathroom at a New York nightclub during an MJQ performance. You might listen to their album *Pyramid* while reading Wilson and Shea's *The Eye in the Pyramid*.

> ("It all depends if the fool has wisdom enough to do it."
> "Quiet, idiot—they can hear us!")

Moon, Simon. A major character in both *Illuminatus!* and *Schrödinger's Cat*. The son of two anarchists, a pacifist mother and a more activist father, Simon becomes an adept of tantra and other Erisian mysteries. He later helps illuminate Joe Malik. In *Schrödinger's Cat* he becomes a gay computer programmer.

Morning Sky, Robert (?–). I heard him at the Prophets Conference in 1997 C.E. on a panel with Bob Wilson. Morning Sky calls himself a "Rebel Apache Warrior" (note the perhaps unintended acronym, RAW). His non-followers (he says he doesn't have followers) wear t-shirts that say "Rebel Apache Warrior." I found it ironic that people calling themselves rebels wore matching t-shirts. Wilson writes about Morning Sky's theories of language, aliens and "primitive" peoples in *Everything Is Under Control*.

Mota, Captain Ernesto Tequila y. The leader of the revolution on Fernando Poo in *Illuminatus!*

Mozart, Wolfgang Amadeus (1756–1791). Sigismundo Celine befriends the nine-year-old Wolfgang and calls him the Monster. Mozart's *Die Zauberfluete* (*The Magic Flute*) deals with Masonic themes.

When I visited Ingolstadt on July 23, 1985, my train from Munich to Ingolstadt passed Dachau. I decided to visit the concentration camp there the next day. I did, and it left me feeling despair about the human condition. I wandered around Munich and saw that a theater had Ingmar Bergman's film of *The Magic Flute* playing. I figured I had just enough time to see it and run to the train station to catch my midnight train to Georgia, er, Vienna. I knew a bit of the story of the opera, so with my limited German I found I could follow the film, in Swedish with German subtitles. Well, I thought the singer who played Sarastro looked like I hoped I might look when I got older, and the experience of Mozart's music and Bergman's visuals helped to restore my hope for the future.

Muss es sein? From Joseph Kerman's *The Beethoven Quartets*, pages 362–363:

> There is a comic canon by Beethoven using the Es muss sein! tag, and an anecdote to go along with it. A certain Ignaz Dembscher, who held quartet parties in his house, had not subscribed to the premiere of Op. 130 in March 1826. So Beethoven refused to lend him the parts until he paid up. When Dembscher heard this, he moaned "Wenn es sein muss!"; the remark caught Beethoven's fancy, and he tossed off a feeble canon with the words "Es muss sein! ja ja ja! Heraus mit dem Beutel!" Thayer suggested that the quartet theme might have been in his head already, and the words clicked right in with it. However, the form of the theme in the quartet differs from that in the canon, and improves upon it.
>
> And there is another comic canon tied up with a major work by Beethoven, as everyone knows: the canon about Lieber Maezel of metronome fame and the Allegretto of the Eighth Symphony (another F-major composition, another conspicuous classical evocation). No metaphysical overtones have been discerned in that movement, so far as I know, in the way that this has been done with the present Finale. Rolland put the case with circumspection and charm:
>
> > It is a common tendency of the German mind to wring a sententious and general signification out of an ordinary word in some daily use (I noted this in Jean-Christophe): so—your good German, when his servant brings him the mustard after dinner is over, and when he says—simply enough— "Too

late," catches himself and adds philosophically (I have heard him!) "Too late: as ever in life!" Beethoven re-read that "Es muss sein!" under a much more general interpretation. And the trivial response evoked the serious question, in an altogether different tone of voice—a question that surged from the very depths of the Beethovenian soul: "Should it be? Must it be?" Must what be?—all that you desire; all that commands your thought and weighs upon it; "the difficult decision," the order of Destiny, the acceptance of life…"

— *Les Derniers Quatuors,* pp. 299–300

Who is being the good metaphysical German here, though— the author of Op. 135 or the author of Jean-Christophe? If a choice were required, I would think that those sections of the movement which develop the Muss es sein? motif sound more like a farcical depiction of an old miser's discomfiture than like any deep serious speculation. Rolland admits that the resolution of the question, in the sections using the Es muss sein! motif, offers "no character of accepted Necessity, not even of 'the difficult decision' according to the title, but of a gay determination…" Beethoven makes light of all previous decision-making perplexities.

— Kerman, *The Beethoven Quartets,* pg. 362–363

(In the above section I quote the musicologist Kerman quoting the musicologist Rolland. Wilson uses these sorts of loops within loops to model the mathematics of Gödel and G. Spencer Brown, as well as to illuminate the recursive nature of consciousness.)

Muldoon, Barney. A character in *Illuminatus!* He teams up with Saul Goodman to save the world, playing a reluctant Watson to Saul's Sherlock Holmes. Of course, Hugh Kenner and Robert Anton Wilson have both compared James Joyce's analytical, intensely observant intelligence with Sherlock Holmes, which might make Muldoon isomorphic with a reluctant Samuel Beckett to Saul's James James. Does that mean Saul and Rebecca's daughter might fall in love with Barney before going insane? And where do purple dinosaurs fit into this picture?

Muldoon, Father James Augustine. Barney Muldoon's brother, who helps Barney and his partner Saul Goodman in *Illuminatus!*

My favorite Wilson book. I would say the original uncut *Schrödinger's Cat*. The one volume *Schrödinger's Cat* has about 212 pages cut, plus some slight revisions. The out-of-print three-volume set has lots of fun stuff. I still heartily recommend the one volume edition if you can't find the originals.

I think Wilson's writing improved between the writing of *Cosmic Trigger* and *Schrödinger's Cat*, which I think has a richer style than *Illuminatus!* I think Wilson's writing continued to improve with the Swiftian precision of *Nature's Law* and the E-prime experiments during the reign of George I. Wilson read all of Swift while living in Ireland in the 80's. His intelligence continued to increase, and I think his 80's non-fiction shows a greater precision than his 70's prose, from the seminal *Prometheus Rising* to *The New Inquisition* and *Nature's God*.

He wrote *Quantum Psychology* in E-prime, and I think his experiments with E-prime, along with his continually increasing intelligence, have caused his writing to continue to improve. I hope future Wilson novels will top even *Schrödinger's Cat*. I think the tragedy of his daughter's death also shapes *Schrödinger's Cat*. Many characters in that book (and the narrative voices) seek to overcome unspeakable tragedy.

Nanokabbalah. Many readers of Wilson and Crowley have expressed a desire to deepen their understanding of Kabbalah. I thought of this technique for deepening my own understanding of the Kabbalah while watching the Portland Trailblazers playing the Phoenix Suns during the 1989–1990 C.E. season. I saw an amazing dunk by Portland's #22 Clyde Drexler, and a bunch of synchronicities occurred to me. For instance, Eric Drexler wrote about nanotechnologies, the possibilities of computers and other machines the size of molecules, and the tarot has 22 trumps, which may correspond with the 22 letters of the Hebrew alphabet. To explore these possible connections between my passion for basketball and my passion for the Kabbalah, I spent a week studying each letter of the Hebrew alphabet and the correspondences Aleister Crowley associates with them, using his book *777*. I would go through the correspondences once each day. I found this technique very liberating, and felt I got deeper into the Kabbalah than ever before. I later expanded this technique, spending 23 days on each letter, which took 529 days. You might

give either version a try, especially if you find yourself stuck trying to learn about the Kabbalah or trying to understand the writings of Aleister Crowley. I have certainly found myself stuck
from time to time. I've found that practicing nanokabbalah helps
me understand Crowley's notions of the Kabbalah, which helps
me understand his books.

Neurolinguistic Programming (NLP). Check out purenlp.com,
which defines NLP as "The Study of the Structure of Subjective
Experience and what can be calculated from it." Wilson did a
number of seminars with NLP founder Richard Bandler in the
90's, and Wilson mentions NLP in the introduction to *The Walls
Came Tumbling Down* and in the article on "Language as Conspiracy" in *Everything is Under Control*

"Never, never, never, never, never." A line from Shakespeare's *King Lear* that Wilson often quotes. (For example, *The
Earth Will Shake*, pg. 268, when John Babcock reflects on
Epicene Wildeblood's suicide.) King Lear's beloved Cordelia
has just died when he uttered this line of five trochees. (A
trochee has the accent pattern long short.) Most of the poetry in
the play has the rhythm of iambic pentameter, five feet with the
accent pattern short long.

The ancient Greek drama consisted of one or two actors
accompanied by a chorus. This chorus did little dance steps
while they uttered their lines, hence the term "foot" for units of
two or three syllables.

Iamb	short long	Shall I compare thee to a summer's day?
Trochee	long short	Once upon a midnight dreary
Anapest	short short long	On a day I will never forget
Dactyl	long short short	Malachi Mulligan (a double dactyl)

A line of iambic pentameter has ten syllables, or five feet
(hence the penta). Imagine the experience of seeing "King Lear"
and having that iambic rhythm drilled into your head for four
hours. Then, at the emotional climax of the story, this trochaic
line "Never, never, never, never, never" goes against that

rhythm, emphasizing Lear's knowledge that he will never see his daughter again, never make things right with her.

Nietzsche, Frederick (1844–1900). German philosopher who has greatly influenced Wilson. Bob says he rereads some Nietzsche every year. Nietzsche said of himself, "I'm a tough nut to crack"; his work does not lend itself to complete understanding on a single reading. Bob included Nietzsche on both of his reading lists (see **Appendix Resh**).

Nine basic winner-loser scripts. Wilson has frequently used William S. Burroughs' cut-up technique. Here we have this technique applied to some of Bob's definitions of the nine basic winner scripts and the nine basic loser scripts from *Illuminati Papers.*

1. I I will don't live know forever how to or die defend trying myself.

2. I am free; you They are free; we can all have our separate trips intimidate or we can have me the same trip.

3. I am I learning more can't about everything, solve including how my to learn problems more.

4. "Love," Everything, and I do like what is thou illegal, wilt "immoral, (Anon. or of fattening." Ibid)

5. How I I can't feel help depends the on way my I neurological feel knowhow.

6. I make Why my do own I coincidences, have synchronicities, such luck, lousy and luck? Destiny.

7. Future Evolution evolution is depends. Blind on and my impersonal decisions. Now.

8. Lilly Dr. John I experiment. experience and am by be learned not to certain limits psychic, within becomes true and or is true, I true to be doubt believed what is anyone mind the of is province in the

9. riverrun, past Eve and Adams, from swerve of shore to bend of bay brings us by a commodius vicus of recirculation oink to Howth Castle and Environs.

1999. When Hagbard blasted off for the stars along with Peter Jackson, according to *Illuminatus!* Appendix Nun.

Ninth Circuit. Mark Johnston, publisher of *The Mind-Blaster*, once asked me, "Why only eight circuits?" Well, eight nicely fits a four and four, right/left symmetry, as well as fitting in with ideas like the octave and the Noble Eightfold Path. Wilson has written extensively about the eight-dimension/circuit/system model. He has, however, suggested the possibility of more dimensions/circuits/systems. I do always like to look beyond, however. "Gate gate paragate, parasamgate bodhi svaha." (Beyond, beyond, beyond the beyond, hail thee who goes, or "On Beyond Zebra" as Dr. Seuss suggested.) If I wanted to explore the idea of a ninth circuit, I would get deeply into Dante, composer Roscoe Mitchell and John Lennon, all of whom had a fascination with the number nine. Wilson has often associated the final movement of Beethoven's Ninth Symphony with the eight circuit. Perhaps a more holistic look at the Ninth might give some clues, as well as Mahler, Bruckner, Dvorak and Shostakovich's Ninth Symphonies. Arnold Schönberg says this about Mahler's Ninth Symphony:

> His Ninth is most strange. In it, the author hardly speaks as an individual any longer. It almost seems as though this work must have a concealed author who used Mahler merely as his spokesman, as his mouthpiece. This symphony is no longer couched in the personal tone. It consists, so to speak, of objective, almost passionless statements of a beauty which becomes perceptible only to one who can dispense with animal warmth and feels at home in spiritual coolness. We shall know as little about what his Tenth (for which, as also in the case of Beethoven, sketches exist) would have said as we know about Beethoven's or Bruckner's. It seems that the Ninth is a limit. he who wants to go beyond it must pass away. It seems as if something might be imparted to us in the Tenth which we ought not yet to know, for which we are not yet ready. Those who have written a Ninth stood too near to the hereafter. Perhaps the riddles of this world would be solved, if one of those who knew them were to write a Tenth. And that is probably not to take place.
>
> — Schönberg, *Style and Idea*, pg. 470

If that intrigues you, you might want to check out the rest of Schönberg's essay on Mahler from which this paragraph comes.

Some might find this number-mysticism nonsense (as well as much else in this book). I think poems can communicate with their sound and what they evoke, in addition to or in spite of their meaning, following the thought of Louis Zukofsky. I think one can communicate in a similar fashion using numbers. I do not *believe* in numerology; I do like exploring the poetry of numbers.

Nuit, a.k.a. Nut. Egyptian sky goddess. Very important to Crowley. Wilson practiced devotional bhakti yoga to her as described in *Cosmic Trigger I.* He associates her with Glinda the Good in *The Wizard of Oz*, who descends from the sky in a bubble in the film. He also associates her with female aliens encountered by UFO contactees. See the works of Jacques Vallee.

I don't think Thelonious Monk intended his song "Nutty" as a paean to Her, but you may if you'd like. Wilson tells of a dream of dancing to the music of Thelonious Monk with his wife in *TSOG.*

O'Brien, Flann (a.k.a. Brian Ó Nualláin) (1911–1966). Irish novelist and essayist, author of *The Third Policeman, The Dalkey Archive*, etc. He wrote an essay on *Finnegans Wake* called "A Bash in the Tunnel" and created the character DeSelby who plays a role in Wilson's *The Widow's Son*, et al.

O'Neil, Gerard (1927–1992). A scientist who suggested that planetside civilization didn't seem like the ideal location for a post-industrial, information-age society. He suggested instead self-supporting space colonies. Both Wilson and Leary have enthusiastically supported this idea. Wilson includes such colonies in *Schrödinger's Cat.*

Orfali, Abraham. A wonderful character from the *Historical Illuminati* novels, especially *The Earth Will Shake*. He seems to me the purest picture of wisdom and gentleness Wilson has created. A Jewish healer, kabbalist and Mason, he guides young Sigismundo on his torturous path through Chapel Perilous, aided by Sigismundo's uncle Pietro, another wise and not-quite-so-gentle fellow.

Osiris. A black god. A death and resurrection god, whom Jung might associate with the same archetype as Jesus and Dionysus. Wilson has suggested that he originated as a rabbit god. See also **Isis.**

Ovid (43 B.C.E.–17 C.E.). A Roman poet, author of *The Metamorphosis*, probably Shakespeare's favorite poet. Pound considered *The Metamorphosis* a holy book, and he considered Arthur Golding's sixteenth century translation "the most beautiful book in English." Wilson mentions *The Metamorphosis* in the final chapter of *Ishtar Rising*, and he includes Ovid in his *Trajectories* "Brain Books" list.

Parapsychology. The study of the possibility the mind can manifest itself in ways seemingly at odds with the "laws of science." Wilson has written extensively on possible scientific models for such extra-sensory perception in the realm of quantum psychology. He has also written about attacks by self-proclaimed "skeptics" on parapsychologists in *The New Inquisition* and *Right Where You Are Sitting Now*.

Pataphysics. An invention of the French pre-surrealist writer Alfred Jarry. The onomatopoetic Greek prefix "pata" means "bang!" "Bang!-physics" deals with the physics of non-repeatable events. Jarry's concept of pataphysics inspired Bob's creation of patapsychology in *The Widow's Son*.

Patapsychology. An invention of DeSelby in Wilson's novel *The Widow's Son*, the psychology of non-repeating psychological states. Flann O'Brien introduced the character of DeSelby in his novel *The Third Policeman*, which Wilson called the finest Irish novel since *Finnegans Wake*. Wilson satirizes the "skeptics'" attacks on parapsychology with similar attacks in *The Widow's Son* on patapsychology, as well as satirizing Joyce criticism and many other things, all using a footnote technique developed from that used by Flann O'Brien in *The Third Policeman*. Wilson has called *The Widow's Son* his favorite of his books.

Patterns. Well, Gary Snyder had a dream in which poet Lew Welch told him to tell young people "about the patterns." Gary and Lew both played a role in the beat movement, which influenced the Grateful Dead, who knew Neal Cassidy, whose son Bob Wilson mentions in *TSOG*. Snyder has a long friendship with Robert Creeley and Allan Ginsberg, both of whom I met at the Ezra Pound centennial in 1985 in Orono, Maine. Wilson's work introduced me to Ezra Pound. Spider Robinson's review of Illuminati Papers in *Analog* in 1981 helped lead me to Wilson's writing. Spider also turned me on to *CoEvolution Quarterly* (now *Whole Earth Review*), founded by Prankster Stewart Brand, who also knew the Dead in the early years. Stewart Brand raved about a book called *A Pattern Language* in a *Whole Earth Catalogue*, in the section following reviews of Bucky Fuller's books. Both Wilson and Pound knew Bucky. My college roommate Mike Welnick married an architect. She owned a copy of a *Pattern Language,* which she recommended and lent to me. Mike's cousin, Vince Welnick, used to play in the Grateful Dead. Jerry Garcia liked *Illuminatus!*, especially the concept of the catma (less dogmatic than a dogma), and Jerry's physician now treats Bob's post polio sequelae.

Playboy **Magazine.** A magazine where Robert Anton Wilson used to work editing the *Playboy Forum*. Wilson satirizes publisher Hugh Hefner in *The Trick Top Hat*.

Plurabella, Anna Livia. See **Anna Livia Plurabella.**

Poe, Edgar Allan (1809–1849). Mentioned in *Everything Is Under Control* as an influence on Lovecraft's early prose style. In Clint Eastwood's film *A Perfect World* the escaped convict played by Kevin Costner uses the name Edgar Poe. Eastwood's film *Play Misty of Me* used Poe's "Annabel Lee" to great effect. Wilson has a great passion for Clint Eastwood's films.

Portinari, Miss Beatrice. Named after Dante's beloved, she takes over as spiritual leader of the Lief Erikson when Hagbard Celine resigns the position in *Illuminatus!* That egregious novel also includes part of lecture on the tarot by Miss Portinari, reading through the tarot trumps in reverse order.

Portmanteau Words. "Two meanings packed up into one word" (Carroll, *Annotated Alice* pg. 271), according to Humpty Dumpty in his analysis of "Jabberwocky." For example, " '*Slithy*' means 'lithe and slimy' " (ibid.). Martin Gardner comments that *Finnegans Wake* contains portmanteau words "by the tens of thousands" (ibid.). Bob makes use of portmanteau words in all of his books, especially when he consciously echoes the style of *Finnegans Wake*.

Pound, Ezra (1885–1972). Born in Hailey, Idaho, his family moved shortly to Pennsylvania where his dad worked in the mint. Ezra had an early interest in poetry and Confucius. He took a trip to Europe with a relative, and later decided to know more about poetry than anyone on Earth by the time he reached 30.

He took a Master's degree in Romance Languages and made friends with poets William Carlos Williams and H.D. (Hilda Doolittle). He lost a teaching position due to a female student in his room (during a rainstorm I think). He moved to Europe & wrote and wrote.

Hemingway said he learned more about writing from Ez than from anyone else. Joyce said, "Many owe him a great deal, none more than I do." He edited "The Waste Land" and paid for the publication of T.S. Eliot's first book of poems. He advanced Robert Frost's career at a critical moment. He wanted to live in a time of great writing. He succeeded.

Later generations learned to write from him: e.e. cummings, Zukofsky, Bunting, Ginsberg, Creeley, Donald Hall, Robert Anton Wilson, etc. Eliot called Pound's the "least dispensable body of criticism" of our time. Although university departments of English have tried to dispose of it, it continues to teach people to read and to write, to hear.

Pound had prejudices, which he voiced. He said some terrible things. He also wrote some exquisitely beautiful poetry. He sounded like a damned idiot at least 1% of the time. Most of us do. He had a deep insight into the human condition much of the time. Few of us do that, practically none of us as well and as deeply as Ez did.

He had an ear, "ear for the sea surge and old men's voice's." Listen.

Pranayama. Yogic breathing. Wilson enthusiastically recommends this for quieting and reimprinting the second system/

circuit, as well as for activating the cyber-somatic fifth system/ circuit. Crowley also insists of the value of pranayama. Wilson discusses pranayama in *Prometheus Rising* and mentions pranayama repeatedly in many of his books. You might check out *The Yoga of Breath: A Step-By-Step Guide to Pranayama* by Richard Rosen or *Light on Pranayama the Yogic Art of Breathing* by B.K.S. Iyengar.

Principia Discordia. The sacred text of the Discordian religion, which worships the Greek goddess of chaos Eris and/or her Roman counterpart Discordia. Wilson wrote an introduction for this delightful book, and he appears therein as Mordecai the Foul. *Illuminatus!* frequently quotes the *Principia*.

Psychedelics. In *Cosmic Trigger I* Wilson writes that some scientists think that psychedelic drugs like L.S.D. produce an altered state "in which one can reorganize or re-imprint our nervous system for higher functioning" (pg. 21). Other scientists think these drugs produce "an imitation (mime) of psychosis" (pg. 20), and still other scientists consider "the new mental state created by ingestion is considered a hallucinatory experience, but not quite a psychosis" (pg. 21).

Prose evolution. I think Wilson's writing gets better and better. I hope he lives to write and write and write. The early *Playboy* books have a certain style, full of Joycean multiple meanings, 60's whimsy and Brooklyn savvy. *Illuminatus!* moves from that style to a post-1973 Sirius Illumination-rich prose. *Schrödinger's Cat* moves further still, marking a deeper understanding of quantum mechanics and a response to the tragedy of the death of his daughter, Luna.

Bob's move to Ireland in 1982 C.E. marked a further evolution, from the subtleties of *The Earth Will Shake* to the pataphysical footnotes of *The Widow's Son*. His continuing concern for semantics marks the wonderfully brisk writing of *Nature's God*, *The New Inquisition* and *Coincidance*.

His interest in selling screenplays (which spurred a rethinking of the role of film—especially Orson Welles'—in his life) and a fascination with E-Prime helped him evolve further as a writer, as marked in *Quantum Psychology*, *Cosmic Trigger III* and the rewrite of *Prometheus Rising*.

His sense of humor keeps getting better, I think, and I look forward to more gems following the hypertextual lead of *Everything Is Under Control* and *TSOG* as he writes in a post-cyber future.

Pynchon, Thomas (1937–). A contemporary writer, author of *Slow Learner*, *V*, *The Crying of Lot 49*, *Gravity's Rainbow*, *Vineland* and *Mason and Dixon*, etc. A major influence on Tim Leary and a lesser influence on Bob Wilson. I think Wilson influenced Pynchon's *Mason and Dixon*, which seems to me reminiscent of Wilson's *Nature's God*. Pynchon's work deals with many similar themes as Wilson's work, although Pynchon doesn't seem as optimistic as Bob. Leary first read Pynchon in prison, where he read *Gravity's Rainbow* in about 23 hours, which had a profound effect on him. Leary once commented that he saw *Gravity's Rainbow* as the Old Testament of the Information Age and William Gibson's *Neuromancer* as the New Testament.

(I particularly love Pynchon's *Vineland*, which I found easier to read than any of Pynchon's other books. *The Crying of Lot 49* also reads pretty easily and doesn't have that many pages.) I recommend buying a copy of *Gravity's Rainbow* and giving it a try. It took me about four years to get through it. Author John Gardner said he thought that *Gravity's Rainbow* would double your intelligence if you understood it. Leary and William Gibson discuss Pynchon in Leary's *Chaos and Cyberculture*, which Wilson includes on his recommended reading list at rawilson.com. Wilson's *Everything Is Under Control* includes an entry on Pynchon's *The Crying of Lot 49*.

Quantum Mechanics. The study of the interactions of very small quantities (quanta) of matter and/or energy. Quantum mechanics revolutionized physics during the first third of the roaring twentieth century. Quantum mechanics has deeply influenced all of Bob's books, especially since *Cosmic Trigger I*.

Quo modo longe, Magna Cucurbita, quo modo longe? "How long, Great Pumpkin, how long?" in Latin. Wilson often ends his emails with this profound saying, and he included it in his tender, sensitive narrative *TSOG: The Thing That Ate the Constitution*. Charles Schultz wrote a book in his own ideogramatic style entitled *How Long, Great Pumpkin, How Long*? The Great Pumpkin, who rises once a year, seems akin to the agricultural death and resurrection Gods discussed in Fraser's *The Golden Bough*, much beloved by Crowley. One can see the winged globes and hearts pictured in *Cosmic Trigger* as winged pumpkins, wondering how long the Great Pumpkin cult may have persisted in secret.

Rabinowitz Factor. Back in 1988 C.E., I came to the realization that Wilson had learned a lot of interesting stuff by exploring where others had warned him not to explore: negative comments about Ezra Pound, *Finnegans Wake* and Aleister Crowley, etc., had spurred him on to learn more. I decided to turn that idea on its head and explore areas where Wilson had voiced criticism. For example, Martin Gardner's intolerance falls under attack in many of Wilson's books, especially *The New Inquisition* and *Wilhelm Reich in Hell*. Wilson based the character Hebert Sharper in *The Widow's Son* on Gardner. Sharper, along with Charles Nagas (Sagan spelled backwards), express "skepticism" of the existence of meteors in that eighteenth century novel, just as Gardner expresses "skepticism" for all varieties of the "paranormal" in the twentieth.

So, I decided to read some Gardner. Wilson had commented that he enjoyed Gardner's mathematical puzzles, although he didn't like Gardner's unscientific attitudes about science. Gardner seems to prefer verbal rebuttal of ideas like those of Wilhelm Reich, rather than the experimental method. Well, reading an essay about quantum mechanics by Gardner, I saw his obvious intelligence and wit in describing the subatomic world. However, I noted a definite style change when he began discussing the possibility of quantum weirdity on the macroscopic level. It seemed to me the wit metamorphosized into a strident and dogmatic tone denouncing the idea that the macroscopic world could possibly bear any resemblance to the microscopic world. He didn't cite any experimental evidence to support his views.

It struck me that perhaps Gardner really believed in these inflexible attitudes, but on the other hand, perhaps he only wanted us to think so. Perhaps he had some ulterior motive for seeming to oppose radical new scientific ideas. With this in mind I formed the Society of Gardner and appointed myself Inquisitive

General. I decided that seeing both sides of a question seemed an inadequate response to the post-quantum world. It seemed like four viewpoints would provide a better basic orientation. Oftentimes we find ourselves looking at a problem from two seemingly opposed points of view, and, thinking "we've looked at both sides," we stop looking for new viewpoints. (Think of the big-endians and little-endians in *Gulliver's Travels*, for example, who get perturbed arguing over which end of an egg to crack. A third point of view would see the question as irrelevant, and a fourth [Swift's] would think of this argument as a wonderful illustration of the absurdity of much human discourse. A fifth point of view might relate the egg to Humpty Dumpty, the Orphic Egg, *Finnegans Wake* and other poetic associations. A sixth might use it in a book about multiple viewpoints, Robert Anton Wilson and Jonathan Swift, etc. A seventh might think of the tar baby parable and wonder if the tar baby became emotionally attached to whatever attacked it and whether the egg cared at which end it became cracked. Etc.)

I decided to call the basic unit of perception 1 Rashomon, after the famous movie which told the same story from four points of view. Seeing one point of view would correspond with 0.25 Rashomons. Seeing "both sides" of a question would yield 0.5 R, and exploring four viewpoints or models would give 1 R. Seeing eight contradictory viewpoints would yield 2 R, or R R, which I named "the Rabinowitz Factor" after my friend, the composer Robert Rabinowitz, leader of the Nine Unknown Men. As an exercise, whenever I see an R R (on a railroad crossing sign for instance), I try to look at whatever challenges I have in my life from eight viewpoints or models.

Rand, Ayn (1905–1982). (First name pronounced like the German "ein" or the Hebrew "ain," with a long i sound.) Author of *Atlas Shrugged, The Fountainhead, Anthem,* etc. Wilson and Shea satirize her in *Illuminatus!* with *Telemachus Sneezed* by Atlanta Hope, with the first line "What is John Guilt," which parallels *Atlas Shrugged's* "Who is John Galt?" The plot of *Telemachus Sneezed* mixes elements of *Atlas Shrugged* and *The Fountainhead.*

Reality Tunnel. The reality constructed by a nervous system. You and I have different reality tunnels, although parts of them probably overlap. The areas which seem to exist in one person's reality tunnel and not in another's tend to lead to conflict, whether in a marriage or international relations, or anywhere conflicting visions of reality collide. Bob has made frequent use of this term coined by Tim Leary.

Regardie, Israel (1907–1985). Aleister Crowley's former secretary, who wrote many wonderful books on magick, the kabbalah, healing, etc. He wrote the introduction for Wilson's *Prometheus Rising*, and Bob wrote an introduction for Regardie's *The Eye in the Triangle. The Eye in the Triangle*, which Wilson read at the recommendation of Alan Watts, introduced Wilson to the world of Aleister Crowley.

Robot. *Illuminatus!* uses the metaphor of the robot for mindless human behavior and/or for the mammal level of the brain/body system. One might think of 99.999% of our behavior as automatic, robotic. One can decrease this percentage and increase one's neurological freedom. For a post-hippie musical derobotizing experience, check out Beachwood Sparks' EP "Make the Cowboy Robots Cry." (Sunday nights from 8–11 PM L.A. time, check out "The Music Never Stops" for Grateful Dead and contemporary jam rock and derobotizing raps from our imaginary friend Barry Smolin at mrsmolin.com, 90.7 in SoCal.)

Robot Animal Within, Rebel Apache Warrior. These share Robert Anton Wilson's initials (RAW). Wilson inserts these into his texts sometimes (such as *The Homing Pigeons,* pg. 184). Similarly, Humphrey Chimpden Earwicker's initials HCE recur over and over again in *Finnegans Wake*. This can indicate the dreamer's (HCE's) ego trying to emerge in the dreamworld of that novel. Phillip Jose Farmer, like Wilson a big fan of *Finnegans Wake,* often uses protagonists who share his initials: Peter Jarius Frigate, Paul Janus Finnegan and Philias Fogg (of *Around the World in 80 Days* fame).

(Wilson once attended Orson Welles' famous production of *Around the World in 80 Days.*)

Wilson suggests the HCE character with his characters Hagbard Celine, Hugh Crane and Harry Coin. When the Yellow

Submarine rescued George Dorn in *The Homing Pigeons*, "Captain Hagbard Celine (who looked a lot like Hugh Crane the magician, when you stopped to think about it, and a little bit like Harry Coin, the crazy assassin, and somewhat like Everyman) took his hand. 'Good to have you back aboard, George.'" The E in Everyman completes the HCE.

Rumi, Jalaladin (1207–1273). A Sufi poet. Check out Idries Shah's books for an introduction to Rumi's writings. Shah contends that non-Sufi translations of Sufi poets tend to miss the true meanings of the poems. Shah's books, and Sufi thought in general, has greatly influenced Bob.

Russell, Bertrand (1872–1970). A philosopher and mathematician, etc., whom Wilson frequently mentions. In *Quantum Mechanics* Wilson suggests Russell's optimism contributed to his longevity. Wilson frequently refers to Russell's work as a mathematician.

S.H., H.M. In *Illuminatus!*, Hagbard Celine includes these initials after his name in his book within a book, *Never Whistle While You're Pissing: A Guide to Self-Liberation*. They stand for "Shit Head, Holy Man," according to *Zen Without Zen Masters* by Camden Benares, New Falcon Publications, 1985.

Sabbah, Hassan i (1034–1124). The Old Man of the Mountain, whom Marco Polo encountered on his way to China, the head of the Ismaelian sect of Islam, as well as the head of the Order of Assassins. Some people claim that both the words "assassin" and "hashish" come from his name. Some of the sources in *Illuminatus!* trace the Illuminati back to Hassan.

Sartre, Jean Paul (1905–1980). Wilson discusses his philosophy and the importance of dating observations in *Quantum Psychology*. For instance, instead of saying "Hermes is a thief" one could say "Hermes stole some oxen at the age of 5 in 1127 B.C.E." Malaclypse the Elder appears looking like Sartre at the Ingolstadt Festival.

Saucer Smear. A delightful UFO-zine which deals mostly with bickering within the UFO world. Check out their great web site at www.martiansgohome.com/smear/. Wilson frequently writes letters of comment to the zine, and he mentions it in his books as well, especially *Everything Is Under Control* and *Chaos and Beyond.*

Scholem, Gershom (1897–1982). A great scholar of Jewish mysticism, especially the kabbalah. He didn't think much of Aleister Crowley and modern occult kabbalah in general, but his work provides great historical background for the development of European occult philosophy. Israel Regardie recommended reading Scholem's books on the kabbalah, and Regardie has greatly influenced Wilson.

Secret Societies. Groups who keep their membership, their activities, and/or their very existence a secret. Oftentimes governments forbid membership in these groups, such as the Freemasons at various times in history in some countries. Wilson has a particular fascination for secret societies within secret societies. For instance, in the 1770's C.E. the Bavarian Illuminati only allowed members who already belonged to the Freemasons. In the 1970's in Italy, P2 only recruited third degree members of the Grand Orient Lodge of Egyptian Freemasonry.

Wilson has written extensively about a wide variety of secret societies in many of his books. *Everything Is Under Control* provides a terrific introduction to many of the real and imagined secret societies which have fascinated Dr. Wilson, such as the Assassins, the Bilderbirgers, the Council on Foreign Relations, the Discordians, the Elders of Zion, Freemasonry, the Golden Dawn, Heaven's Gate, da Illuminati, the Knights Templar, LAWCAP, the Mafia, Noon Blue Apples, Ordo Templi Orientis, the Priory of Sion, Rosicrucianism, Skull and Bones, the Trilateral Commission, Wicca, and the Xists, etc.

Secret to Success (The). Perhaps "Location, location, location" (i.e., Move west or into space). Or maybe "Vocation, vocation, vocation." Bob has written that he knew he wanted to become a writer from an earlier age. He attributes his success to writing, writing, writing. He says that the only sensible rules for writer's came from Robert Heinlein: You must write; you must finish what you write; and you must keep sending it out until it sells.

Seem Here Now. E-Prime version of *Be Here Now,* by Baba Ram Dass, formerly Richard Alpert, who participated with Bob's sometime collaborator Timothy Leary in various LSD experiments.

Semper as oxhousehumper. A line from *Finnegans Wake* which Wilson used as the title for an essay in *Coincidance.* The first three letters of the Hebrew alphabet, aleph, beth and gimel, mean "ox," "house" and "camel" in English. The line from the *Wake* can mean "Simple as A, B, G," or, since semper means "always" in Latin, "Always as A, B, G," which I associate with Aleister Crowley's advice to always relate everything to the Kabbalah. Of course, Hebrew reads right to left, so one would see the first three letters as G, B, A, the initials of one of my favorite organizations, Gamma-irradiated Beings Anonymous.

In the Hulk comic books, Bruce Banner got exposed to a gamma bomb, which causes him to turn into the incredible Hulk. Sundry other folk have gotten exposed to gamma radiation in the Marvel comics world as well, creating the Abomination, She-Hulk, the Leader, etc. In one Hulk comic written by the amazing Peter David, the Hulk and Bruce's wife Betty come to the understanding that they both play a role in Bruce's life. They say that this dialog about acceptance sounds like something from a twelve step group, Gamma-irradiated Beings Anonymous (G.B.A.), where the Hulk, the Abomination, etc., sit in a circle on folding chairs, and the folding chairs collapse under them. Bob has not discussed G.B.A., although he has mentioned occultist Louis Culling who discusses the G.B.L. (Great Body of Light). Perhaps there are some secrets even Wilson won't reveal...

Sephiroth. Ten lights which form the structure of the kabbalistic Tree of Life, along with 22 paths corresponding with the letters of the Hebrew alphabet. Modern occult kabbalists like Aleister Crowley associate the sephiroth with the small cards of the Tarot (the cards numbered one through ten in the suits of Wands, Cups, Swords and Pentacles). They associate the paths with the 22 Tarot trumps. Wilson and Shea based the ten trips of *Illuminatus!* on the ten sephiroth of the Tree of Life. See **Appendix Samech.**

Servix, Mary Lou. A character in *Illuminatus!*, an undercover cop who has tantric sex with Simon Moon. She chooses not to follow Hagbard Celine's path in a long monologue patterned on Molly Bloom's final monologue in James Joyce's *Ulysses*. Mary Lou's monologue centers on the word "No," while Molly's monologue centered on "Yes."

Shah, Sayed Idris (1924–). A great Sufi writer, whom Wilson frequently quotes. Shah's Mulla Nasrudin books gained a certain underground popularity in the 60's.

Shea, Robert (1933–1994). Co-author of *Illuminatus!* He also wrote *Shike, All Things Are Lights, The Saracen, Shaman,* etc. He worked at *Playboy* while Wilson worked there. The two became friends and decided to write together. You can read Wilson's moving tribute to Shea in *Cosmic Trigger III*.

Sheldrake, Rupert (1942–). A biologist who suggested in his book *A New Science of Life* that non-local fields similar to those in quantum theory communicate between cells. He calls them morphogenetic fields, leading Robert Anton Wilson to rename the seventh "neurogenetic" circuit/system the "morphogenetic system" in *Quantum Psychology* (pg. 191).

Sombunall. A word coined by Wilson meaning "some but not all."

Spartacus (?–71 B.C.E.). Leader of Roman slave rebellion (73– 71 B.C.E.), subject of a film directed by Stanley Kubrick, although Kubrick came to the project late and didn't consider the film completely his own. Wilson discusses this film in an essay on "Barry Lyndon" in *The Illuminati Papers*. Many slaves were crucified after Spartacus' rebellion, as mentioned in *The Earth Will Shake*.

Adam Weishaupt used Spartacus as a code name, and *The Widow's Son* mentions pamphlets from pre-Revolutionary Paris by another "Spartacus."

Stapledon, Olaf (1886–1950). A visionary science fiction writers, two of whose books, *First and Last Men* and *Last Men in the Moon*, Wilson included in his Brain Books list in *Trajectories*.

Stella. Or, as she sometimes calls herself, Stella Only. A character in *Illuminatus!* and *Schrödinger's Cat* (where she practices pranayama at an orgy). See also **Mavis**.

Stephens, James (1882–1950). Irish writer, whom Joyce selected to finish *Finnegans Wake* if Joyce's health would not permit Joyce to finish it. Stephens, an orphan, selected February 2, 1882, Candlemas, as his birthday, not knowing his "real" birthday. He selected the name James Stephens in honor of the Irish patriot, Fenian leader James Stephens. Wilson discusses the later Stephens in *Coincidance* on pages 5 and 6. Joyce selected Stephens to finish the Wake not only because of Stephens' skill as a writer, but also because Joyce thought they shared the same date of birth in the same city with the same first name. Also Stephens' last name resembles the first name of Joyce's fictional mask "Stephen Dedalus." (Hugh Kenner says Richard Ellmann's "standard" biography of Joyce conflates the fictional Dedalus with the "real" Joyce. See **Beckett, Samuel**.)

Also, Joyce thought Stephens had written a book under a pseudonym which Stephens claims he didn't write (although he provided an introduction to a later edition of the book in question). Stephens wrote a contemporary account of the Easter 1916 rebellion, several novels and books of poems, and some terrific literary essays, including some on Yeats, another of his acquaintances.

Students for a Democratic Society (SDS). A New Left political group from the 1960's. *Illuminatus!* contains many references to SDS.

Superman. Translation of Nietzsche's *Ubermensch*, which Walter Kaufmann chooses to translate as "Overman." Saul Goodman calls his wife Rebecca from a phone booth with a sticker on the door:

THIS PHONE BOOTH RESERVED FOR CLARK KENT

(*Illuminatus!* pg. 23, yes, you read that right, **23!**) August Personage, who perhaps made an obscene phone call to Rebecca, probably left this sticker.

El Hajj Stackerlee Mohammed leads a rock band called Clark Kent and his Supermen in *Illuminatus!* They perform "Rock Around the Clock," whose lyric runs through the first trip of that illustrious novel.

System Pyramid. When discussing the eight circuit (system) model of the brain, Wilson writes that "yoga, like brainwashing, begins from the bottom up, working on the more primitive and older circuits first." (*Prometheus Rising,* pg. 273) (The Church of the Sub-Genius regards 273 as their sacred number. Go figure.) One develops the first circuit, and then develops the second, while still developing the first, and so forth. The lower circuits support the higher ones. Perhaps secret passageways exist.

Leary warned that activation of the higher circuits without stability in the lower circuits might lead to an unbalanced personality.

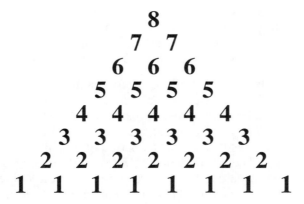

Taming of the Shrew (The). An interesting early play by Shakespeare. It begins with an "Induction" which deals with brainwashing a poor single man into thinking of himself as a rich married man, using a play as one of the brainwashing tools. It almost makes one think of a hypnotic induction, either of the poor man or perhaps the audience. (Prospero's magickal ability to put his daughter Miranda to sleep in *The Tempest* also suggests hypnosis.) The play itself deals with Petruccio's attempts to brainwash Kate into becoming his ideal wife, controlling her eating, establishing himself as top dog, controlling her semantic environment, basically following the brainwashing process outlined in Wilson's *Prometheus Rising* and Leary and Wilson's *Neuropolitique*. Shea and Wilson allude to his play when Mavis kneels to kiss Hagbard's instep after he announces their engagement. (*Illuminatus!*, pg. 616) (Seeing this page number as an allusion to *Ulysses* might seem going too far.)

Swift, Jonathan (1667–1745). Irish writer, author of *Gulliver's Travels*, *A Tale of a Tub*, "A Modest Proposal," *The Drapier Letters*, etc., noted for his satire. A major influence on both James Joyce and Robert Anton Wilson. While living in Ireland, Wilson discovered that his local library had almost everything Swift had written, so he began reading his way through it, one volume at a time. Wilson can see the particular influence of Swift on his books *The New Inquisition* and *Nature's Law*, according to *Robert Anton Wilson Explains Everything*.

Tantra. A branch of Buddhism, some of whose followers practice meditative sexuality, prolonging the sexual act to achieve radically altered states of conscience. Wilson writes about this in almost all of his books, especially in *Sex, Drugs and Magick*.

Tarot. A collection of cards used for mediation and fortune telling, etc. The deck usually includes 78 cards. Wilson makes use of tarot references in most of his books. Aleister Crowley's vision of the tarot greatly influenced Wilson. Wilson mentioned in *Cosmic Trigger I* that he spent a period of time doing frequent tarot readings. The sections of *The Earth Will Shake* take their titles from tarot cards, which correspond with the contents of each section. For example the section called the World includes Sigismundo Celine's first travels outside of Italy, to Spain, France and Germany. Also, Crowley associates the World card (which he calls The Universe) with crocodiles, and Wilson mentions crocodiles in passing in this section of the novel. This section also illuminates how each of us lives in our own neurological Universe. Wilson illustrates this through Sigismundo's encounter with the Spanish boys, as well as in Sigismundo's experience reading David Hume. Sigismundo concludes "we are all walled cities shouting at each other over the armaments of our perceptions." (*The Earth Will Shake*, pg. 226) Earlier in the section Sigismundo had contemplated the importance of building castles on hills during the Middle Ages, which contributes to the individual/World/city/castle complex.

The fourth system/circuit chapter in *Prometheus Rising* includes a discussion of the tarot court cards. *The Game of Life* by Leary (with help from Wilson) associates the twenty-four brains of the human nervous system (three for each system) with the tarot trumps, adding two not included in the 22 standard tarot trumps. Miss Portinari calls the tarot "the most important book in the world" (*Illuminatus!*, pg. 716).

Note that the Hebrew alphabet has 22 letters, and many occultists, including Crowley, associate each trump with a letter of the alphabet, although they often disagree about which trump goes with which letter. Wilson makes use of the associations in *Masks of the Illuminati*. Coincidentally, Ishmael Reed suggests there exist 22 hoodoo loas in *Mumbo Jumbo*. Reed, born February 22, calls himself Agent 22 and works 22 into many of his works.

Thomas, Dylan (1914–1953). Welsh poet. Wilson has said Dylan Thomas's poetry provides a poetic analogue for what Joyce did in prose in *Finnegans Wake*. Bob Dylan changed his name in homage to Dylan Thomas. Thomas's poem "Do Not Go Gentle into that Good Night" has achieved great popularity. Donald Hall's *Their Ancient Glittering Eyes Are Gay* contains a chapter on his encounters with Thomas, as well as sections on Ezra Pound and T.S. Eliot, etc. Wilson fans will especially appreciate the section on Pound.

Thornley, Kerry (1938–1998). A founder of the Discordian Society. Jim Garrison suspected Thornley of involvement in the John Kennedy assassination. Thornley served in the marines with Lee Harvey Oswald.

Tolkien, J.R.R. (1892–1973) Author of *The Hobbit*, *The Lord of the Rings*, and *The Simarillion*. According to *Illuminatus!*, J.F.C. Moore claims that Tolkein created these works for the British government to combat Nazi mystic beliefs. (*Illuminatus!*, pg. 147) Mama Sutra incorporates the story of *The Lord of the Rings* into a Lovecraftian history of the Illuminati where Phroto challenges Zaurn instead of Frodo challenging Sauron. (*Illuminatus!*, pg. 531) Bands with Tolkien-inspired names like

the Entwives and Frodo Baggins and His Ring attend the Ingolstadt rock festival in *Illuminatus!*

Tucker, Benjamin (1854–1939). Joyce called Tucker the sanest
mind ever to write on politics. Tucker advocated competing
currencies and no copyrights or patents. He has greatly influenced Wilson's thoughts on economics.

**Twain, Mark (a.k.a. Samuel Langhorne Clemens). (1835–
1910).** Or Mark the Twy as Joyce calls him in *Finnegans Wake,*
which deals with Finn again, going down the long river Mrs.
Liffey. Twain's use of humor and development of his own personal style of writing have greatly influenced Wilson.

23. Novelist William S. Burroughs began collecting coincidences
involving the number 23, and Wilson continued this process. He
weaves the number 23 into all of his books, and *Illuminatus!*
became a symphony of 23's. Wilson shows how each individual
can edit their perceptions so as to become more or less aware of
various aspects of their environment. Wilson's reader's often
become hyper-aware of the number 23. After reading somebunall
of this book, you will probably notice a few more 23's than
usual. Perhaps a lot more. Just a coincidence, I suspect.

273. Sacred number of the Church of the Sub-Genius. Sub-
Genius numerology owes a great deal to Wilson. Note the 2 and
3 in 273.

Vallee, Jacques (1939–). A computer scientist and astronomer
whose writings on UFO's have greatly influenced Wilson as
discussed in *Cosmic Trigger I* and *Everything is Under Control.*
The film *Close Encounters of the Third Kind* contains a
character, a French ufologist, based on Vallee.

Verne, Jules (1828-1905). Author of *Around the World in 80
Days*; *20,000 Leagues Beneath the Sea*; *Journey to the Center of
the Earth*; *From the Earth to the Moon*; etc. Wilson has made
reference to Michael Lame's book *Jules Verne, initiate et initia-
teur,* which suggests that Verne's novels actually served as Illuminati recruiting manuals. Check out "The Horror on Howth
Hill" at deepleafproductions.com/wilsonlibrary/texts/raw-howth.
html.

Vico, Giambattista (1668–1744). A Neapolitan writer. His *New Science*, published in 1735 C.E., proved a major influence on *Finnegans Wake* and Wilson's *TSOG: The Thing That Ate the Constitution* with what Wilson calls Vico's "concept of language as Class Warfare" (*TSOG*, pg. 205). Vico's ideas also influenced Sigismundo Celine in the *Historical Illuminati* books.

Vivaldi, Antonio (1675?–1741). Baroque composer. Ezra Pound championed his music. Much of Vivaldi's music remained out of print during the 1930's. Joe Malik has Vivaldi on the radio before he sees the fnords. (*Illuminatus!*, pg. 438) *Schrödinger's Cat* mentions a recording of Vivaldi's "Four Seasons" on traditional Japanese koto. In *The Historical Illuminatus Chronicles* Sigismundo Celine prefers Scarlatti's music to Vivaldi's, but as he gets older he comes to appreciate "the red-headed priest."

J.S. Bach studied the openings of Vivaldi's concertos, copying them out. Luigi Dallapiccola claimed that Vivaldi wrote not five hundred concertos but the same concerto five hundred times (Rosen, *Critical Entertainments*, pg. 55). Charles Rosen turns that on its head, commenting that "Vivaldi had five hundred ideas for a concerto, and that none of them ever was fully worked out. It is only after his wonderful opening bars, his extraordinary beginnings (which taught J.S. Bach so much), that his concertos begin to resemble each other in the deployment of harmonic cliches." (ibid.) For readers who wanted to more deeply appreciate the classical music which shapes Robert Anton Wilson's books, I highly recommend Charles Rosen and Joseph Kerman's books.

Vonnegut, Kurt (1922–). Author of *Slaughterhouse Five*; *Mother Night*; *The Sirens of Titan*; *Cat's Cradle*; *Breakfast of Champions*; *Deadeye Dick* and many other wonderful books.

Wilson concludes his great essay "Ten Good Reasons to Get Out of Bed in the Morning" with the following paragraphs:

> As Kurt Vonnegut says, "A great swindle of our time is the assumption that science has made religion obsolete. All science has damaged is the story of Adam and Eve and the story of Jonah and the whale." Vonnegut goes on to say that there is nothing in science that contradicts the works of mercy recommended by Saint Thomas Aquinas, which include: to teach the

ignorant, to console the sad, to bear with the oppressive and the troublesome, to feed the hungry, to shelter the homeless, to visit prisoners and the sick, and to pray for us all.

If we can see and act on the wisdom of those suggestions, we can greet life with the bravery and joy it deserves.

— *Illuminati Papers* pg. 57

Wagner, Eric (1962–). Poet friend of Wilson's, referred to in *Chaos and Beyond, Cosmic Trigger III* and *TSOG*.

Walker, Evan Harris (?–). A quantum physicist, whose "The Compleat Quantum Anthropologist" Wilson frequently cites. That paper discusses the possibility that quantum events allow some ESP and telekinesis. Nick Herbert's *Elemental Mind: Human Consciousness and the New Physics* discusses this model. You might also check out Evan Harris Walker's *The Physics of Consciousness: The Quantum Mind and the Meaning of Life.* I will leave it to students of synchronicity to explain the George Herbert Walker Bush connection.

Walpurgisnacht. April 30. The old pagan religions in Europe often thought that the door to the next world open most widely twice a year: Walpurgisnacht (the eve of May Day, the day Weishaupt would later found the Illuminati in 1776) and Halloween (the eve of what would later become All Saint's Day). May 1 and November 1 served as important dates for cattle raising cultures which migrated due to the changes in the weather, hence the phrase "till the cows come home." The cult of the Great Pumpkin celebrates Halloween as its high holy day. The rock festival in *Illuminatus!* culminates on Walpurgisnacht.

Wayne, Bruce. A minor character in Thomas Pynchon's *Gravity's Rainbow*. He fights crime. Timothy Leary had a huge affection for *Gravity's Rainbow* and Wilson frequently mentions it.

Weishaupt, Adam (1748–1811). Heap big mystery. An ex-Jesuit professor of canon law at Ingolstadt University, he founded the Bavarian Illuminati on May 1, 1776. I remember thinking of him and his wife Eve and the opening line of *Finnegans Wake* on Maybe Day, July 23, 1985 C.E., looking out over the river Donau in Ingolstadt, "riverrun, past Eve and

Adams..." Weishaupt plays a central role in *Illuminatus!* and Wilson mentions him in many of his other books.

Welles, Orson (1915–1985). A great motion picture director, radio director, stage director, actor, etc., and a radical influence on Wilson. Welles' "War of the Worlds" broadcast terrified a nation in 1938 C.E., and his films, especially *Citizen Kane*, changed cinema forever. Wilson has written extensively on Welles, especially his *F for Fake*, which he discusses at length in *Cosmic Trigger III*.

What's up? Common greeting. One might model "up" as an adverb or preposition. Wilson has noted that Bucky Fuller recommended thinking of "up" as "out," as in "out into space," since "up" and "down" suggest a pre-Copernican flat Earth.

Wheeler, John A (1911–). A very influential quantum physicist. He co-authored the Everett-Wheeler-Graham model which suggests that whenever the possibility arises for an electron to exist in two different states, the electron exists in both states simultaneously, except in different universes. In other words, the electron exists in one state in one universe and in the other state in an otherwise identical universe "next door." This leads to the constant creation of multiple universes. This model provides the form for Wilson's *The Universe Next Door*.

White, T.H. (1906–1964) Author of *The Once and Future King*, the basis for the Disney film *The Sword in the Stone*. Wilson and/or Shea often quote the lines "everything not forbidden is compulsory" and "everything not compulsory is forbidden." (For example, *Illuminatus!*, pg. 623, quoting Hagbard Celine's *Never Whistle While You're Pissing*.)

Wiener, Norbert (1894–1964). A mathematician and one of the principal developers of cybernetics. He studied under David Hilbert, about whom Thomas Pynchon may have a book coming out. Wilson has frequently mentioned Wiener's book *The Human Uses of Human Beings*.

Wigner, Eugene (1902–1995). A quantum physicist who provided a new wrinkle on the Schrödinger's Cat paradox, the "Wigner's Friend" thought-experiment. Imagine on the day of the Super Bowl you miss the game and don't know who won. The question of who won remains in the "maybe state" for you until you find out who won, even though many other people may know the result of the game. In the same way, in the Schrödinger's Cat thought-experiment, when an experimenter discovers whether the cat has lived through the experiment, the fate of the cat remains in the "maybe state" for the experimenter's friend outside the lab until the experimenter tells the friend.

In *Schrödinger's Cat* a novel exists in the universe next door called *Wigner's Friend*. This chilling science fiction novel deals with the life of Richard Nixon (who had not become President in that universe, which readers in that universe find entertaining but fortunately unbelievable).

Wilde, Oscar (1854–1900). Irish novelist, playwright, etc. Wilson frequently mentions his essay "The Truth of Masks," which deals with costumes in Shakespeare, as well as the play between masks and reality. Wilson frequently mentions Wilde in his works. For many funny stories about Wilde, check out *Four Dubliners* by Richard Ellmann, or Ellmann's huge biography of Wilde.

Wilde's *The Importance of Being Earnest* plays with the relationship between names and reality (as does Faulkner's *The Sound and the Fury*). One character calls going on sexual adventures "bunburying." Wilson included the film *The Picture of Dorian Gray*, based on Wilde's novel, on his website's recommended viewing list.

Wildeblood, Mary Margaret. S/He started out as Epicene Wildeblood in *Illuminatus!*, a book reviewer for *Confrontation* magazine who writes a blistering critique of *Illuminatus!* inside of *Illuminatus!* In *Schrödinger's Cat* s/he has a sex change operation, and his surgically removed penis makes an epic voyage around the world in that novel until finally returning home to Wildeblood, now surgically attached to Markoff Chaney who makes love to Mary Margaret in a weird marriage of the *Odyssey* and *Finnegans Wake*.

Wilson, Arlen Riley (1925–1999). Robert Anton Wilson's wife of 42 years. She provided him with love, inspiration and support for everything Bob has written and will write. I feel lucky to have talked with her on a the phone a few times, and she sent me a wonderful letter once when Bob's health would not allow him to correspond. I like to think she would enjoy this book.

Wilson, (Patricia) Luna (1961–1976). Bob and Arlen's daughter, about whose life and murder Bob wrote so movingly in *Cosmic Trigger I*. I think much of the power of the *Schrödinger's Cat* comes from Bob attempting to deal with the tragedy of her death.

Wizard of Oz (The). Saul Goodman thinks, "We're off to see the wizard" in the Fourth Trip in *Illuminatus!*, and Fission Chips encounters the Cowardly Lion, the Tinman, the Scarecrow, Dorothy and Toto in the Eighth Trip. Wilson also mentions the impact the film *The Wizard of Oz* had on him as a child in *Cosmic Trigger II*. The Oz characters nicely fit the eight system model: the Lion for the first approach/run away dialectic, the Tinman for the emotional system, the Scarecrow for the intellect, and Dorothy with her desire to go home for the socio/sexual. The Wizard, the two evil Witches and Glinda (as well as Toto for the Sirius connection) might map onto the higher systems.

In *Schrödinger's Cat*, people come out of concerts by the Civic Monster "catching odd fugitive glimpses into fairyland and Oz...," influenced by lead singer Rhoda Chief's "mutation of old-fashioned Dixieland 'scat singing'" with fragments of the Enochian keys. For more on the Enochian keys, see *Gems from the Equinox* by Crowley, *The Eye in the Triangle* by Israel Regardie (with a great Introduction by Wilson) and *The Complete Golden Dawn System of Magic*, compiled by Regardie.

In *The Homing Pigeons* when Frank Dashwood uses magick to escape the cops, he passes through a series of visions, including the Tin Woodsman, accompanied by "some of the boys from the Heavy Metal Mob" (pg. 183).

In *Natural Law* the chapter "Natural Law as Ventriloquism" begins with the quote, "Pay no attention to that man behind the curtain," attributed to "Oz the Omnipotent." Note how many times "Oz occurs in the following quote attributed to Jesus in the *Pistis Sophia* (*The Homing Pigeons*, pg. 41):

"AAAOOOOZORAZAZZAIEOAZAEIIIOZAKHOEOOOY
THOEAZAEAAOZOKHOZAKHEYTYXAALETHYKH
—This is the Name which you must speak in the interior
world."

TSOG: The Thing That Ate the Constitution contains the line
"Tsarists and Nazis and spooks, oh my!"
The Modern Jazz Quartet recorded "Over the Rainbow" on
their wonderful album *Fontessa*. My friend Phil Strange also
recorded "Over the Rainbow" on his album *Quiet* [plug! plug!].

Wodehouse, P.G. (1881–1975). A wonderful writer of humorous novels and creator of the character of Jeeves the butler, pictured at the Askjeeves.com website. Wilson told me that Orson
Welles and W.C. Fields once conceived a film version of Jeeves,
starring Fields, and written and directed by Welles, which never
came to fruition. Welles did once use the pen name O.W. Jeeves,
and Fields used the pen name Mahatma Kane Jeeves.

Yeats, William Butler (1865–1939). A great poet, a member of
the Golden Dawn along with Aleister Crowley, and a minor
character in *Masks of the Illuminati.* He lived at Stone Cottage
with Ezra, and he actually got better as a poet as he got older. (At
least I think so. Ezra selected mostly earlier poetry by Yeats for
his great anthology *From Confucius to cummings.* Boy, did I
have to fight to get that anthology approved as a world literature
text at the high school where I teach. Remind me to tell you
about it some time.) Richard Ellmann's *Four Dubliners* has a
terrific discussion of Oscar Wilde, William Butler Yeats, James
Joyce and Samuel Beckett. Wilson read and enjoyed Hugh
Kenner's book on modern Irish literature, *A Colder Eye*, which
discusses Synge, Yeats, Joyce, Beckett and others. It takes its
title from a poem by Yeats (which appears on his gravestone).
Shea and Wilson allude to Yeats' "Lapis Lazuli" when they refer
to Marilyn Monroe's "ancient glittering eyes so gay." (*Illuminatus!*, pg. 714)
   Yeats had this to say about making your own reality, discussing the Irish philosopher Bishop George Berkeley:

And God appointed Berkeley, who proved all things a dream,
That pragmatical, preposterous pig of a world, its farrow that so
   solid seem,
Must vanish on the instant, if the mind but change its theme.

T.S. Eliot's essay on Yeats in *On Poetry and Poets* emphasizes how Yeats transformed himself from an anthology poet to a
great poet as he grew older. I plan to explore this more fully
(hopefully). Pound in *Guide to Kultur* says he wants to enable
the reader to know more at 50 than Pound did. A female character in Thomas King's *Green Grass, Running Water* says that
most men don't start to get intelligent until after 40. As a 42-
year-old poet, these three themes interest me.

Yippies. The Youth International Party founded by Abbie Hoffman, Paul Krassner and Jerry Rubin. They ran the pig Pigasus
for President in 1968 C.E. They play a role in *Illuminatus!*
Krassner, incidentally, published Bob's first article and many
others over the years in *The Realist*, and Bob dedicated *TSOG* to
Krassner.

Yogis, mathematicians and musicians. "Seem more inclined to
develop meta-programming consciousness than most of humanity." (*Prometheus Rising*, pg. 223) Sigismundo Celine, a musician, becomes more and more obsessed with mathematics on
page **273** of *The Earth Will Shake*. He practices analogs of yoga
in 1760's CE Napoli.

Yoknapatawpha diet. If you feel like eating something unhealthy, get in your car instead, listen to a Faulkner book on tape
and get something healthy to eat. Walk for about three hours a
week, seeing everything around you as an interconnecting web
of humanity, as in Faulkner's books. Wonder who built the
buildings, planted the trees, cut the grass. Wonder about the stories of the people in the cars who pass you by. Decide to play the
role of "that kind person with the great sense of humor who lost
all that weight." Wilson has written on his great love for Faulkner's Yoknapatawpha books. He especially enjoys them on tape.
   If you eat something unhealthy, refuse to accept the inevita-
bility of failure. Remember Christ fell three times and decide to
eat better. Think about the overweight doctor in Faulkner's

novel, *Sartoris.* You could even read about fat in Deuteronomy 32.

(Do you really think Caddy, the character from Faulkner's *The Sound and the Fury,* had an affair with a German general?)

In *Quantum Psychology* Wilson suggests that David Bohm's model of the implicate order "seems to undermine our traditional dualism of 'consciousness' and 'matter.'" (*Quantum Psychology*, pg. 185) One might model the seeming "matter" of someone's excess body fat as "consciousness" or part of the "matter/consciousness continuum." One might say the same about donuts, pizza, etc. Like William Faulkner, we can transform matter/consciousness into a magnificent tool for human understanding and cooperation, each in our own way. This idea reminds me of Crowley's idea of the True Will.

Zukofsky, Louis (1904–1978). Great American poet born January 23, 1904, to whom Ezra Pound dedicated his *Guide to Kulchur* along with British poet Basil Bunting. 1/23/4 (2004) marks his centennial. Wilson mentions both Bunting and Zukofsky in *TSOG* (pg. 211).

APPENDIX SAMEKH

Illuminatus!

Wilson and Shea constructed the novel *Illuminatus!* using the kabbalistic Tree of Life as a model. The Tree of Life contains ten Sephiroth and thirty-two Paths which one may interpret as thirty-two aspects of reality and/or thirty-two levels of consciousness. The books of Gershom Scholem, Aleister Crowley and Israel Regardie provide a huge amount of material on this subject. *Illuminatus!* contains ten "Trips" and it originally contained 22 appendices to correspond with the Sephiroth. This Appendix contains an analysis of the use of this kabbalistic structure in *Illuminatus!* In the preface to the New Falcon edition of *Cosmic Trigger I*, Wilson implores his readers to memorize the following quote from Aleister Crowley:

> IN THIS BOOK IT IS SPOKEN OF THE SEPHIROTH & THE PATHS, OF SPIRITS & CONJURATIONS, OF GODS, SPHERES, PLANES & MANY OTHER THINGS WHICH MAY OR MAY NOT EXIST. IT IS IMMATERIAL WHETHER THEY EXIST OR NOT. BY DOING CERTAIN THINGS CERTAIN RESULTS FOLLOW; STUDENTS ARE MOST EARNESTLY WARNED AGAINST ATTRIBUTING OBJECTIVE REALITY OR PHILOSOPHICAL VALIDITY TO ANY OF THEM.

BOOK ONE:
VERWIRRUNG, OR CHAOS

Kether: The First Trip. Last word: point. Wilson and Shea use the last words of each trip to show the expansion from the point to the line to the plane, etc. Kether means crown in

Hebrew, giving "Crown Point," Simon Moon's first words in the novel. John Dillinger escaped from Crown Point Jail. In Arabic, Aleister Crowley associates Kether with "the three last fathers." (*777*, TABLE OF CORRESPONDENCES, pg. 14) Simon Moon mourns his dead father throughout *Illuminatus!* My father would have celebrated his 69th birthday today (July 27, 2001 C.E.). As for the third, perhaps the thunder god Blake called Nobodaddy. (Crowley associates Kether with thunder gods like Zeus and "God, the 3 in 1." The 1 points back to Kether as well. Of course, the first date to appear in the book, April 1, contains the phallic 1 as well. It also suggests not to take all this too siriusly. (Oops, seriously.) The narrator says, "that crown sits uneasily on my head (if I have a head)" on page 8 of *Illuminatus!*

Wilson and Shea chose the final words in the first five trips in keeping with Crowley's Naples arrangement, as discussed in his *Book of Thoth*. The final words of the remaining trips reflect a more personal interpretation the tree of life and its interrelation with the novel. Crowley begins his discussion with three veils of nothingness, corresponding with Ain, Ain Soph and Ain Soph Auer, (the three veils of nothingness in the Kabbalah) and then he arrives at the point, Kether, the first sephiroth. Hence the first trip ends with the word "point." Chokmah, the second sephiroth, gives us the line, the first dimension. Binah, the third sephiroth, gives us the plane, or two dimensions. Then after the abyss we get Chesed, the fourth sephiroth, the solid in three dimensions, and Geburah, the fifth sephiroth, gives us motion, which indicates time or the fourth dimension.

Crowley calls Kether the "home of the 12 stars." The Greeks had a system of 12 deities, six female and six male. One could think of *Illuminatus!* as a film with 12 stars: Stella/Mavis, Mao Tu Tsi, Miss Portinari, Mary Lou, Eris, Leviathan, Hagbard Celine, Joe Malik, Simon Moon, George Dorn, Malaclypse the Elder and FUCK-UP. Of course, one could select another list of 12. Pound used for the twelve Greek deities as the basis for his post scriptum Ulysses calendar (starting with November: Hephestus, Zeus, Saturn, Hermes, Ares, Phoebus, Kupris, Juno, Athena, Hestia, Artemis, Demeter.) Pound frequently refers to Aphrodite as Kupris in the *Cantos*. Wilson discusses this calendar in *Cosmic Trigger III*.

The narrator spends the opening ten pages of the novel jumping from viewpoint to viewpoint, in a fashion somewhat similar to the Wandering Rocks chapter of *Ulysses* by James Joyce. Then "I find and identify a body, a self, a task." The narrator and the novel arrive in Saul and Rebecca Goodman's bedroom. The "I" suggests the number 1 as well as the phallus or the ego or Kether itself. The novel moves into the third person, but, again like *Ulysses* as Hugh Kenner pointed out in *Joyce's Voices*, the third person narrator often takes on vocabulary and attitudes from the characters on stage at the moment. Kenner calls this the Uncle Charles Principal, after the way the character Uncle Charles influences the narrative voice at one point in Joyce's *Portrait of the Artist as a Young Man*. The narrative voice of *Illuminatus!* seems to belong primarily to the computer FUCK-UP, but in FUCK-UP's attempts to comprehend Universe it uses a variety of voices (sort of like the voice shifting used in Ericksonian hypnosis). FUCK-UP fully enters the form of each character. When becoming Saul Goodman, the fluid narrative voice comments, "any notions about being a stranger in this body have vanished with my dreams into air. Into thin air."

Similarly, *The Homing Pigeons* has deep structure of perhaps existing as a drug vision of George Dorn, or as a necessary hallucination as George functions as an extraterrestrial intelligence agent before returning to the center of our galaxy (the homing pigeon image). In the novel George's ego transforms into Frank Dashwood, John Disk and others. Perhaps. The whole novel has the form of non-objectivity according to the glossary. Interestingly, the one-volume edition of *Schrödinger's Cat* removed the lines in the glossary which indicated the forms of the three novels which compose *Schrödinger's Cat* (non-objectivity for *The Homing Pigeons*, Bell's Theorem for *The Trick Top Hat* and the Everett-Wheeler-Graham model for *The Universe Next Door*). Non-objectivity in quantum mechanics suggests that acts of observation create Universe. According to John A. Wheeler, only observations at the subatomic level participate in this creation. Wilson would expand that model. See *Quantum Theory and Measure* edited by Wheeler for a technical discussion and Nick Herbert's *Quantum Realities* for a non-technical discussion.

Chokmah: Paris' choice of Aphrodite over Athena and Hera led to the Trojan War. The choice of deity shapes the metastructure of our perceived reality. Many characters in *Illuminatus!* select Eris, Goddess of Chaos, as their deity. (Athena, Goddess of Wisdom, perhaps looks over this trip since Chokmah means wisdom in Hebrew.) If one had Aphrodite, the Great Pumpkin, Nuit, Anna Livia Plurabella or the Virgin Mary as one's shordurpersav (short duration personal savior in the Sub-Genius terminology) or middurpersav (mid-duration personal savior), one would shape one's perceptions in very different ways. Imagine traveling through the Louvre. With Aphrodite as one's middurpersav, the Venus de Milo might seem the main object of interest. If one had chosen (or gotten chosen by) Nuit, the Egyptian antiquities might shine with a special radiance. The choice of Eris guides the choices of action by many of the characters in *Illuminatus!* as well as that of its authors.

This trip ends with the word "line," adding a dimension to the first trip's "point." Appropriately, we meet Buckminster Fuller on the first page of this trip, which opens with a reference to "Spaceship Earth," a phrase coined by that wise critter. Also a voice George Dorn hears during this trip says, *"It all depends on whether the fool has wisdom enough to repeat it"* (*Illuminatus!*, pg. 68) when he hears the words "Hail Eris!" (See **Modern Jazz Quartet.**)

Crowley associates Chokmah with hashish. In this trip George remembers a sexual encounter on hashish. (*Illuminatus!*, pg. 74)

Binah: The Third Trip. Final word: plane. Meaning of Binah in Hebrew: Understanding. Crowley calls Binah the Great Mother, so naturally Goddess worship plays a great role in this trip. Also, Binah refers to the sea, so the undersea adventures of Hagbard and friends in their yellow submarine also fit in nicely. This trip completes Book One. The first three sephiroth in the tree of life reside above the abyss. In the Naples arrangement we get point, line and plane. Only with the fourth dimension do we get dynamics, movement, time, etc. The opening quote to this trip refers to the yoni and "Our Lady," both attributes of Binah. Crowley refers to silence as the virtue associated with Binah. This trip contains the line, "They drove for a while in silence."

(*Illuminatus!*, pg. 124) (Trivia? Well, these little things add up, or least it seems that way on this side of the Abyss.)

Binah has the same numerical value (67) as the Hebrew word for "to embalm." We must beware embalming the text through over analysis. Heh, heh, heh.

BOOK TWO:
ZWEITRACHT, OR DISCORD

Chesed: The Fourth Trip. Final word: solid. Now we have moved below the Abyss and have reached the world of solid matter. This trip has the subtitle "Jesus Christ on a Bicycle." The bicycle has a number of interesting associations for the Roaring Twentieth Century (as Timothy Leary calls it). *Butch Cassidy and the Sundance Kid* has a few wonderful scenes concerning bicycles, where a salescritter takes over a crowd gathered to listen to someone trying to form a posse to catch the outlaws. Sales overtaking vengeance seems a theme for the importance of capitalism and advertising in the Roaring Twentieth Century. Note that *Ulysses'* Leopold Bloom and the Church of the Sub-Genius's J.R. "Bob" Dobbs both played the role of salescritters. Later in *Butch Cassidy* the bicycle plays a romantic role, with "Raindrops Keep Falling on My Head" playing. Finally, Butch casts the bike away, consciously rejecting the future.

The surrealists used many bicycle images.

Albert Hoffman accidentally discovered LSD and took a bicycle ride he would never forget.

When the computer Hal dies in *2001: A Space Odyssey*, he sings about a bicycle built for two. Wilson and Shea divide the five phases of the Illuminati vision of history into the bicycle and the tricycle. They also model the 1968 protests at the National Democratic Convention in Chicago using Alfred Jarry's presurrealist "The Crucifixion of Christ Considered as an Uphill Bike Race."

The fourth trip of *Illuminatus!* begins with a discussion of the Assassins, who used the symbol of an upside down four. This also suggests the shape of the upside down Hanged Man in the twelfth tarot trump. A little later in this trip Hagbard encounters the word SNAFU ("Situation normal, all fucked up") that suits this sephiroth perfectly; i.e., little in the material world seems perfect. We live in a burning house, as the Buddha said. I wonder if the Talking Heads' "Burning Down the House" refers to this. Of course beth means house in Hebrew, and the path of beth lies above the abyss, leading from Chokmah to Kether. Timothy Leary loved the music of Talking Heads' David Byrne, and he interviews him in his book *Chaos and Cyberculture*, which Wilson includes on his website's Recommended Reading list.

In this trip Simon thinks of Chicago Mayor Richard Daley (1902–1976) as the ringmaster during a meditation on the microcosm and the macrocosm during the 1968 police debacle. This echoes the discussion of the ringmaster in the first trip as well illustrating the crossing of the abyss: in the first trip the discussion of the ringmaster focuses on a rodent in central park, a somewhat idyllic scene. In the material world we get cops Macing folks for poor use of the First Amendment. Simon thinks, "Conclusion: Mayor Daley, in a small way, is what Krishna is, in a large way. QED." (*Illuminatus!*, pg. 148)

Also, this trip quotes Ted Zatlyn from the *Los Angeles Free Press* on the John Birch Society's view of the goal of the Illuminati: "Their evil goal is to transcend materiality." (*Illuminatus!*, pg. 151) This fits with the theme of Chesed and suggests the desire of the Illuminati to cross the abyss.

Wilson has written how one may view Lovecraft's visions of Cthulhu as looking at the abyss from below, fearing to cross it. The Campus Crusade for Cthulhu pictures Cthulhu as looking something like a cosmic octopus. In this trip Saul Goodman describes the Illuminati as a million-armed octopus, and from below the abyss many view the Illuminati with a similar horror to that with which Lovecraft viewed Cthulhu. One might view the history of Universe as an overlong story based on a simple joke, a short of Shaggai dog story, if you will.

Father James Augustine Muldoon's discussion of Gnosticism further illuminates the nature of existence beneath the abyss. The Manicheans called the God of this world *panurgia*, "which has the connotations of a kind of blind, stupid blundering force rather than a truly intelligent being. The realm which their god inhabits is pure spirit of pure light." (*Illuminatus!*, pg. 169) Once again this trips presents us with a below the abyss/above the abyss double picture. One can see why the Church condemned Scotus Erigina, who said, "*Qui sunt omnia sunt*" ("all things that are, are lights"), as a Manichean, as Ezra Pound has discussed. Robert Shea took the title of his book about the Cathars, etc., *All Things Are Lights*, from that quote.

The fourth trip concludes with Hagbard Celine about to choose whether or not to take sentient life, whether to kill the people he imagines on board the Illuminati ships. This signals the shift from mercy to severity, from trip four, Chesed, to trip five, Geburah.

Geburah: The Fifth Trip. Final word: motion. Now we have the space-time four-dimensional world of three space dimensions and a dimension of time. Geburah usually gets translated as strength, but Crowley translates it as courage in *777*. (*Sepher Sephiroth*, pg. 27) Perhaps the Wizard can give us some. Geburah has the numerical value of 216, and the Hebrew word for lion also adds up to 216. Curiouser and curiouser. Both the courage and lion associations fit the role of this sephiroth as the sphere of Mars. 216 equals six cubed, which might relate to *The Book of the Law*'s "Love under will." (Six relates to the tarot trump, The Lovers.) Plus, for 23 lovers, 216 equals two cubed times three cubed. Twenty-three skidoo! The Cowardly Lion also fits in with this trip's examination of George Dorn perception of himself as "yellow."

This trip begins with a discussion of Hitler and the Holocaust, plunging the reader into Geburah's world of severity. Next the authors present a surreal examination of the events surrounding the 1968 C.E. Democratic Convention in Chicago.

This trip also includes Epicene Wildeblood's discussion of his review of *Illuminatus!* as if the novel already existed within the world of the novel. In other words, we have a discussion of the review of a novel within the novel itself. The four dimensional world of Geburah allows this sort of postmodern recursion.

Trip Five also includes a description of Adam Weishaupt discovering the law of fives, realizing that the more you look for the number five, the more you will find it. This corresponds with the self-referentiality of Wildeblood's discussion of his review of one of the novels in which he exists. Markoff Chaney discovers his tarot deck has the Five of Pentacles missing, leaving 77 cards. (Oz adds to 77 in Hebrew. Crowley associates the ruby with Geburah, as in Ruby Slippers. He says the ruby represents "flaming energy.")

One can see Geburah receiving the energy of Binah via the path of Cheth (Hebrew for fence), the Chariot. I've always associated the Chariot with Reich's muscular armor. The armored human bears the Grail, the energy from Binah. In this trip Saul curses Gruad the Grayfaced. Grayface represents the armored human who denies the Grail within, the energy from Binah, which Joyce called Anna Livia Plurabella, the "everliving" and the "bringer of plurabilities."

BOOK THREE:
UNORDNUNG, OR CONFUSION

On the page before this book begins, the authors include Aleister Crowley's *Liber OZ*.

Tipareth: The Sixth Trip. Final word: Rebecca. Tipareth, which means beauty in Hebrew, represents the heart of the tree of life, and one might see this trip as the heart of *Illuminatus!* Appropriately, the sequence of final words changes from the geometrical to the more human "Rebecca," Saul Goodman's wife. Trump six of the tarot has the title "The Lovers." "Love is the law, love under will," as *The Book of the Law* says. For 23 fans, the Hebrew word Tipareth adds up to 1081, which equals the sum of the first 46 (2 x 23) integers. Crowley also calls Tipareth the sphere of Sol, the sun. Sol sounds kind of like Saul. Heh, heh, heh.

With Tipareth's central place on the Tree, this trip emphasizes the role of balance, opening with a quote about balance from the *Principia Discordia*, and including Hagbard's discussion of the balance of order and chaos. Also, Tipareth alone of the sephiroth below the Abyss communicates directly with Kether, the crown. This accounts for this trip's discussion of communication with disembodied beings, which takes on a dark form in the discussion of "Hitler's Master" and the intelligent beings that preexisted humanity in Arthur Machen's fictions. Crowley associates Tipareth with the Knowledge and Conversation of the Holy Guardian Angel, a contact with Higher Intelligence.

For Wilson and Shea, however, the non-hierarchical human-to-human contact seems more important than the Kether-Tipareth connection. Although the book deals speculatively with contact with "higher beings," the message that "Communication is only possible between equals" seems to have a higher place in their hierarchy of values. Robert Putney Drake bemoans his lack of serious human contact before his death, despite his tremendous wealth, power and sexual conquests. The reunion of Saul and Rebecca and their lovemaking appropriately climax this trip.

Of course, one can also interpret Crowley's metaphor of the Knowledge and Conversation of the Holy Guardian Angel as an individual realizing their true will, manifesting their potential. This accounts for Drake's meditation on Dutch Schultz's last words in this trip. Drake realizes that "if a cheap hoodlum like Dutch Schultz had a great poet buried in him, what might be released if any man looked the old whore Death in the eye?" (*Illuminatus!*, pg. 354) Here one can see the Higher Intelligence contacted as within the individual. This also corresponds with the discussion of the impact of the tomato juice in this trip. The tomato juice contains a drug which changes neophobes (those who fear the new) into neophiles (those who love the new). One might say that the love of new ideas initiates the contact with Higher Intelligences within the individual.

Note that in the introduction to *The Walls Came Tumbling Down* Wilson changes these terms to infophobes (those who fear information) and infophiles (those who love information).

Information. Information.
You won't get it.
By hook or by crook, we will. I am the new Number Two.
Who is Number One?
You are Number Six.
I am not a number, I am free man!
      — From the television series, *The Prisoner*

At the conclusion of Trip Six, Saul, having connected with his Higher Intelligences, shares them with Rebecca, helping her connect with her own Higher Intelligences, or their Higher Intelligences, if you'd prefer. Above the Abyss ideas like personal possession seems to get a bit tangled. Saul seems to connect with non-local mind, in some way. Who knows how much of that resides in his own skull and how much elsewhere/elsewhen?

Netzach: The Seventh Trip. Final word: end. Meaning of Netzach in Hebrew: Victory; attributions: Venus, bliss. In this trip Hagbard hands over spiritual leadership to Miss Portinari, named after Beatrice Portinari, the inspiration for Dante's *Commedia*. Hagbard even plays with a quote from Dante when he hands over the spiritual leadership of the Leif Erickson to Miss Portinari. The transfer to female leadership goes along with the Venus attribution, as does the party for the nude plastic martini and the sex scenes. Note the lack of spiritual fulfillment in the sex scenes, which signify "victory" as in "scoring" but not the personal union in the sex scene from the end of trip six. However, Crowley does associate Netzach with the Garden of Delights, the epitome of purely physical pleasure. See Wilson's *The Trick Top Hat* and *Prometheus Rising* for an exploration of this cyber-somatic Garden. This also fits in with the discussion of Hassan i Sabbah in this trip. (For how Bucky Fuller's ideas fit in with this, perhaps I'll write *Synergetic Magick: The Eye in the Tetrahedron*.) The metaphor of "the most manicured and artificial garden" (*Illuminatus!*, pg. 401) also corresponds with the Garden of Delight.

Markoff Chaney's sexual frustration also corresponds with the sexual aspect of Netzach. This trip also deals with Markoff's own kind of victory in his war against the Illuminati and the idea of "normalcy."

Crowley emphasizes that the path of nun, corresponding with the trump Death, links Tipareth and Netzach. *The Book of Lies* deals with sexual aspects of the death metaphor ("chapters I, VIII, XV, XVI, etc., etc."). Trip Eight of *Illuminatus!* ends with FUCK-UP predicting the final victory of the Illuminati, the extinction of the human race, the end. Of course, Crowley discusses illumination as the "extinction" of normal consciousness, so double meanings abound.

This sephiroth relates to the 37 sequence.

0: O tell me all about Anna...; the Cosmic Egg (Humpty Dumpty).

37: A prime number, man's crown.

74: Lamed (ox-goad), the Hebrew letter associated with the tarot trump Adjustment (a.k.a. Justice); also the Hebrew word for circuit adds to 74, as does the Hebrew word for "all the way."

111: The Hebrew value of A (1) + L (30) + P (80). Joyce uses this number a lot in *Finnegans Wake* because of its connection with Anna Livia Plurabella, the goddess of that book, as well as the river Liffey in Dublin and the dreamer HCE's wife, etc., etc. The Hebrew letter aleph (ox), which corresponds with the tarot trump the Fool, adds to 111, and Crowley frequently uses this number as well, calling it "priceless." It also means "Thick darkness" and "Sudden death." (*777*, pg. 45). Louis Zukofsky wrote a long poem titled "*A*". His book *A Test of Poetry* seems to me a powerful magickal text for training the ear, the heart and the mind.

148: The Hebrew value of this sephiroth, Netzach. One could see this as the victory of Netzach over the first two circuits (74 + 74). The Hebrew word for "glutton and drunkard" also adds to 148: someone who overindulges in the first circuit/ system (glutton) and someone who overindulges in the second (drunkard). Maznim, the Hebrew word for the Scales of Justice, also adds to 148, relating to Libra, the scales.

185: ? Crowley notes: "I have not yet worked out all the numbers of this important scale." (*777*, pg. 44) Scales, of course, relate to Libra, 148, 37 x 4.

222: Ishmael Reed's birthday (2/22). This number "may one day be of value" according to Uncle Al. (*777*, pg. 46)

259: ?

296: ?

333: Choronzon, denizen of the Abyss.

370: "Most venerable," according to Crowley. "It delivers the secret of creation into the hand of the magician." (*777*, pg. 46) Also shalom, peace, adds to 370.

666: The sum of the numbers 1 to 36. Aleister Crowley added his name up to the Number of the Beast in various ways. (Robert Heinlein's novel, *The Number of the Beast,* interpreted the Biblical 666 as six to the sixth power, to the sixth power. That novel also includes a trip to Oz. Really.)

703: The sum of the numbers 1 to 37.

777: The total number of paths on the Tree of Life; a sacred number of Las Vegas; the *Flaming Sword* that drove Eve and

Adam out of the Garden, riverrun from swerve of shore to bend of bay, leads by a comodious vicus of recirculation back to...; the World of Shells.

Just as victory marks the end of a game, this victory trip ends with the word "end."

BOOK FOUR:
BEAMTENHERRSHAFT OR BUREAUCRACY

(Aleister Crowley wrote a book called *Book Four* which played a big role in *Masks of the Illuminati*. It contains a great kabbalistic analysis of Mother Goose. First Crowley book I read, I think.)

Hod: The Eighth Trip. Final word: ALIVE... Meaning of Hod in Hebrew: Splendor. Kabbalistic attribution: Mercury, Thoth, the point's idea of intellection. Hagbard's notion of the logogram and the biogram seems central to this trip. A lot of stuff in this chapter sounds like Neurolinguistic Programming (NLP), from Hagbard's encounters with the cops to the discussion of redundancy and flexibility in social situations. Also, Fission Chips encounters with the characters from *The Wizard of Oz* and *Alice's Adventures in Wonderland*, and his contemplation of the link between writer's imaginations and reality fits Hod's intellectual world. The Dealy Lama story about the Laurel and Hardy archetypes seems like the intellectual center of the novel. The fourth Laurel and Hardy vision deals with the Hegelian world, whose dualities seem particularly appropriate to Hod. For a thorough destruction of Hegelian (and Platonic and Marxist) realities, see *The Open Society and Its Enemies* by Karl Popper, which greatly influenced Robert Anton Wilson.

In this trip Mama Sutra gives a psychic reading in which she picks up pieces of the film *Manhattan Melodrama*, starring Clark Gable and Myrna Loy, the film John Dillinger saw the night of his supposed assassination. This film became a hit due to the publicity around the death of Johnny D., and this success propelled Myrna Loy to stardom. Loy felt guilty that her big break came from a man's death. Clark Gable served as the basis for Bugs Bunny a few years later, in particular a scene of him eating a carrot from *It Happened One Night*.

Myrna Loy entitled her autobiography *Being and Becoming*, an expression from Søren Kierkegaard, whom Wilson discusses in the introduction to *Quantum Psychology*. Loy gained her greatest fame with William Powell playing Nora and Nick Charles in the *Thin Man* films. Nick and Nora's names both have Joycean referents: Joyce calls the devil Nick to St. Michael's Mick in *Finnegans Wake,* and Joyce spent most of his life living with Nora Barnacle. Cynthia Heimel's *But Enough about You* has a wonderful article called "When in Doubt, Act Like Myrna Loy."

The reading by Mama Sutra also relates to the mercurial nature of Hod. The human mind (mercury) tends to jump to premature certainty, and as Wilson has frequently remarked, quoting Nietzsche, we tend to forget the artistic power of our brains. ("We are all greater artists than we think." — Friedrich Wilhelm Nietzsche.) Mama Sutra weaves a magnificent yarn for detective Danny Pricefixer, never realizing that her own nervous system has concocted this particular reality, using all of her perceptions and life experiences. Mercury can move quickly to answer all questions without too much contemplation, explaining away all data that doesn't fit the model of choice. Of course, the use of the verb "to be" helps this jump to premature certainty. Also, Mama Sutra's portrayal of the Illuminati as followers of the light of reason fits the mercurial nature of this trip. Sutra's model does, however, reveal the anti-rational bias of most (all?) organized religion.

This trip also has an homage to author Robert E. Howard (1906–1936), mixing his stories of Kull and Conan the Barbarian with the Lovecraftian history of the Illuminati, as well as elements of *The Lord of the Rings*. This mixing of literature and history fits in with the mercurial nature of Hod. Mercury symbolizes the ever-changing nature of human thought, and Mama Sutra's vision of history reveals history as a creation of human nervous systems. We sometimes speak about the "facts" of history, but each mind selects its "facts" and shapes them into a particular narrative. And speaking of Hod as intellect, we get a wonderful satire of Ayn Rand's *Atlas Shrugged* as *Telemachus Sneezed* in this trip. Its protagonist focuses on Heraclitus rather than Aristotle. *Telemachus Sneezed* includes a Captain Clark who pilots a plane which crashes, a nod to William Burroughs.

Simon Moon reads this novel on a trans-Atlantic flights, and when he reads about Captain Clark in the novel, he asks the name of the captain of his flight. You guessed it, Captain Clark, Heathcliffe Clark. This ties in with what Crowley calls the double mercurial current of Hod. Simon, who always has Joyce on the brain, thinks of "weathering heights" as he returns to the novel within the novel. *Telemachus Sneezed* also includes a Captain Howard Cork, based on Hagbard Celine, with a dash of Captain Ahab. Amidst all this mercurial literary satire, the Ringmaster begins to recognize itself as the author of the text and/or as the computer FUCK-UP. One might see the occasional partial awakening as parallel to the partial awakenings of HCE in *Finnegans Wake*.

Speaking of double currents, someone once told Wilson he had previously lived as Baron Knigge, a member of Weishaupt's Illuminati. A paragraph in this trip mentions Knigge and alludes to the possibility that Robert Putney Drake considered himself a reincarnation of his ancestor Sir Francis Drake. The double current theme also relates to Harry Coin's double memories. (And all these H.C. initials serve as an homage to *Finnegans Wake*'s H.C.E.'s.)

Wilson also intended an homage to Philip Jose Farmer in Hagbard Celine's family tree, although most of the evidence may have gotten trimmed when Dell cut 500 pages from *Illuminatus!* Farmer created a family tree of fictional characters, mostly adventure characters like Tarzan, Doc Savage, the Scarlet Pimpernel, Sherlock Holmes, etc., in books such as *Tarzan Alive* and *Doc Savage: His Apocalyptic Life*. Farmer hypothesizes that a meteor fell near Wold-Newton in England in the late eighteenth century, which mutated the genes of Percy Blakely (the Pimpernel), among others. The descendants of these individuals have exceptional physical abilities, great minds and, usually, gray eyes. Farmer goes so far as to include Joyce's Leopold Bloom in his "Wold-Newton" family tree. Wilson links his characters explicitly with the Wold-Newton families in *Masks of the Illuminati*. This makes Hagbard a distant relative of Leopold Bloom, appropriately enough. James Joyce features Leopold Bloom in *Ulysses*. Both Phillip Jose Farmer and Robert Anton Wilson love Joyce's books.

On page 543, FUCK-UP recognizes itself as the ringmaster, just as it did in the first trip. The mind (Hod) can see things clearly on occasion, for instance listening to a tape of Alan Watts talking. Suddenly the linear mind catches a glimpse of a cosmic order (or cosmic disorder).

The mind, Hod, can take itself very seriously. In addition to sending up Ayn Rand in this trip, Wilson and Shea also jibe at philosopher Mortimer Adler in the wonderful discussion of "The Great Tradition" as privilege or private law. It seems appropriate to discuss economic matters below (after) the sphere of Tiphareth/Beauty.

In *Illuminati Papers* (pg. 104) Wilson says of Ezra Pound:

> Pound refers to a celebrated drinking cup said to be molded directly from the right breast of Helen of Troy and, therefore, the most beautiful cup in the ancient world. Decent government is important, he is saying, but a lovely woman is more important.

Both Hod and Netzach point back to Tiphareth. Hod yearns for victory and beauty. These yearnings also lead to the next sphere down the tree of life, a return to the middle pillar and the sphere of Yesod, the moon, sex.

Yesod: Hebrew meaning: Foundation. Last word: Ra! This sephiroth returns us to the middle pillar. Appropriately, this trip begins with a recapitulation of events of the novel so far, mixed with names of bands attending Woodstock Europa. These include the Entwives (a Tolkien reference whose bittersweet romance fits this sephiroth) and The Horse of Another Color, a *Wizard of Oz* reference. Interestingly, the film of *The Wizard of Oz* and *Finnegans Wake* both came out in 1939 C.E.

Crowley says the Tree of Life has its root in Yesod, and that Malkuth merely serves as a pendant. In the same way, this Trip climaxes the novel with the triumph of Eris, and the final Trip serves appropriately as Aftermath or pendant. The final word "Ra!" seems a word of triumph and humor, as well as emphasizing the Sun as the center or root of our solar system and Egypt as the root of Western Civilization. The exclamation point suggests the phallus, as Crowley points out (so to speak) in *The Book of Lies*. This fits the sexual nature of Yesod.

In the Naples arrangement Crowley calls Yesod "the point's idea of being." In this trip Mary Lou Servix "felt herself dwindling to a point and approaching absolute zero." (*Illuminatus!*, pg. 635) This occurs just after Simon's dead father tells him, "Kether. Right here in the middle of Malkuth," echoing the kabbalistic structure of the book as well as *Hamlet*. (The point's idea of "to be" or not.) Then Mary Lou observes "the point was giving off light and energy, my light and my energy but God's also." She connects this with Bucky Fuller's concept of the omnidirectional halo. In the same paragraph she remembers her abortion, suggesting a parallel between the point and the single cell which grows into a complete human body-mind metasystem. This also echoes the idea of Ra!, the Sun as a point of light and/or as the phallus. Also, Crowley associates the Hebrew letter Yod with both the shape of the spermatozoa and tarot Trump IX, The Hermit. That IX fits in with Trip Nine, even though it has Yesod as a primary association. The Hermit, Virgo, suggest hidden mystery, and he holds a lantern containing a light, perhaps the glowing point Mary Lou saw, an image of Ra! Mary Lou's whole monologue, which runs intermittently throughout this chapter, echoes Molly Bloom's monologue at the end of *Ulysses*, but where Molly's monologue finishes with a section focused on the word "Yes," Mary Lou's climaxes with a section (in the Tenth Trip) focused on the word "No." As the monologue progresses Shea and Wilson cease using punctuation (almost— they use a "-" for emphasis on page 692, as well as some quotation marks, and two question marks on page 714), just as Joyce did throughout Molly Bloom's soliloquy. This gives a sense of the river-like flow of the internal monologue. *Ulysses* monologue continues uninterrupted, while that of *Illuminatus!* cuts back and forth with other elements of the story. The paragraphs which end with parts of the monologue have no terminal punctuation. Wilson has said that D.W. Griffith's *Intolerance*, with its four interspersed story-lines, inspired the form of *Illuminatus! Illuminatus!*, of course, has many more interlinking plot lines.

Robert Pearson refers to Hagbard as "my ace." As George Strait sang, "You've got to have an ace in the hole, a little secret that nobody knows." In his song "Ace in the Hole," Paul Simon sang,

> Some people say Jesus is the ace in the hole.
> I never met the man, so I don't really know.
> Maybe some Christmas when I sick and alone,
> He'll look up my number, and call me on the phone.

As Mary Lou's monologue continues, she thinks of "throne after cast down into the void." This echoes the thrones in Dante's *Commedia* and the Thrones book of Pound's *Cantos*. Plus the Hebrew word for throne (Exodus XVIII, 16) adds up to 80, as does Yesod. When Winifred (one of the leaders of the Illuminati), looks into the apple of discord she sees her heart's desire, the throne of the world. Crowley associates the tarot trump the Tower Struck by Lightning with the letter *peh,* which also has the value of 80, and Mary Lou certainly seems to go through a Tower experience in this Trip. Perhaps the growing glowing point Mary Lou observed turned into the giant orb Eris carries at the climax of this Trip. Fittingly the Nine Unknown Men chant the ending to the Trip.

BOOK FIVE:
GRUMMET OR AFTERMATH

Malkuth: Has the value 496 (M 40 + L 30 + K 20 + U 6 + Th 400), the same as Leviathan, in the Kabbalah, hence Leviathan's appearance in this trip. 496 also serves as the mystic number of Shin (the sum of the numbers 1 through 31), representing Saturn and fire in Crowley's system. This links with the final word of this trip (and of the novel proper), "cracked." This suggests that the world functions as a non-static process, a complex set of verbs and not a noun. Incidentally, Malkuth has the mystic number 55 (the sum of 1 through 10), the same value as the Hebrew word for noon. Malkuth represents the world, the earth, a noon blue apple seen from space. In *777* Crowley says, "Earth appears for the first time in Malkuth." This relates to the characters in the novel seeing themselves in the novel form. The fiction has descended into our world. The reader plays the role of Dorothy, awakening in their familiar world (Malkuth), but seeing the archetypes from the novel all around them (along with some 23's): "You were there, and you and you!"

The fish smell from dead Egyptian mouth-breeders occurs in both the First and Tenth Trips, humorously suggesting Kether's presence in Malkuth. Perri the squirrel from the First Trip also reappears. Hagbard tells Joe Malik that the ultimate weapon seems the ability of the individual to say "no." Mary Lou's monologue emphasizes this, as does Satan's "non serviam" (I will not serve). The gospels call Satan the king of this world, a.k.a. Malkuth. This Trip reveals the Dealy Lama as both Satan and Prometheus, as well as Gracchus Gruad.

In the Naples arrangement Crowley sees Malkuth as "The Point's Idea of Itself fulfilled in its complement." This relates to the meeting of Leviathan and FUCK-UP. Leviathan, as a huge one celled organism, plays the role of the point throughout the novel in its parallels with the Naples Arrangement, from the Point as ringmaster in Kether to the alchemical marriage in Malkuth. FUCK-UP awakens to his role as the ringmaster, and they all lived happily ever after.

Appendix Aleph: George Washington, the Fool. If Washington parallels the first trump, perhaps each president parallels another, trump: John Adams the Magus, etc. (In *The Game of Life,* Leary and Wilson reverse the positions of the third and fourth trumps, so Jefferson would correspond to the Empress. P.G. Wodehouse's later Blandings Castle novels featuring a prize winning pig named Empress. This corresponds with the pig-Bacon-Shakespeare-HAMlet theme in *Finnegans Wake*.) Washington as the Fool suggests an American set of trumps, with the stoned fool leading us to initial military victory. Thomas Pynchon includes a hemp smoking George Washington in *Mason and Dixon*, a novel with many parallels with Wilson's *Historical Illuminatus* series. I suspect Pynchon has read Wilson and learned from him.

Appendix Ayin

Joyce's Influence on
Masks of the Illuminati

James Joyce has exerted considerable influence over novelist Robert Anton Wilson. Wilson says, "My style derives directly from Ezra Pound, James Joyce, Raymond Chandler, H.L. Menken, William S. Burroughs, Benjamin Tucker, and *Elephant Doody Comix*[2], in approximately that order of importance." (*Illuminati Papers*, pg. 66) Wilson frequently mentions Joyce in his nonfiction as well as in his fiction. He even made Joyce a major character in his novel *Masks of the Illuminati* and Joyce shows up in various guises in other of Wilson's novels. Wilson has used stylistic devices from *Finnegans Wake* and elsewhere in the Joyce corpus, as well as structural devices from *Ulysses* and the *Wake*.

I first read Wilson's *Masks of the Illuminati* in 1982. At the time I knew next to nothing about James Joyce. Wilson introduced me to Joyce's personality, his techniques, and his work, all at the same time. Over the last 22 years I have continued to read Wilson's work with a great deal of pleasure. In addition, I have delved deeper and deeper into the worlds of James Joyce, Ezra Pound and others. Wilson has served as a constant mentor. As Hugh Kenner said about *Ulysses*, "A mentor is advisable: not an unreasonable prerequisite for one of the key books of the space-time age." (Kenner, intro to Budgen, *James Joyce and the Making of Ulysses* pg. ix) Robert Anton Wilson has mentored me and many others through the worlds of *Finnegans Wake*, *Ulysses*, *The Cantos* and beyond.

---

[2] A comic from Wilson's youth.

Wilson's non-fiction over the last forty-five years has frequently focused on Joyce. These interests carry over into his fiction. Wilson has looked at Joyce's work through the lenses of various psychological theories, from those of Freud and Jung to those of Wilhelm Reich and Timothy Leary. Wilson has also mentioned a variety of writers on Joyce, from Samuel Beckett to Hugh Kenner and Richard Ellmann. For Wilson, Joyce brings relativity to literature. Joyce provides a kaleidoscope of viewpoints and techniques to his novels, eliminating the single viewpoint narrator of nineteenth century realistic fiction. Joyce moves from the Newtonian paradigm to one more in tune with the umwelt of Einstein and quantum mechanics. Like the multiple viewpoints of the cubists, Joyce presents incidents and characters from multiple viewpoints, revealing them in a dynamic ever-changing universe through literary parallax. Wilson uses these techniques in *Masks of the Illuminati* to reflect on the characters of both Einstein and Joyce, as well as to present multiple views of all of the novel's characters.

Hugh Kenner, discussing *Ulysses*, commented:

> But toward the end, working on 'Penelope' and 'Ithaca' together, James Joyce seems to have gone farther, divining—no, not the cosmos of Picasso, Einstein, Heisenberg and Gödel, his visual taste being banal, his science but a smattering of terms, his very arithmetic deplorable—divining rather something of what they intuited and modeled in their own idiom, their own arts; for that the human experience is homogenous, that innovators in diverse fields are assuredly one another's contemporaries without necessity of interaction, is one of the exhilarating truths of history.
> — Kenner, *Ulysses*, pg. 153

Wilson illuminates this in his novel *Masks of the Illuminati*, making Einstein, Joyce, Aleister Crowley, Carl Jung, Ezra Pound, William Butler Yeats and Lenin, et al, characters whose fictitious and actual interactions reflect the parallels between their innovations. Wilson describes his "Major theme as I worked: Relativity as illustrated by Einstein's physics, Joyce's art and Crowley's 'magic.'" (Wilson, 10/20/2001 email) The title itself links the book with Wilson's vision of Joyce's Irish tradition. Wilson has frequently discussed Oscar Wilde's essay "The Truth of Masks," which he links with the notion of Mask and Counter-Mask in Yeats' *A Vision*. Wilson even called the two parts of his *Cosmic Trigger Volume III* "The Masks of Reality" and "The Reality of Masks." Wilde's original essay dealt with costuming in Shakespeare, but Wilson suggests it also suggests the masks worn by homosexuals in Victorian England and the masks worn by conquered peoples in colonized nations, especially the Irish. He links this with Stephen Dedalus' "silence, exile and cunning." Silence seeming a powerful Joycean mask, the "presence of the absent." (*Coincidance*, pg. 87)

In his 1977 *Cosmic Trigger*, Wilson says:

> "Reality" is a word in the English language which happens to be (a) a **noun** and (b) **singular**. Thinking in the English language (and in cognate Indo-European languages) therefore subliminally programs us to conceptualize "reality" as one block-like entity, sort of like a huge New York skyscraper, in which every part is just another "room" within the same building. This linguistic program is so pervasive that most people cannot "think" outside it at all, and when one tries to offer a different perspective they imagine one is talking gibberish.
> — *Cosmic Trigger,* pg. iii

Wilson presents myriad relative realities in *Masks of the Illuminati*, using methods derived from the relativities of Einstein, Joyce, Crowley and Pound while incorporating Einstein, Joyce, Crowley and Pound as characters. In addition, Wilson makes Einstein and Joyce into amateur detectives. Wilson had commented on the similarities between Joyce's method of almost obsessive observation with that of Sherlock Holmes in his *Schrödinger's Cat* trilogy. Hugh Kenner refers to Sherlock Holmes as "our mentor" in his book on *Ulysses*, since Holmes also serves as a model for the observer looking at Joyce's fictional worlds (Kenner, *Ulysses*, pg. 143). Leopold Bloom had an overdue library book by Conan Doyle, which the "real" Dublin library declared "missing" in 1906 (ibid.).

Masks of the Illuminati begins with a newspaper article dated April 23, 1914 (Shakespeare's birthday). Numbers play a poetic role in Wilson's work, especially the number 23 which haunts this and all of his novels. Using methods learned from Aleister Crowley, William S. Burroughs and Joyce (*Finnegans Wake's* use of the numbers 1132, 111, 1001, etc.), Wilson almost makes the numbers characters in the book. Emerson said every word contains a fossil poem, and Joyce allowed the poems in certain numbers to blossom in the *Wake*. Similarly Wilson uses 23 as a leitmotif in *Masks*. The opening article also mentions Conan Doyle, anticipating Joyce's role as a detective in the novel and evoking Wilson's comparison of Joyce and Sherlock Holmes in *Schrödinger's Cat*, wherein Joyce in a parallel universe become Pope Stephen and an obituary compares him with Holmes. Of course, Joyce made use of a journalistic style in one section of *Ulysses*, the first of many parallels between *Ulysses* and *Masks*. The opening section of *Masks* concludes with a fragment of a film script, a device Joyce didn't include in *Ulysses*, although he did write the Nighttown chapter in the form of a play.

One could see *Masks* as the portrait of a magician as a young man. Sir John Babcock becomes fascinated with the occult and eventually ends up interacting with members of the Golden Dawn such as Yeats and Crowley. Wilson uses devices from *Ulysses* and *Finnegans Wake* to bring to life various altered states of consciousness Babcock encounters and endures during his occult adventures.

In the novel, Sir John Babcock arrives in Zurich, pursued he thinks by Satanists. He bursts into a bar where he coincidentally runs into Joyce and Einstein. They play the role of Good Samaritans and Babcock tells them about his initiation into a secret society and how his life has turned into chaos. (Incidentally, Wilson sees the parable of the Good Samaritan underlying *Ulysses*, with Samaritan Leopold Bloom rescuing Stephen Dedalus in the Nighttown episode.) Joyce and Einstein apply their considerable observational and reasoning powers to bear on Babcock's conundrum that night and over the next two days. When they finally reach the conclusion that his nemesis Aleister Crowley has manipulated all the events which have terrified Sir John, supposedly for Sir John's own benefit, Aleister himself shows up at the door. He congratulates the scientific detectives with champagne.

I imagine, Einstein said staring fixedly at his pipe ash glittering, that your original plan for Sir John's rite of passage had
some dramatic climax. I hope we haven't ruined it by explaining the tricks to him prematurely.

    Have some more wine, Babcock, Crowley said pouring. As
a matter of fact, the climax of the drama will be much as I
planned except of course that there will be three candidates
instead of one.

— Masks of the Illuminati, pg. 320

    Of course, Aleister has spiked the champagne with a psyche-
delic drug.

    The reader first encounters Einstein and Joyce in a pub in
Zurich in a passage based on the first chapter of *Ulysses*.
"Stately, plump Albert Einstein" plays the role of Buck Mulligan
while Joyce once again plays Stephen Dedalus. While the first
sentence in *Ulysses* begins with "Stately" and ends with
"crossed," indicating the two tyrants Dedalus must escape (the
state of England and the Catholic Church), *Masks* gives us
"Stately, plump Albert Einstein came from the gloom-domed
Lorelei barroom bearing a paleyellow tray on which two mugs of
beer stood carefully balanced, erect." (*Masks of the Illuminati*,
pg. 12) This suggests the more frankly sexual nature of this
book, as well as the particular concerns of both the character
Joyce and Sir John. The first sentence of *Ulysses* has 22 words,
suggesting the number of letters in the Hebrew alphabet and the
number of trumps in the tarot deck some commentators believe.
Wilson's parallel sentence has 24 words. In *The Game of Life*
Wilson and Timothy Leary add two new trumps to their post-
modern tarot deck. The word "paleyellow" in the Wilson sentence suggests the style of first chapter of *Ulysses*. Wilson has
Joyce use "yellowbrown" a few pages later. (Wilson, *Masks*,
pg. 15)

    Next Wilson provides a series of questions and answers
about Joyce and Einstein's conversation in the style of the Ithaca
chapter of *Ulysses*. Wilson suggests that

> Joyce had escaped from the normal constrictions of ego by
> pondering deeply what it feels like to be a woman. Einstein
> had escaped from the normal constrictions of ego by ponder-
> ing deeply what it feels like to be a photon. Joyce approached

art with the methodology of a scientist; Einstein practiced
science with the intuition of an artist.
                              — *Masks of the Illuminati,* pg. 14

Wilson draws a similar parallel between Beethoven and
Einstein in his *Illuminati Papers,* calling Beethoven "The
World's Greatest Sound Engineer" and Einstein "The World's
Greatest Intuitive Artist." (*Illuminati Papers,* pg. 143) Joyce's
contemplation of life as a woman would enable him to write
Molly Bloom's section of *Ulysses.*

Throughout the novel Wilson has Joyce think about the
possibility that his mistress Nora Barnacle had had an affair with
his brother Stanislaus. In the Scylla and Charibdis chapter of
Ulysses, Joyce has Stephen Dedalus present the case that Shakespeare thought his wife had cuckolded him with his brother.
Wilson presents an obsessed Joyce similar to the obsessed
Shakespeare Joyce himself has Stephen Dedalus present. This
theme occurs in the internal monologue of the character Joyce
throughout *Masks of the Illuminati,* just as Leopold Bloom's
thoughts return again and again to Blazes Boylan and Molly
Bloom in the Leopold Bloom chapters of *Ulysses.* However,
where Leopold avoids the thoughts of the (probably actual) infidelity of Molly and Blazes, the character Joyce dwells on the
(probably false) infidelity of Nora and Stanislaus. This theme of
Joyce's fear of Nora's infidelity first appears in the mock-Ithaca
section of *Masks of the Illuminati* and continues to reappear
throughout the book.

Also in the mock-Ithaca section of *Masks* Wilson writes a
passage locating Bahnhofstrasse in space-time, similar to a passage locating Stephen Dedalus in space-time in *Portrait of the
Artist as a Young Man.* Wilson provides a few more scientific
details in his version, fitting with the plethora of scientific details
in the novel. The mock-Ithaca pattern of questions and answers
in the text of *Masks* recurs several times in the novel.

Many details of the novel illuminate coincidences. Samuel
Beckett saw coincidence as the main theme in *Finnegans Wake.*
Wilson even brings Carl Jung as a minor character in the novel.
Jung writing with physicist Wolfgang Pauli called some coinci-
dences "synchronicities," and Wilson combines the notion of
synchronicity with Joyce's ideas of coincidence in *Masks.* Jung

thought patients going through periods of radical change tended to experience more coincidences then average. Joyce came to coincidence from an angle suggested by Giordano Bruno. Bruno saw reality as a coincidence of opposites. Joyce constructed the world of *Finnegans Wake* (and to a lesser extent *Ulysses*) from these coinciding opposites. Wilson combines the Jungian and the Joycean views of coincidence. As the character Sir John Babcock in *Masks* gets deeper into his personal transformation, he encounters more and more coincidences. He also comes to see the world more and more in a Brunoesque fashion, as a deeply interrelated web of coinciding opposites. However, the character Einstein discovers at the end of the novel that Babcock's initiators have manufactured many of these coincidences. This undercutting of the proliferation of coincidences by human agency suggests the central role of human intelligence in the process of perception, one of Wilson's central themes. Of course, this also demonstrates Bruno's ideas. A web of spontaneously occurring, interrelating synchronicities coincides with a net of manufactured coincidences.

Wilson includes the forms of radio broadcasts, game shows and film scripts at various times in the novel. This use of fragments of various genres follows and expands Joyce's example. Wilson even includes four pictures of tarot cards on pages 72 and 73, and a drawing of an alien (or perhaps a time-traveler) on page 165.

At various points in *Masks* Wilson includes Sir John's dreams, always written in a style reminiscent of *Finnegans Wake*. This blossoms into the full blown Wakean-style prose which represents altered states of consciousness in the drug scene at the end of the novel. Of course, Wilson does not limit himself to a Joyce pastiche. He combines Joyce's use of portmanteau words, lists, puns, jokes and acronyms with Crowleyean Golden Dawn kabbalah, Burroughs' cut-up technique and Wilson's unique sense of humor. (The cut-up technique involves taking pages of text, cutting them up and rearranging the pieces. Then the writer can take passages from the cut up text and use them as they see fit. Artist Brion Gysin invented this technique, and Williams S. Burroughs developed it over several decades.)

Using a variety of Joycean techniques, Wilson presents the climactic drug scene in language reminiscent of *Finnegans Wake*:

> Hawk-like man, Joyce reflects. Ascending from the labyrinth old father old artificer the moocow in the beginning.
> Come back to Erin, mavourneen.
> *Merde*, said General Canbronne. A toll telled of shame and scorn.
> — *Masks of the Illuminati,* pg. 326

The "labyrinth" points to its builder Daedelus, who of course links with Stephen Dedalus. The "old father" suggests the Christian God as well as Daedalus' relationship with Icarus. The "moocow" points to the first line of Joyce's *Portrait of the Artist as a Young Man*: "Once upon a time and a very good time it was there was a moocow coming down along the road and this moocow that was coming down along the road met a nicens little boy named baby tuckoo...." (*Portable Joyce*, pg. 245) Of course the character Stephen Dedalus hallucinates the beginning of *Portrait* while sick in the hospital, whereas the character James Joyce hallucinates this allusion to the *Portrait* while intoxicated at the end of *Masks of the Illuminati.*

General Canbronne replied *"merde"* when asked to surrender at Waterloo. This anecdote recurs many times in *Finnegans Wake*. "A toll telled of shame and scorn" echoes the *Wake*'s refrain "a tale told of Shaun and Shem." This climatic drug scene lasts thirty pages, filled with this sort of Joycean wordplay.

At the novel's end the character Joyce feels he has a better idea of the huge novel he wants to write, patterned on Homer and Hamlet as well as the Good Samaritan (*Ulysses*). Wilson has used Joyce's methods to help him shape his narrative. Wilson has also used the character Joyce to unravel those narrative strands and to piece together the underlying patterns. Wilson has used Joyce's methods to present the character Joyce, and he has used the process of presenting the character Joyce to better understand James Joyce, both as an artist and as a human being.

APPENDIX PEH

An Interview with Robert Anton Wilson

July 23, 2000 C.E. Athena 23, 79 p.s.U., Anaheim, CA

EW: One modification you seem to have made to the progression through the circuits, as we get it from Aleister Crowley[3], seems to suggest that martial arts training can reimprint the first circuit. You suggest this in a couple of books. I was curious about your experience with that.

RAW: I don't have any experience with the martial arts. Well, a little, damned little. But my daughter Christina has a black belt in both kung fu and karate, and, watching the changes in her personality while she was in training, completing the training, I would say that she has less anxiety than anybody I know. I think she completely reimprinted that circuit. I think the kung fu helped even more than the karate. She also is on the board of directors of the Obsessive Compulsive Foundation in Connecticut, and her American Express card, says Christina Pearson, Obsessive Compulsive. They didn't have room for the whole title.

EW: You've written about the efficacy of pranayama. I know that some yoga teachers have hesitancy about teaching that before the mastery of asana. I have the impression that you feel

---

[3] Yes, I know Tim Leary came up with the circuit theory. However, Aleister Crowley suggested practicing asana, pranayama, mantra, etc., which Wilson connects with the reimprinting of the circuits. In *Prometheus Rising* and elsewhere, Wilson suggests that martial arts training can reimprint the first circuit more quickly than asana.

143

you've gotten benefits from it without necessarily having mastered asana.

RAW: I've never thought about it that way, but I agree that it's probably better to work on asana before you try pranayama. Because, the way I see it, asana deals with the first circuit and pranayama with the second, and you should build from the ground up. Howsoever, I did a lot of asana, although I never got very good at it. I got better results from pranayama.

EW: You talk about the kabbalistic structure of *Illuminatus!* It seems as though a lot of your approach to kabbalah has come through your study of Aleister Crowley. I wonder where else you have found stuff that you've found beneficial about kabbalah.

RAW: Well you know, Crowley has served as a major source for me. Another was one of Crowley's dissident disciples, Charles Stanford Jones; I have a couple of his books which I thought were very illuminating; and I read a Sufi book on kabbalah, which I thought was very good, but I don't remember the name of the author. And I read a few other books on kabbalah by folks whose names I don't remember either. And, of course, Israel Regardie is very good too, but I'd say I read about ten books on kabbalah not by Crowley; all the rest were by Crowley. He's affects me more than any of the others, except that one Sufi book I read so long ago I can't remember the author's name. But it's very hard for me to remember Arabic names, since I don't know how to pronounce them and they're all spelled five different ways, from being transliterated into European alphabets. For all I know Jalaladin Rumi will be spelled a new way.

EW: I remember Idries Shah writes about kabbalah, suggesting it was derived from Sufi practice, although I know that people like Gershom Scholem disagree with that.

RAW: Well, Idries Shah seems to claim everything is derived from Sufi practice, even Zen Buddhism in one of his books.

EW: Well, the humor of the Three Stooges, of course...

RAW: Very Sufi. Goofy Sufi.

EW: Very, very Sufi. It also seems that thinking back on the circuit model, Crowley's work and thinking definitely helped shape your perceptions about how to the master the fourth circuit.

RAW: Oh yeah.

EW: As well, it's interesting there's a line in *Prometheus Rising* where you talk about permanent fifth circuit, and I had forgotten that in *Cosmic Trigger* you talk about the mixture of marijuana and sex magick *ala* Crowley being a way to rapidly have a permanent fifth circuit imprint. I was curious in the year 2000 with your recent bout of studying Pound and Joyce, has your perspective on Uncle Al changed?

RAW: No, not really. I still regard Uncle Al as one of the most fascinating, humorous, instructive, entertaining, illuminating and puzzling characters who ever lived. I still can't figure him out. But then I knew Timothy Leary fairly well, and I still haven't figured him out either. I suspect that beyond a certain level, people reach a High plateau beyond which you can't understand them until you're on that plateau, too.

EW: I guess, thinking about Dr. Leary, it seems similar to me, I can imagine sitting down to have dinner with Tim, but I can't imagine what it would be like to have dinner with Aleister Crowley.

RAW: Oh I'd love to try that experiment. I've had dinner with Tim several times. I'd also like to have dinner with Hannibal Lecter. But I want to tell him that the menu should not include any of his specialties. I prefer something a little more orthodox.

EW: Somehow with Lecter and Crowley, I think there are a lot of similarities.

RAW: Yeah, they're both entirely outside the moral categories of the Western world. They're outside *all* moral categories. They're subject to debate endlessly. Hannibal chooses his victims very carefully. Hannibal is not your typical serial killer. There is not one type he is after all the time, acting out some kind of compulsive ritual, something to do with some childhood trauma. Hannibal isn't that type at all. The people he decides to bump off are people who've offended his aesthetic sensibilities, or his sense of propriety. He's taking the place of the God he doesn't believe in. And he's also serving as a Darwinian agent, ridding the gene pool of people who he thinks shouldn't populate the world any more than they already do.

EW: In that way he reminds me somewhat of Sigismundo Malatesta, especially as you portrayed him in *The Earth Will Shake*, as someone unwilling to be bound by the conventions of his day.

RAW: Yeah. Of course, Sigismundo Malatesta may not have done any of the monstrous things the Inquisition accused him of. Historians are still debating that.

EW: Along the lines of outside the boundaries, in your books talk you talk about Timothy Leary's Eight Circuit Model, and the sixth and seventh circuits ping-pong a little bit.

RAW: Yeah, Tim ping-ponged a little bit. As a matter of fact, I think I influenced him a little bit. And in one of his later books, the neuroelectric circuit has disappeared entirely, replaced by the metaprogramming circuit which he got from *Prometheus Rising*. So we influenced each other somewhat.

EW: Absolutely, and my theory of that: it seems again that we haven't had adequate scientific exploration, especially with the ban on certain drugs, so that people have to deal with their own experiences and the experiences they read about, so it's not enough to know what comes first, whether it's the metaprogramming or the neurogenetic, and what the nature of these are.

RAW: Yeah, that is to me the second major scientific tragedy of the twentieth century. The major scientific tragedy is the development of nuclear energy. The second one was the government's taking over the role of the Holy Inquisition, and determining what scientists may or may not investigate. The ban on orgone research, on LSD research. I feel as sure as I am of anything, which is about nine out of ten, that the future will look back with absolute shock and horror. "These people seem so enlightened in so many ways, yet they let the government ban scientific research? What, did they think they were living in the Middle Ages?"

EW: Speaking of scientific research, you talk about the Physics/Consciousness Research Group in the seventies. It seems as if that worked synergistically with your background in math and physics in university to create a certain view of quantum mechanics and consciousness, which you put forward in *Cosmic*

Trigger I. I wonder, 23 years later, about your thoughts about consciousness and quantum mechanics.

RAW: Well, I still basically hold to the Copenhagen view, which is that whatever model we create, we should always remember we created it, and not bow down and worship it, like I say in *New Inquisition*. But of all the models, I feel that the one that seems most convincing to me is David Bohm, and then Evan Harris Walker and Nick Herbert, who all hold that mind is non-local. That seems to encompass all of the data of parapsychology, and for all varieties of mystical experience, and out-of-body-experience. And it seems to make sense in terms of interpreting quantum mechanics too, so I like that model a lot. But I don't want to be committed to it dogmatically. Oh, by the way, in one of the later *Cantos* Ezra Pound says, "As for the dogmatic, they must lie occasionally to maintain conformity." That's the way I feel about dogmatists. I don't trust anybody who's too dogmatic, even if they're an expert in their field. That's why I like [Orson Welles'] *F for Fake*, because it raises the question, "Are the art experts surviving mostly on bluff?"

EW: I wonder if the sciences survive by bluff as well. Einstein has become such a popular figure, I wonder if in the next century we'll see Bohr and Heisenberg join him. I know there's a popular play now called "Copenhagen" that's playing in New York and London, about Bohr and Heisenberg. I haven't seen it. But apparently it's got a debate about the Copenhagen Interpretation.

RAW: Really?

EW: Yeah.

RAW: There's a play about that? Wow.

EW: Yeah, I wanted to see it, but didn't see it when I was in London.

RAW: My God, I'm a prophet again.

EW: Amen.

RAW: I was the first one to put that in fictional form. Now they're doing a play about it. And there's a play about Bucky Fuller in San Francisco. And you were telling me something that's going on here.

EW: A musical of "The Dead."

RAW: Oh yeah. Somebody's going to do a film of *Finnegans Wake* next.

EW: Absolutely. I find it interesting in the years since *Schrödinger's Cat* that so many themes that you wrote about there have become ubiquitous, whether it's Immortalism, or your proto-cyberpunk in *The Homing Pigeons*; you, like Phil Dick, seem to have connected with the culture and made valid predictions.

RAW: Some of them were based on scientific probabilities, the direction that research was going and so on. Some of them amaze even me. When I filled the United States of the 1980's with homeless people wandering the streets, there was nothing like that going on, and where I got that idea from I'm not entirely sure. But when it started to manifest, I felt like I was partly responsible for imagining it. What I did was really a satire on landlords. You ever notice that in all discussions of the homeless problem you never see the words "landlord" or "mortgage"?

EW: You've written about the westward movement of capital, and new ideas. The origins, or some of the earliest examples of this, seem the capital centering around Cambodia, at the beginning of the Bronze Age. We now see a growth in the Asian economy, where this may be coming full circle, and perhaps capital moving out away from the earth.

RAW: Yeah.

EW: It seems interesting to me that both you and Dr. Leary wrote about this, but never chose to move to Asia. I wondered did that ever cross your mind?

RAW: I've always wanted to visit Asia. I always hoped I'd get a lecture gig in Japan. I'd even accept one in China. I'm a little nervous about that, but, yeah, I would like to see more of Asia. As for moving there, I sort of agree with—what the hell's that anthropologist's name? Lewis Harmon? The guy who wrote *The Pacific Rim*. Oh hell, he's a very important writer; too bad neither of us can remember his name. He also wrote *The Sound of Falling Bodies When They Light*. Still don't know?

EW: I do not. I will look him up. I know of whom you speak, but I do not know his name.[4]

RAW: I get his name mixed up because I think of Willis Harmon, and that's not his name, but it's close to his name. Anyway, he claims that there's a culture that is forming and has already to some extent formed, that includes California, Oregon, Washington, British Columbia, Alaska, the Hawaiian Islands, Australia, Japan, and increasingly China. He calls it the Pacific Rim Culture. And he claims this is different from eastern United States and Europe, as well as the difference between Chinese and American eco-sphere. That's another reason the *Cantos* are important. I think they will help parts of the Pacific Rim to understand each other better.

EW: You know, it's something, that, and also your works that deal with the shift of capital—

RAW: Do you know who originated that idea?

EW: I know Samuel Johnson wrote about it, and I know Brooks Adams wrote about it.

RAW: Brooks Adams I got it from. The first one that suggested it was Sir William Temple, who was one of [Jonathan] Swift's close friends, the father of one of Swift's girlfriends, I forget which one. No he wasn't the father, he was the guardian. He was the model for the King in Brobdingnag.

EW: I do not know about that. The transition from London and Europe as the center of world capital to New York and Washington as the center of economic power in the world seems decisively to have taken place during the Second World War.

RAW: Yeah.

EW: It seems to me that Herman Wouk's *Winds of War* and *War and Remembrance*, and Thomas Pynchon in *Gravity's Rainbow*, in his more poetic way, deal with this shift of world capital. Do you think that that sort of massive bloodshed will inhere in the shift of capital from the western United States towards Asia?

---

[4] William Irwin Thompson wrote *Pacific Shift* and *The Time Falling Bodies Take to Light*.

RAW: I certainly hope not. That doesn't look very likely right now. I think, I hate to make gloomy predictions, but I think there is going to be a certain, there is already, and there will probably be some more, I hope very little, bloodshed in the shift from north to south. The south, the southern hemisphere, wants to get out from under the domination of the northern powers, and they will get out, it just depends on: Will there be an outbreak of sanity among our rulers, comparable to the one in the Union of South Africa, where they suddenly decided this can't go on? Or they can go on fighting for a long, long time while they dominate the whole globe. I don't know, but I think Internet is accelerating the process of non-centralized globalization. All these people protesting globalization, I wish they would think more clearly. Globalization seems inevitable to me. The question is what form of globalization: centralized in one place or decentralized.

EW: Well, it seems interesting to me if one looks at the shift from Egypt to Athens to Rome to Florence to Venice to Paris to London, one often sees a single center, but with the shift from London to New York with economic power, and Washington with political power.

RAW: And Boston with financial power.

EW: Yeah. And the shift westward is even more diversified. From—

RAW: Yeah!

EW: Silicon Valley to Texas oil, L.A. entertainment and Japanese banking. It seems not nearly as city-centered as the Renaissance.

RAW: Yeah, there's a movement towards decentralization. I was talking to a friend who just got back from Japan. She said everyday life in Japan has so much more high-tech than here in the States. That's another indication that this movement has circled the whole globe and has nowhere to go now but out, where the rats have also gone. That's why I'm so fascinated with rats. Rats started out in Southeast Asia, now they're all over the globe. They're even seen on jet airliners. So I figure the first space colony will be infested by rats within ten years after it's built. They'll find a way. They've got a program for ubiquity just like we do.

EW: I've lost the question. I had two final questions. After the Bible and Shakespeare, *The Wizard of Oz* seems the most alluded-to work in America. Some would see this as a sign of decline in religious values. You have alluded certainly a great deal to Shakespeare and *The Wizard of Oz* in your work. What works do you see becoming central to education in the next century? I know you've mentioned Pound before. Do you think Shakespeare will continue to be seen as central?

RAW: Yeah. Shakespeare is being performed everyday somewhere in the world. He has reached every continent except Antarctica. And when the penguins learn to read, they'll be doing Shakespeare, too.

EW: I guess we'll have a zero gravity Falstaff before too long. Thank you Dr. Wilson.

RAW: That's all?

EW: It's getting late. I'm not sure if I'm going to include this.

RAW: What is this for, by the way?

EW: I'm finishing my *Lazy Entity's Guide to Robert Anton Wilson*, which I've been working on, and the writing is not coming quickly. I have a good facility when writing poetry, but prose comes very slowly to me. Pound talks about, "Go read forty novels by Henry James," which I haven't done yet.

RAW: Uh-huh. I'd say, Read *Ulysses* forty times.

EW: But I'm slowly learning how to write this book. What would you like to see in a book about yourself?

RAW: I don't think the influence of Joyce has been noticed by most reviewers. As a matter of fact, I don't think most reviewers have ever read Joyce—most reviewers of my books anyway. I get reviewed in weird places, although I have seen a few references to my works on a James Joyce website.

EW: I know James Joyce shows up in Simon Moon's *Finnegans Wake* discussion in *Illuminatus!* that continues in *Schrödinger's Cat*. And also in *Illuminatus!* you talk about the five-fold structure of *Portrait of the Artist as a Young Man* and the four fold structure of *Finnegans Wake*, and of course in *Coincidance* you write a great deal about Joyce. What do you think you've learned from Joyce that helps you write?

RAW: Well, the possibility of writing on several levels at the same time. I didn't discover Crowley until about twenty, twenty-five years after [discovering] Joyce. Crowley does a lot of the same type of multiple meanings, but I learned it from Joyce first.

EW: It seems to me that you had some early influences who wrote in a very popular style, in that they wrote to make money to pay their bills. They may have been wonderful writers, but they don't have the high-brow reputation, say, that Joyce has in comparison with Robert Heinlein. And I think that, like Heinlein, you do very *avant garde* things, but you do them in such an entertaining fashion that people don't notice.

RAW: Well, I hope they're entertaining. They haven't been entertaining enough that I've had a bestseller yet.

EW: But I think that, whereas Joyce might pack several levels of meaning into one paragraph, with a surface that eludes understanding by many readers, a lot of your narratives still...the surface level is followable.

RAW: For a large enough audience to keep me alive, but, hell, I've seen reviews of people who've given up after 10 pages. They couldn't make head nor tails out of if. They decided it was all gibberish. That's what the first readers of *Ulysses* thought, too.

EW: It always surprises me that your work isn't more popular. I find it so thoroughly entertaining and thought-provoking. RMJon23 (who posts at alt.fan.rawilson), and I've been talking about this. I think there's something very revolutionary in your writing, that you have an optimism and a pragmatic notion about how to change society, that is a little threatening, and is one of the reasons that you haven't been as popular as, say, Pynchon, who shares some of your background, but is not as overtly gleeful about the possibility of changing the world for the better.

RAW: Yeah, well, it's finally a matter of...the only way to get famous as a writer is to get praised by really important New York reviewers. None of whom have ever admitted I exist... They not only haven't liked my books, they haven't even panned them; they just simply ignore them. I've never been reviewed in any of the major New York publications. I finally decided, after years of brooding, that this makes me quite satisfied. If they ever discover me they'll come after me with pickaxes and toma-hawks. Like they did with Marshall McLuhan, after they discov-ered him. So I'm just as happy that they should go on ignoring me, at least until after I die. And the other thing about popularity: I'm always amazed at how popular I am.

EW: Oh, yes.

RAW: You know, I mean, for a writer who's never been reviewed in any major publications, I keep running into fans in the damnedest places. I get fan mail from Russia, Hong Kong, the damnedest places.

EW: Again to realize how decentralized publishing has become in America. And then, while certainly you have large publica-tions and large readerships, other publications exist. I first encountered you in *Science Fiction Review* and in a review in *Analog* science fiction magazine that Spider Robinson did. Those are whole worlds that are ignored by the *New York Review of Books*.

RAW: Oh yeah.

EW: But there are millions of readers learning from and enjoy-ing *Illuminatus!* for over twenty-three years now.

RAW: Twenty-five.

EW: I just wanted to throw the twenty-three in there. It shows no sign of stopping.

RAW: The fact that I don't get reviewed in important publica-tions—whenever I think about that, there's also the thought that, hell, most of my books from the seventies are still in print. Most of my books from the eighties are still in print. There's only one book from the seventies that's out of print. And only three from the eighties. And anything of mine that's gone out of print hasn't stayed out of print for long. Very few writers have their books stay in print as long as mine, unless they're being really heavily promoted by the New York media. So my career is based entirely on word of mouth, which I think is probably the strongest type of advertisement. So I'm quite satisfied with the way things are going. I know exactly what *The New York Review of Books* would say about me. The same things they say about Leary and John Lilly and Marshall McLuhan. And Faulkner before he won the Nobel.

EW: To finish off, you have made a number of references to McLuhan in recent e-mail. Umberto Eco suggested that McLuhan's vision of the internet was totally false. I take it that you think that McLuhan still has something to offer us.

RAW: Oh yeah, I think that a lot of what McLuhan wrote about television was really about internet, only internet didn't exist yet. He was imaging it out of television, he was projecting forward.

EW: Thank you very much.

RAW: You're welcome.

APPENDIX HEH

Style and Form in *The Homing Pigeons*

In this section I intend to examine the style and form of Robert Anton Wilson's novels through the example of *The Homing Pigeons*. This novel originally appeared in 1981 as *Schrödinger's Cat III: The Homing Pigeons*. Wilson's *Schrödinger's Cat* novels took three different interpretations of the equations of quantum mechanics and used those interpretations to give form to the fictional narratives. Each book appeared with a preface with the heading "CAVEAT LECTER" stating that the reader did not have to read the novels in sequence. *The Homing Pigeons* takes on the "Brownian form" of "non-objectivity" according to Wilson in the glossary to the novel. This refers to *The Laws of Form* by mathematician G. Spencer Brown and the theory of the non-objective, observer-created universe posited by physicist John A. Wheeler. In this section I would like to observe how the macrocosmic form of the novel relates with the vernacular style of the novel. Note that the novel's glossary has the subtitle "A Guide for the Perplexed." This alludes to the Jewish thinker Moses Maimonides, whom Leopold Bloom mentions in *Ulysses*. Wilson's allusive, intertextual style reinforces the idea of interconnectedness from quantum mechanics that shapes the form of this novel.

Some readers have called *The Homing Pigeons* the first "cyberpunk" novel for its references to computers and networks, although others cite the work of Rudy Rucker or even *The Sheep Look Up* by John Brunner as the "first cyberpunk novel." The priority depends on how one defines cyberpunk. Cyberpunk emerged in the mid-eighties as a movement in science fiction which emphasized the growing role of computers in our everyday lives. Wilson uses stylistic devices from the world of science fiction: alternative universes, informal diction combined with technical vocabulary, and references to other science fiction writers such as Robert Heinlein and Olaf Stapleton. However, Wilson, especially in the *Schrödinger's Cat* books, eschews linear narrative and also includes sections using William S. Burroughs' cut-up technique and portmanteau words in the style of *Finnegans Wake*. These later stylistic traits have tended to limit Wilson's popularity among traditional science fiction fans, although one can see similarities in the work of writers like Philip Jose Farmer and Philip K. Dick. (Note that Burroughs' cut-up technique involves cutting up pages of text and rearranging the sections. The author then picks out portions of the collage-like arrangement to include in the text. Wilson has said that he has used the cut-up or similar methods in all of his novels. One can see evidence of this in drug scenes and dream sequences particularly.)

Certainly computers play a unique role in *The Homing Pigeons*. The novel consists of three "loops," a term borrowed from Douglas Hofstader's notion of "strange loops" in logic, as well as to the idea of nested algorithms in computer science. The "Second Loop" deals with a variety of subjects including the radical theology of Pope Stephen, a.k.a. James Augusta Joyce, in a parallel universe. Again, Wilson uses conversational language to discuss rather esoteric subjects such as the aesthetics of Pope Stephen, quantum mechanics and the meaning of Beethoven's "Hammerklavier" sonata. All of these discussions keep coming back to the idea of "esse est percepi," the observer creating their perceived universe, lending credence to Wilson's claim that the form of the novel comes from Wheeler's idea of non-objectivity.

Above these loops and discussions Wilson has also outlined the plot of Homer's *Odyssey*, but with a typically Wilsonian twist. Many characters from Robert Shea and Robert Anton Wilson's *Illuminatus!* appear in the *Schrödinger's Cat* novels, including Epicene Wildeblood, a book reviewer who panned *Illuminatus!* within the text of *Illuminatus!* (a unique post-modern feat). Well, in *Schrödinger's Cat I: The Universe Next Door* Epicene has a sex change operation, becoming Mary Margaret Wildebloode. Mary Margaret has the amputated member (which she/he had named Ulysses long ago) stuffed and mounted in her living room. It gets stolen and has a long odyssey before it eventually returns to her, paralleling the plot of both the *Odyssey* and Joyce's *Ulysses*, but only if the reader chooses to read the trilogy in the order one, two, three. Reading the trilogy in other orders allows for other details to rise to the surface. This also supports the "esse est percepi" structure of the form of the novels.

The Homing Pigeons has deep structure of perhaps existing as a drug vision of George Dorn, or as a necessary hallucination as George functions as an extraterrestrial intelligence agent before returning to the center of our galaxy (the homing pigeon image). In the novel, George's ego transforms into Frank Dashwood, John Disk and others. Perhaps, or perhaps not, since the whole novel has the form of non-objectivity according to the glossary. Interestingly, the later 1988 one-volume edition of *Schrödinger's Cat* removed the lines in the glossary that indicated the forms of the three novels which compose *Schrödinger's Cat* (non-objectivity for *The Homing Pigeons*, Bell's Theorem for *The Trick Top Hat* and the Everett-Wheeler-Graham model for *The Universe Next Door*). Non-objectivity in quantum mechanics suggests that Universe gets created by acts of observation. According to John A. Wheeler, only observations at the subatomic level participate in this creation. Wilson would expand that model. See *Quantum Theory and Measure* edited by Wheeler for a technical discussion or Nick Herbert's *Quantum Realities* for a non-technical discussion.

> The Stephenites called themselves "Seekers of the Real" and were always watching very closely to see what was going on. They all had posters in their rooms with the sainted Pope's famous remark: "If you don't pay attention to *every little detail*, you miss most of the jokes."
> — *The Homing Pigeons*, pg. 104

This passage deals with an alternative reality where James Joyce has become Pope Stephen. The Pope's message to "pay attention to *every little detail*" certainly seems an invitation to stylistic analysis, so let us look a little closer. Note the presence of "seeing" words like "Seekers," "watching," and "to see," complemented by "hearing" words like "called" and "remark." James Joyce had terrible vision, and T.S. Eliot, among others, have

remarked on the intensely auditory nature of Joyce's work, perhaps a consequence of Joyce's near blindness. Expressions such
as "what was going on" and "pay attention" can apply to both the
visual and the auditory world and suggest a synthesis. ("Pay no
attention to the man behind the curtain," as someone once
remarked.)

The quoted passage above contains four capitalized nouns,
two plural (Stephenites and Seekers) and two singular (Real and
Pope). Ironically, this passage suggests the underlying plural
nature of both of those singular nouns. The novel as a whole
suggests the presence of multiple realities, different perceived
realities seen and heard by different characters, as well as the
possibility of multiple universes in the Everett-Wheeler-Graham
hypothesis of quantum mechanics. This would allow for a
universe where Joyce became not only a priest as he had once
contemplated, but the Pope himself. This would also allow for
multiple Popes in multiple universes. (In other works Wilson
discusses a religion, the Paratheometamystichood of Eris Esoteric, in which every member becomes a Pope.)

When hearing of all the serious discussion of his *Ulysses*,
Joyce commented that he wished someone would remark what a
damn funny book it was. Wilson may allude to this in his linking
of perception and humor. Typically Wilson mixes technical
vocabulary from a variety of fields with a casual, vernacular
style. This mix of high and low culture typifies Wilson's art. The
surreal humor of the novels also contributes to the reader's
appreciation of the idea of non-objectivity.

The second loop of the novel begins with the following
quotes: "Art imitates nature" (Aristotle) and "Nature imitates art"
(Oscar Wilde). This snark chase of art and nature imitating each
other suggests the world of Heisenbergian physics where the
observer interacts with the observed. John Wheeler suggests that
observations in the subatomic world can effect changes in the
universe, even causing effects outside of time, at least according
to Bell's inequality. (Bell suggested that any hidden variable
would have to have a grossly non-local character.) Wilson juxtaposes the heading "The Second Loop" with the quotes from Aristotle and Wilde suggesting the links between physics, aesthetics
and computers. Wilson has attributed his use of this "ideogra-

matic method" of juxtaposition of images to his long study of
Ezra Pound.

In *The Illuminati Papers* Wilson states:

My style derives directly from Ezra Pound, James Joyce,
Raymond Chandler, H.L. Menken, William S.
Burroughs, Benjamin Tucker, and *Elephant Doody Comix*, in approximately that order of importance. Chandler has also influenced
my way of telling stories; all my fiction tends to follow the
Chandler mythos of the skeptical Knight seeking Truth in a
world of false fronts and manipulated deceptions. (Of course,
this is also my biography, or that of any shaman.) [pg. 66]

Even in this list of stylistic influences one can see Wilson's
mixture of the literary and the popular for humorous effect with
the inclusion of *Elephant Doody Comix*. The breadth of Wilson's
influences helps him to paint a picture of a multifaceted,
observer-created cosmos.

The second loop continues with the heading "What—Me
Infallible?" (*The Homing Pigeons*, pg. 97) This allusion to *Mad
Magazine's* Alfred E. Newman and the Catholic doctrine of
papal infallibility introduces the theme of Stephen's pontificate,
as well as emphasizing the ludic nature of the non-objective
model. Next Wilson provides a "quote" from Pope Stephen's
Encyclical *Integritas, Consonantia, Claritas*. This title comes
from St. Thomas Aquinas' definition of beauty upon which
Stephen Dedalus bases his aesthetics in Joyce's *Portrait of the
Artist as a Young Man*, "*ad pulchritudinem tria requiruntur:
integritas, consonantia, claritas.*" Wilson follows this with Dr.
Dashwood scanning his mail, beginning with a scatological chain
letter. (The novel later suggests that Dr. Dashwood only exists as
a hallucination of George Dorn's.) Once again the juxtaposition
of Aquinas with a chain letter suggests the broad variety of tex-
tual styles we encounter and endure in our day-to-day life, as
well as the multifaceted nature of an observer-created world. The
signers of the chain letter include:

Budweiser N. Kief
2323 N. Clark
Chicago, Illinois 60611

Occupant
P.O. Box 666
Bad Ass, Texas 23023

G. Neil's Artificial Life & Pipe Storage Co.
401 N. 27th
Billings, Montana 59101

Mystery Whizz and Whats-It Works
210 E. Olive
Bozeman, Montana 59715

Dynamite Dave's Phosphate Soda and Kangaroo Stand
Kibbutz Palmahim
Doar Rishaon, Israel

Ethyl's Chocolate Shoppe & Nonphenomena Foundation
242 West Lincoln,
Anaheim, California 92805

Dr. Dashwood made a mistake. He assumed that this was
another hoax by the enigmatic Ezra Pound.
— *The Homing Pigeons,* pg. 98

(The character Markoff Chaney has used the name Ezra
Pound for some of his communications with Dashwood in the
novel.) Wilson typically charges numbers with meaning in his
work. He learned of William S. Burroughs' fascination with the
number 23 back in the 1960's, and he has incorporated that into
all of his books. Burroughs frequently associates the name
Captain Clark with 23, which leads to the first address above.
This again suggests the observer-created model. Gerard O'Neil
suggested the viability of living in space colonies, an idea
supported by Wilson. One can see the influence of the surrealists
on Wilson's combination of kangaroos and a kibbutz. Wilson
learned a lot about the poetic use of numbers from the writings
of Aleister Crowley, whose favorite number, 666, Wilson
humorously combines with Bad Ass, Texas. Crowley developed
his use of numbers through his study of the kabbalah, as did
Wilson. Of course, the first name on the list suggests two intoxi-
cants, once again pointing to the idea that the whole novel might

exist in George Dorn's imagination. Lewis Carroll might have provided inspiration here. In fact, one might see the whole novel as parallel with *Alice's Adventures in Wonderland*, with the reader in the role of Alice. Wilson uses the techniques described in this Appendix to keep the reader off balance, confronted with weird combinations and off-kilter humor to make the reader feel "curiouser and curiouser."

After a discussion of Pope Stephen, the loop continues with Dr. Dashwood confronted by "Joseph K," a character out of Kafka's *The Trial*. Wilson has Joseph utter Kafkaesque statements like "What are the charges against me?" and "They have established so many rules, and recorded them in archives that the ordinary citizen cannot consult, that we must all, the most loyal and decent of us, stumble on a mere technicality occasionally" (*The Homing Pigeons*, pgs. 104–105). Cleverly, Wilson has Joseph outline an argument similar to Gödel's proof in mathematics that all non-trivial systems must contain contradictions. Gödel shows this for mathematical systems, and Wilson reveals how Kafka illuminates the same process in bureaucracy. Wilson book, *Quantum Psychology,* utilizes the story of the door of the law from *The Trial*, likely influenced by Orson Welles' film of *The Trial*. Wilson has frequently cited Welles as a major influence.

This scene from *The Homing Pigeons* concludes with Joseph calling Dr. Dashwood "George." When Dashwood asserts his identity, Joseph replies, "You claim that you are not George Dorn? How clever of them, although I can't imagine how they persuaded you, but of course a man of your moral principles would not be *bribed*, certainly." (*The Homing Pigeons*, pg. 105) Here Wilson provides an imitation of Kafka's style with a long sentence with hints of paranoia and bureaucracy which also asserts the formal concerns of the novel: i.e., non-objectivity and the role of the observer in shaping their perceptions.

Next Wilson provides an interlude dealing with a new school of art, pararealism. This pays homage to the influence of surrealism on his style, as well as providing another angle of perception for his central themes.

> We are delighted that Pluto, Mickey and Goofy are all at odd angles from the plane of the eight inner planets. We are

thrilled with Bohr's great principle of Relativity, which shows
that to look out into space is also to look backwards in time.
WE ARE THE DAY AFTER YESTERDAY!!!
— *The Homing Pigeons,* pg. 108

Here Wilson uses a style reminiscent of Artaud, with the editorial "we," a whole final sentence capitalized, and extra exclamation points. Wilson discusses Artaud's *There Is No More
Firmament* in his *Cosmic Trigger I.* In the world of *The Homing
Pigeons,* astronomers have two new planets named Mickey and
Goofy, providing a Poundian shift from the ancient to the modern at Pluto, which ambiguously inhabits both the world of
Roman myth and Disney cartoons. Also, Wilson has Bohr as the
discoverer of Einstein's theory of relativity. In our world Bohr
posited the theory of complementarity. Wilson posits Bohr and
Einstein as complements, much as Bohr presented the particle
and wave models as complements. Hence, by replacing Einstein
with Bohr, Wilson demonstrates both Bohr's complementarity
and a perceptual analog of Einstein's relativity. At the same time
he satirizes pretentious writing about art. This section concludes:

It reads better in the original French. But it would have been a
top news story if it hadn't been eclipsed by the singularly
obscene "miracle" at Canterbury Cathedral that week.
— *The Homing Pigeons,* pg. 109

That "miracle" involved the amputated "Ulysses" which
keeps popping up in the novel.

After the discussion of the "miracle," Wilson provides a
section entitled "GALACTIC ARCHIVES." Here scholars from
the future discuss the question of the identity of Robert Anton
Wilson. "It is also said that he lived in faithful monogamy with a
simple peasant woman from Galway whom he never married due
to his distaste for Organized Religion and the primitive, brutal
States of that period." Here Wilson has these future scholars con-
fusing his biography with that of James Joyce. Also, through the
extra capital letters in the sentence Wilson echoes the first line of
Joyce's *Ulysses* which begins "Stately" and ends "crossed" (for
"Organized Religion").

As the second loop progresses, Wilson introduces a young man named John Disk. A religious fanatic, Disk begins hearing a "seductive female voice" saying "YOU ARE GEORGE DORN YOU ARE GEORGE DORN YOU ARE GEORGE DORN." (*The Homing Pigeons*, pg. 118) Here Wilson uses capitalization, along with repetition and the absence of punctuation, to suggest mental illness. Of course, the fact that both Frank Dashwood and John Disk face challenges to their identity involving George Dorn suggest the surreal/non-objective nature of the narrative as well as the notion that the whole narrative takes place in George Dorn's imagination. Deeper still one might posit that this meta-narrative takes place in the reader's imagination. Wilson might suggest that the Wheeler non-objectivity model suggests that all our apparent "realities" take place largely in our imaginations. This echoes Blake's "Mind-forged manacles" which Wilson quotes elsewhere.

As the loop continues, Wilson uses the line "Things were coming to a head" repeatedly. (*The Homing Pigeons*, pgs. 119, 124, 125, etc.) This use of repetition plays with a sexual pun as well as suggesting the acronym H.E.A.D. for Hedonic Engineering and Development, which Wilson uses in many of his books when he describes the H.E.A.D. Revolution. The repetition also shows the loop coming to a climax.

"Ulysses" ends up on a safari in Africa right out of Hemingway's "Short Happy Life of Francis Macomer," except that the couple here consists of two wealthy lesbians. Hemingway's story had a Robert Wilson who reappears in *The Homing Pigeons*, unhappy at his displacement. Wilson here satirizes Hemingway's style, bringing in dialog from "The Hills Like White Elephants," where one woman says to Wilson "The hills in the distance... They look like white rhinoceri." (*The Homing Pigeons*, pg. 129) The loop concludes with "Ulysses" getting stolen again, spending a brief period as an object of worship in a temple in India as the Shivalingam.

The third loop begins with the quote, "Forget it, Jake. It's Chinatown." Chinatown serves as a model for Chapel Perilous, which Wilson discussed above in reference to Raymond Chandler and Wilson's own style. Chinatown represents the breakdown of all rules, similar to the discussion of Gödel and Kafka above. In this trip, an astronomer discusses black holes as a place where all rules break down, and suggests a parallel with Beethoven's "Hammerklavier" sonata, where Beethoven pushes the language of the classical style to its limits, or perhaps past its limits. The film, *Chinatown,* suggests Chinatown as a place of asymptotic complexity, where Jake cannot resolve the film's conflicts. This closely parallels Kafka's parable of the door of law, especially as presented by Welles and Wilson.

The third loop continues with a character with the absurd name of Clem Cotex "programming himself into the head space of the First Bank of Religiosophy." Here Wilson takes the radical economics of Pound, Bucky Fuller, Benjamin Tucker and Silvio Gesell, and turns it into a get rich quick scheme. Note the phrase "head space." This echoes the "things are coming to a head" from the second trip, as well as suggesting the 1960's use of "head" as denoting a member of the youth culture (as in "head shop," etc.) The use of the word "programming" suggests computer programming as well as John Lilly's book on LSD, *Programming and Metaprogramming in the Human Metacomputer,* a book which Wilson frequently cites. After his experiment, Clem Cotex tells another character, Blake Williams, "Money is the Schrödinger's Cat of economics." (*The Homing Pigeons,* pg. 139) This line echoes Silvio Gesell's "Money is the football of economics," as well as connecting economic theory with the non-objectivity theme of the novel. (Gesell suggested in his advocacy of paper money that money serves as the tool with which we play the economic game, just as we use the football to play the game of football.)

The character Blake Williams' name derives from that of poet and painter William Blake, whose line about discovering "infinity in a grain of sand" Wilson frequently quotes. The line also parallels the fractillic nature of the text of both *The Homing Pigeons* and *Finnegans Wake,* in that the elements of both novels constantly reflect each other, revealing an infinite labyrinth of relations.

The First Bank of Religiosophy calls Bad Ass, Texas, its home, echoing the reference to that fair city earlier in the text, as well as in Shea and Wilson's *Illuminatus!*

In the third loop Buckminster Fuller (one of the sources for "Religiosophy") becomes President, but quickly resigns. This parallels Joyce becoming Pope in the second loop, and also provides a complement for Nixon's resignation in a Bohr sense. Fuller provides a model for a "good" president as opposed to Nixon. On resigning, President Fuller remarks, "The synergetic interlock or real time vectors in Universe cannot be augmented from here." (*The Homing Pigeons*, pg. 141) Here Wilson provides superb presentation of Fuller's style. Note the absence of "the" before Universe, characteristic of Fuller's prose. Fuller considers Universe "plural and at minimum three," which goes along the multiple universe theme of *Schrödinger's Cat*. Fuller has asserted that real change does not come from politicians, so it makes sense for the character based on him to resign the presidency. In the novel, the founder of the First Bank of Religiosophy takes "Fuller's monetary theory seriously." (*The Homing Pigeons*, pg. 141)

Wilson then discusses a science-fiction novel called *Wigner's Friend* by Timothy Leary (a fictitious novel that only exists in one of the universes of *The Homing Pigeons*) about a bad president named Noxin who resigns. This idea of a novel set in a parallel universe wherein a novelist writes about our universe echoes Philip K. Dick's *The Man in the High Castle*, but Wilson takes the concept to another level. Timothy Leary really did write a book called *Diary of a Hope Fiend*, which in *The Homing Pigeons* gets written by Sigmund Freud. Leary intended the title as an homage to Aleister Crowley's *Diary of a Dope Fiend*. In *The Homing Pigeons* Crowley gets conflated with his student General Fuller and becomes the Arctic explorer General Crowley.

Interestingly, the Wigner's friend paradox takes the Schrödinger's Cat paradox to another level. In the Schrödinger's Cat paradox, the question of the life or death of a cat hinges on the decay of a subatomic particle. Wigner suggested that if the experimenter had a friend outside of the lab, the state vector for the observer would not collapse until the friend inside the lab notified the friend outside, even if it had already collapsed for the friend inside. To back up for a moment, Schrödinger's posited a thought experiment where a closed box would contain a cat and a device that would release a poison gas pellet if a certain quantum decay took place. The equations yield a fifty percent chance of the decay taking place during a certain length of time. However, the observer in the lab cannot tell whether or not the decay has taken place without opening the door. According to classical mechanics, the mathematics should allow the observer to predict the results, but quantum mechanics only gives percentages. Hence, that cat seems both alive and dead— according to the math—until the observer opens the door. However, Wigner showed that even if the observer opened the door and determined whether the cat had died or not, a friend outside the lab would still perceive the cat in the "alive and/or not alive" mode until notified by the friend inside. This sort of infinite regress suggests the idea of recursion in computer science as well as the odd form of the *Schrödinger's Cat* novel(s).

The third loop names General Crowley as the man who led the communist takeover of Unistat (the name for the United States in the universe next door), who handpicked Franklin Delano Roosevelt. (*The Homing Pigeons*, pg. 143) The third loop continues with a weird twist on the story of the paint forger Elmyr. Blake Williams finances a film about Elmyr directed by Orson Welles called *Art Is What You Can Get Away With.* In our universe Welles directed a film about Elmyr called *F for Fake,* and Wilson wrote a screenplay a few years after *The Homing Pigeons* called *Reality Is What You Can Get Away With.* The Welles film dealt with Elmyr and his biographer, Clifford Irving, who later went to jail due to his attempts to write a supposedly authorized biography of Howard Hughes. Hughes claimed that the contract Irving had contained a forgery of Hughes' signature. Welles bought a documentary about Elmyr and Irving, and filmed additional segments and edited them together with footage of Elmyr and Irving, making a somewhat fake documentary of a somewhat fake biography of a somewhat fake painter. This looping suggests, once again, the form of *The Homing Pigeons.* Wilson has written at length about Elmyr, especially in *Cosmic Trigger III* and *Everything Is Under Control.*

Next, Williams and his friends:

> ...financed a new literary journal, *Passaic Review*, which they advertised so widely that everybody with any pretense to being an intellectual had to read it.
>
> The *Passaic Review* heaped scorn and invective on the established literary idols of the time: Simon Moon, the neo-

surrealist novelist; Gerald Ford, the "country-and-western"
poet; Norman Mailer; Robert Heinlein; Tim Hildebrand; and
so on. They also denounced all the alleged "greats" of the first
part of the century, H.P. Lovecraft, Henry James, T.S. Eliot
and Robert Putney Drake.

They established their own pantheon of "great" writers,
which included William Butler Yeats (an obscure Irish
schoolteacher nobody had ever heard of), Olaf Stapledon,
Arthur Flegenheimer, and Jonathan Latimer.
— *The Homing Pigeons,* pg. 151

Williams "knew that Value was the Schrödinger's Cat in
every equation." (*The Homing Pigeons*, pg. 152) Here Wilson
has fun with canon formation, concluding by connecting the idea
of literary and financial value with the novel's theme of non-
objectivity. Silvio Gesell spends a great deal of time discussing
the nature of value, and both Pound and Wilson have cited
Gesell as an influence. (See *Selected Prose of Ezra Pound*, *Right
Where You Are Sitting Now* by Wilson, and Wilson's recommended reading list on his website at rawilson.com.) In the lists
of writers Wilson includes characters from *Illuminatus!* (Simon
Moon and Robert Putney Drake) with figures from the world of
science fiction (Heinlein and Stapledon), and fantasy (artist Tim
Hildebrand and H.P. Lovecraft). Actually, Lovecraft also appears
in *Illuminatus!,* as do Arthur Flegenheimer (Dutch Schultz) and
Yeats (who appears briefly, talking with James Joyce in the
afterlife). William Burroughs also wrote a book about Flegenheimer, *The Last Words of Dutch Schultz.*

The third loop continues with a visit to the world of Dr. Raus
Elysium and his Invisible Hand Society. The doctor's name
derives from "Tochter als Elysium" from the German writer
Johann Christoph Friedrich von Schiller's "Ode to Joy" which
Beethoven uses in his Choral Symphony (number nine). The first
loop contains a gate which says

FATALITY INC.
Muss. S. Sine, President
S. Muss Sine, Vice-President

This refers to the last movement of Beethoven's string quartet in F, op. 135, which has two themes entitled "Muss es sein?" (Must it be?) and "Es muss sein!" (It must be!) One might see these mottos as representing fatalism, as Wilson's jest suggests. Ironically, musicologist Joseph Kerman relates an anecdote that Beethoven's themes originally suggested the repayment of a debt (must it be? it must), which goes well with *The Homing Pigeon's* economic preoccupations.

Style

Let us return to the passage from the art manifesto.

> We are delighted that Pluto, Mickey and Goofy are all at odd angles from the plane of the eight inner planets. We are thrilled with Bohr's great principle of Relativity, which shows that to look out into space is also to look backwards in time. WE ARE THE DAY AFTER YESTERDAY!!!
> — *The Homing Pigeons*, pg. 108

These three sentences all begin with the editorial "we," followed by the second person plural of the verb "to be." In the first two sentences "are" acts as a helping verb, while in the third sentence it serves as a linking verb. Wilson, a long-time student of Korzybski's General Semantics, tends to pay particular attention to the verb "to be," when he doesn't avoid it all together. (Wilson wrote two books, *Quantum Psychology* and *Cosmic Trigger III*, where the verb "to be" only appeared in quotations.) Korzybski suggested that the "is of identity" (i.e., "is" as linking verb or copula) tends to distort communications. Korzybski suggested that readers tends to confuse the "is of identity" with the mathematical equals sign. In the above passage Wilson satirizes the pompous quality of many artistic and literary manifestos with the repeated use of "We are."

The first sentence has one clause, ending with three prepositional phrases. The second sentence has two clauses, each with two prepositional phrases. The final sentence has only one clause, with one prepositional phrase. The paragraph accelerates: the second sentence has grown longer and more complicated than the first one, and the final sentence has all capital letters as well as three exclamation points. This parallel construction combined with the acceleration helps to give the paragraph power as well as wit.

One can also see Wilson's hedonistic bias with verbs such as "delighted" and "thrilled." The linking of these verbs with scientific ideas suggests the hedonic quality of learning and discovery so central to Wilson's *umwelt*. Also, the planet Pluto has many meanings. It suggests the lord of the underworld as well as the god of wealth. Wilson has commented that all of his books involve a journey through the underworld, an archetypal trip paralleling that of Ishtar, Dante, etc. He has said that the metaphor of Chinatown plays the role of underworld in the *Schrödinger's Cat* books. In addition, Wilson constantly has an awareness of the economic implications of his ideas. The authors of this manifesto within the novel clearly have an idea of the economic worth of their association with the manifesto and the publicity attending it.

Pluto also suggests the dog in the Mickey Mouse cartoons. The naming of the other planets "Mickey" and "Goofy" emphasize this association. The connection between a dog and outer space suggests the dog star Sirius. This star has played a central role in many of Wilson's writings, especially *Cosmic Trigger I*. Interestingly the phrase "the plane of the eight inner planets" suggests an astronomic interpretation, but in the occult context of much of the novel it also suggests astrology and the "planes" of the kabbalah. Wilson, in *Cosmic Trigger I*, draws particular attention to a quote from Aleister Crowley involving these kabbalistic planes, even printing it all in capital letters:

IN THIS BOOK IT IS SPOKEN OF THE SEPHIROTH & THE PATHS, OF SPIRITS & CONJURATIONS, OF GODS, SPHERES, PLANES & MANY OTHER THINGS WHICH MAY OR MAY NOT EXIST. IT IS IMMATERIAL WHETHER THEY EXIST OR NOT. BY DOING CERTAIN THINGS CERTAIN RESULTS FOLLOW; STUDENTS ARE MOST EARNESTLY WARNED AGAINST ATTRIBUTING OBJECTIVE REALITY OR PHILOSOPHICAL VALIDITY TO ANY OF THEM.

— *Cosmic Trigger I*, pg. 18

In the "PREFACE TO THE NEW EDITION" of *Cosmic Trigger I* in 1986 Wilson wrote, "I beg you gentle reader, to memorize the quote from Aleister Crowley at the beginning of Part One and repeat it to yourself if at any point you start thinking that I am bringing you the latest theological revelations from Cosmic Central" (*Cosmic Trigger I*, pg. v).

The naming of the planets after Disney characters demonstrates Wilson's combination of the scientific with the popular and hedonistic. The presence of the extra comma between "Mickey" and "and" shows Wilson mischievously highlighting each Disney name. The ambiguity of Pluto shows Wilson's desire to suggest multiple meanings *ala* Joyce and Crowley. (Wilson alludes to Empson's *Seven Kinds of Ambiguity* elsewhere in the *Schrödinger's Cat* trilogy. He even includes a rock band "The Seven Kinds of Ambiguity" from *Illuminatus!* in the trilogy.) Also, the juxtaposition of the eight inner planets (with Latin deity names) and the outer three planets (with American Disney names) suggests the 8 x 3 structure of the brain suggested by Timothy Leary in *Info-Psychology*, *The Game of Life* (co-written with Wilson), *Neuropolitique* (also co-written with Wilson), and other books. Wilson makes many references, both explicit and oblique, to Leary's model of the brain in *The Homing Pigeons*. Pluto exists both within the Latin god framework and the American Disney framework. This combination within the ambiguous "Pluto" helps to make the passage work effectively. Note also that this close stylistic analysis of Wilson's prose parallels the analysis Wilson makes of Joyce's writing in *The Illuminati Papers* and *Coincidance*. Wilson has frequently spoken of his desire to pack multiple meanings into a paragraph. He says he learned many techniques for doing this from Joyce and Crowley.

In our world Einstein, not Bohr came up with the theories of relativity. The attribution of this archetypal discovery to Bohr demonstrates the meta-relativity between universes, as well as Bohr's own theory of complementarity. Korzybski has commented that Einstein made his great breakthrough by ceasing to separate space and time, and by dealing with space-time instead, since we never encounter space or time without the other. Wilson alludes to this by inserting the words "space" and "time" into parallel positions in the second sentence of the above paragraph

from *The Homing Pigeons.* "Space" appears in the first prepositional phrase in the second clause while "time" appears in the
second prepositional phrase in the second paragraph: "into
space" and "in time." This coincidence between time and space
gets emphasized in the capitalized final sentence. The editorial
"WE" gets identified via the "is" of identity with "THE DAY
AFTER YESTERDAY!!!" The abstract noun "day" does not
usually get associated with a personal pronoun. Korzybski would
suggest that the time measurement "day" relates to the space-
time measurement of the length of time it takes for the earth to
rotate as it orbits the sun. The unusual juxtaposition of the personal pronoun "WE" with the noun "DAY" might jar the reader,
reminding them of the astronomic nature of our perception and
measurement of time. Here, as elsewhere, Wilson combines popular vocabulary with less familiar scientific vocabulary. Relatively (heh-heh) few people have heard of Niels Bohr. Wilson
inserts this name into the passage, linking the art and science
worlds, C.P. Snow's "Two Cultures."

To return to Earth, at least briefly, earlier in the novel
Lemuel Gulliver accosts Dr. Dashwood. At least the man calls
himself Gulliver. The scene parallels the encounters with Joseph
K and Captain Ahab elsewhere in the novel. The confrontation
between Gulliver and Dashwood comes to a head when Dashwood says that the "Race of perfectly Enlightened Beings,"
whom Gulliver describes, "sound like a bunch of damned com-
munists."

"Nay," Gulliver protested. "They live in the State of Nature,
without Bureaucrats or Commissars of any kind. And, I might
add, Sir, their Opinion of our Doctors was based upon my
showing them an ordinary *Medical Bill*, at which they inquir'd
of me the Average Income of the Doctors who present these
Bills and the Average Income of the Unfortunate Patients who
must pay them or be left without Treatment to Die in the
Streets. Their comments on this were of such Disgust and
Anger that I dared not show them a Psychiatrist's Bill, lest
their opinion of our Species, already Low, should sink Lower
than *Whaleburger*, which is, as you may know, at the bottom
of the Ocean."

— *The Homing Pigeons,* pg. 64

"Whaleburger" seems like the most unusual word in this paragraph. Earlier in the novel a future commentator on the novel suggests that proper nouns replace the words for sexual and/or forbidden words in the novel. Hence, the Supreme Court Justice Burger provides the novel's word for "shit," which gives us whaleshit at the bottom of the ocean.

Wilson obviously had a lot of fun writing this passage, an homage to Jonathan Swift, one of his favorite writers. In an article entitled "Brain Books" Wilson wrote, "Swift does a great job of tearing apart conventional ideas about almost everything. He's very, very liberating; almost psychedelic in some passages." ("Brain Books," pg. 29) Here Wilson uses the capitalization of proper nouns to suggest an eighteenth century style, although perhaps more in the style of John Adams than that of Jonathan Swift (or Lemuel Gulliver). In addition, Wilson adds italics to add inflection. This also emphasizes the parallel between the *Medical Bill* and *Whaleburger*. Wilson feels free to add twentieth century vocabulary like Psychiatrist and Commissar, although the capitalization helps them to fit in with the eighteenth century style. The expression "State of Nature" also suggests John Adams, who told the Second Continental Congress they lived in a "State of Nature." The writings of Thomas Jefferson refer to "Nature's God," and Wilson later wrote a novel called *Nature's God* which involved Jefferson and Adams, and one of the characters drew on Swift as a role model.

Note the apostrophe in the word "inquir'd." This helps to give an antiquated feel to the passage, as well as suggesting the "National Enquirer," or, perhaps more to the point, the Inquirer newspapers in Orson Welles' *Citizen Kane*. This long sentence balances references to the rich and the poor much as the earlier example parallels space and time. This paragraph also balances "us" and "them." Gulliver uses the personal possessive pronoun "our" to refer to "our Species" and uses the third person plural pronoun "they" to refer to the outside observer. Of course, references to "observers" in this science-fiction novel suggests Heisenberg's contention that the observer always interacts with the observed. The interaction between Gulliver and Dashwood exemplifies this; the two of them come together in the reference to "our Species." Gulliver doesn't even get a chance, though, to convince Dashwood of Dashwood's "real" identity as George Dorn.

In keeping with Swift's less than hedonic nature, Wilson forgoes the "delighted" and "thrilled" verbs of the earlier passage. Here we have "protested," "Unfortunate," "must pay," "to Die in the Streets," "Disgust and Anger," "dared not," "already Low," "sink Lower" and "*Whaleburger.*" The absurdity of this final negative allows Wilson's ludic sense to peek through this misanthropic mask. "Protested" and "in the Streets" point to Wilson's own political involvement in the sixties, where hedonism and misanthropy collided on occasion, as reported in various of his books.

Later in the novel:

> Dr. Dashwood went out to dinner that night with Dr. Bertha Van Ation, the astronomer from Griffith Observatory who had discovered the two planets beyond Pluto.
>
> They ate at Bernstein's Fish Grotto, the best seafood restaurant in San Francisco, which was becoming famous at that time for giving free meals to writers who plug it in their books, a tradition that had begun a few years earlier when they were prominently featured in the funniest science-fiction novel of 1981.
>
> "Welcome to Bernstein's Fish Grotto," said the waiter. "I hope you enjoy the food."
>
> "I always enjoy the food at BERNSTEIN'S FISH GROTTO!" Dashwood shouted.
>
> "Why are you shouting?" Dr. Van Ation asked.
>
> "I don't know," Dashwood said. "Something just sort of...came over me..."
>
> "Well, *Bernstein's Fish Grotto* is certainly worth shouting about," Dr. Van Ation said, in a low but intense voice.
>
> — *The Homing Pigeons*, pg. 78

Once again Wilson uses italics and capitalization to add to the humor as well as to emphasize to the reader the experience of the act of reading. Characteristically, Wilson follows the word "said" with a period rather than a comma, encouraging the reader to take their time. In this passage the capitalization suggests a raising of voice. Redundantly Wilson uses the verb "shouted." Just as the reader notices the redundancy, Bertha Van Ation asks,

"Why are you shouting?" This brings us back to the novel's theme, *esse est percepi,* "to be is to be perceived." Wilson uses these typographical tools, along with the asides by the characters, to bring the reader into the work.

The absurdity of the name Bertha Van Ation suggests the controversial film "Birth of a Nation," directed by D.W. Griffith. Dr. Van Ation works at Griffith Observatory. Wilson has stated that he and Robert Shea based the structure of *Illuminatus!* on D.W. Griffith's *Intolerance.* Here the prepositional phrase "beyond Pluto" suggests the planets Dr. Van Ation has discovered beyond Pluto, a motive in life beyond money, life after a passage through the underworld/Chinatown or "beyond Pluto" and a culture beyond that of Disney cartoons.

We have a couple of paired superlatives in the next paragraph, the best seafood restaurant and the funniest science-fiction novel. The "funniest science-fiction novel" contains an ironic reference to *The Homing Pigeons* itself. The humor underscores how this self-referential passage reinforces the theme of the novel. The begging quality of this passage also fits in with the general economic orientation of Wilson's work as a whole. This paragraph consists of a single sentence. The opening clause consists of a pronoun, an intransitive verb and a prepositional phrase. The rest of the sentence elaborates on the object of that prepositional phrase. This absurdly back-heavy sentence format supports the absurdity of the passage.

After Dashwood's shouting, Dr. Van Ation continues to plug the restaurant in "a low but intense voice." This low voice parallels the shouting of Dr. Dashwood. The fact that both of these unwitting members of a commercial for a fish restaurant have the title "Doctor" adds to the humor of the scene, as well as its unreality. This also emphasizes the connection between the scientific and the economic. Dr. Van Ation's name also emphasizes the link between science as art, as well as the ludic quality of writing and reading.

In these passages we can see many of the stylistic features that help to make *The Homing Pigeon* the "funniest science-fiction novel of 1981." Wilson likes to mix italics and capitalized words and even to capitalize whole sentences. He feels free to multiply exclamation points for humorous effect. He favors a readable style with occasionally long sentences. He incorporates a variety of parodistic effects, with a surface source as well as subtler references. He often juxtaposes references to science with unusual settings: an art manifesto, a commercial for a fish restaurant, etc. He consistently mixes vernacular vocabulary with more technical vocabulary, especially scientific vocabulary.

These stylistic features complement the ideas from quantum mechanics which Wilson says give form to the novel (and to the other two *Schrödinger's Cat* novels). Wilson's willingness to use typographical devices and humorous names shows that he doesn't see the necessity for a sharp division between "high" and "low" culture. He also appears shameless in his plug for Bernstein's Fish Grotto, begging for free food. This contains an ironic reference to the recursive self-referentiality of both the mathematical and quantum mechanical roots of this novel. Also, this passage supports the novel's commentary about the freelance writer's precarious place in the contemporary American economy. Elsewhere in the novel Wilson has a writer at a party in the novel get drunk and yell and curse at publishers.

Wilson has made a career out of self-referentiality. From Epicene Wildebloode reviewing *Illuminatus!* within the text of *Illuminatus!* itself to the above-mentioned plug for Bernstein's Fish Grotto within "the funniest science-fiction novel of 1981," Wilson uses this and other stylistic tools to help make the reader aware of the creative act of reading. Wilson frequently cites the Zen koan "Who is the master who makes the grass green?" He suggests that we perceive the greenness of the grass through a yoga of our perceptive and cognitive apparatus and the external world (the grass). "Yoga" means union, and Wilson's writing style itself seems a "yoga" of the scientific, the commercial, and the sublime. He learned much of this from Joyce. However, Wilson places a high premium on readability. Even when he brings a variety of sophisticated concepts which might overwhelm some readers, he favors a clear and relatively simple prose style, learned in part from successful non-academic writers like Raymond Chandler, H.P. Lovecraft, George Higgins and others.

Wilson likes to deal with the unity of seeming opposites. Giordano Bruno saw the world as a coincidence of opposites. Wilson likes to take seemingly opposed ideas and juxtapose them in a humorous way, often reflecting on the quantum mechanical roots of his thinking, and his other philosophical orientations as well. These juxtapositions allow the work to deconstruct before the reader's eyes. Wilson makes the reader aware of this deconstruction, as well as of the element of creativity in the very act of reading, and certainly in the act of writing.

APPENDIX QOPH

Space-Time Pyramid

Although Wilson likes to use alternative calendars, I think we can still have some fun with the Gregorian calendar. One can use each of the next few years to nurture and develops the systems of the mind-body. 2003 seems like a great year to develop the third system of Timothy Leary's eight circuit model, 2005 for the fifth, etc. Every time you write the date you can remind yourself to nurture that system of your mind-body. I think this will help make 2006, 2007 and 2008 a blast.

2008
2007 7
2006 6 6
2005 5 5 5
2004 4 4 4 4
2003 3 3 3 3 3
2002 2 2 2 2 2 2
2001 1 1 1 1 1 1 1

APPENDIX RESH

Brain Books
(In Hebrew, Resh means "head")

In *Trajectories* #16/17 (Autumn 1996 C.E., pp. 28–29), Wilson gave "a list of books I wish everyone would read: the ten books I most feel the lack of in people who otherwise seem intelligent. These books would fill anyone's cranium with useful information."

1. *Ulysses* by James Joyce. This surprised some Wilson fans since he has written so much more about Joyce's *Finnegans Wake* than about *Ulysses*. However, Wilson suggests, "Nobody has really entered the 20th century if they haven't digested *Ulysses*. And if they haven't entered the 20th century, they're going to fall pretty far behind pretty soon, as we enter the 21st."
Like Wilson, I prefer the 1961 edition of Ulysses, although many scholars prefer the 1984 "corrected" text edited by Hans Walter Gabbler. Hugh Kenner's short book *Ulysses* provides a good introduction to the novel. David Norris' comic book *Introducing Joyce* and Edna O'Brien's *James Joyce* both provides accessible introductions to Joyce's life and works, but I still consider Wilson's *Masks of the Illuminati* and Joyce's children's story *The Cat and the Devil* the best introductions to Joyce.

2. *The Cantos* by Ezra Pound. I suggest buying a copy and reading it out loud. You can get to know Ezra's personality and learn to appreciate his magnificent sense of humor by reading his prose. You might begin with *How to Read*, included in *Literary Essays*, which also includes a great introduction by Pound's friend T.S. Eliot. The anthology *From Confucius to cummings*,

edited by Pound and Marcella Spahn, seems to me the best anthology of poetry ever put together, and it provides a beautiful summary of Pound's thinking about poetry.

Peter Makin's book *The Cantos* provides a good roadmap to Pound's epic. I also recommend Donald Davies' books on Pound, as well as Hugh Kenner's. Kenner's *The Pound Era* gives a deep and powerful picture of the artistic worlds of Pound, Joyce and Eliot, etc. Also, *A Companion to the Cantos of Ezra Pound* by Carroll Terrell provides invaluable annotations to this multi-lingual work.

3. *Science and Sanity* by Count Alfred Korzybski. This book radically influenced Wilson, as well as Heinlein, Israel Regardie, Bucky Fuller, Gregory Bateson, Richard Bandler and others. It took me years to finish it, but I consider it time well spent. Wilson's books, especially *Cosmic Trigger III* and *Quantum Psychology* provide a good introduction to Korzybski.

4. Ovid. Wilson told me he meant *The Metamorphosis* primarily, but it wouldn't hurt to read all of Ovid. Pound and Shakespeare loved Arthur Golding's sixteenth century translation of *The Metamorphosis*, which Pound called the most beautiful book in the language. Shakespeare lifted parts of Golding's translation and put them in his plays, most notably in *The Tempest*. Pound also highly recommended Christopher Marlowe's sexy and beautiful translation of Ovid's *Art of Love*.

5. *The Canterbury Tales* by Geoffrey Chaucer. Great stuff. I recommend reading it out loud in the original Middle English. My Chaucer professor at Arizona State, Dennis Moran, recommended memorizing ten lines of Chaucer with the correct pronunciation as a tool for learning to read Chaucer for pleasure. I remember he used to come into the bookstore where I worked and correct my Middle English pronunciation. Thank you, Dr. Moran!

6. *Justine* by Comte Donatien Alphonse François de Sade. Not for the squeamish. This book has more torture scenes than any book I've ever read, except perhaps *Without Remorse* by Tom Clancy, although de Sade lacks Clancy's self-righteous justification of torture.

7. *Instead of a Book by a Man Too Busy to Write One* by
Benjamin Tucker. Joyce called Tucker the clearest mind he'd
ever read on politics. Well worth reading. Wilson provides links
to some Tucker essays from this book at rawilson.com.

8. *Progress and Poverty* by Henry George. Wilson writes,
"everyone's heard of Karl Marx and Adam Smith. If you read
Tucker and George, you get the idea that there are more than two
choices." George suggested that the government own all the
land, and that citizens would pay rent as the only form of
taxation.

9. *The Open Society and Its Enemies* by Karl Popper. A big
two-volume book that I had trouble finishing, but, like all the
works on this list, I found it ultimately rewarding. Popper writes
that a society with open communication tends to become
wealthier, and he discusses in great detail the opposition to open
communication in Plato, in the first volume, and Kant, in the
second. He sees Kant's historicism as underlying Marx's
thought. Popper wrote this book during World War II, and it
seems to me an epic tool to oppose totalitarianism of all sorts,
especially fascist and communist.

10. Shakespeare. Who dat? Reading his plays out loud with a
group can help bring out the humor. *Asimov's Guide to
Shakespeare* gives useful historical background information.
Leslie Fiedler's *The Stranger in Shakespeare* examines
Shakespeare's treatment of outsiders, the Woman Joan of Arc in
Henry VI, Part 1, the Jew in *Merchant of Venice*, the Moor in
Othello and the Native in *The Tempest*, etc. A fun book. You
also might enjoy reading Shakespeare's history plays in
chronological sequence, from *King John* to *Henry VIII*. Orson
Welles used to perform some of these plays in sequence, and
Ezra Pound called the Histories our true English epic poem.

In addition to these ten, Wilson recommended Jonathan
Swift (all of *Gulliver's Travels*), Friedrich Nietzsche (*Twilight of
the Idols* and *The Anti-Christ*) and Olaf Stapledon (*First and
Last Men* and *Last Men in London*). Wilson calls Swift "Very,
very liberating; almost psychedelic in some passages." *The
Portable Nietzsche* contains the above two Nietzsche works,

among others, in Walter Kaufman's translation. However, Wilson's reading list at rawilson.com recommends H.L. Menken's translation of *The Anti-Christ*. I had to use interlibrary loan to get the Stapledon books. Leslie Fiedler, one of the first "literary critics" to write about science fiction, wrote a whole book about Stapledon.

Crowley gives 465 as the mystic number of resh. The Hebrew word for kiss or "sweet mouth" adds to 465 as well.

The website rawilson.com has a list of recommended reading which includes some of the above books with a few interesting additions. Wilson describes this list as "the bare minimum of what everybody really needs to chew and digest before they can converse intelligently about the 21st Century."

First comes Wilhelm Reich's *The Mass Psychology of Fascism*. In *TSOG: The Thing That Ate the Constitution,* Wilson calls this book "the best depth analysis of Mystical Tsarism" (e.g., our current U.S. government). I think this book moved to the top of Wilson's recommendations because of the continuing destruction of the U.S. Constitution. You might enjoy reading this in conjunction with Wilson's *Wilhelm Reich in Hell.*

Next we have *Ulysses* and *Finnegans Wake* by Joyce and then *The Cantos*, *Machine Art* and *Selected Prose* by Ezra Pound. *Machine Art* contains some interesting essays, as well as a photo section which Bob particularly likes. It tries to get the reader to see machines with new eyes. *Selected Prose* contains a lot of Ezra's economic writings, as well as his essay on the *Adams/Jefferson Letters*, essays on Confucius and Mencius, and a beautiful obituary for his friend the Possum, T.S. Eliot. Pound wrote, "Who is there now for me to share a joke with?" Also, "I can only repeat, but with the urgency of 50 years ago: READ HIM." (Pound, *Selected Prose,* pg. 464) A university library will likely have tons of Pound, as well as books about Possum and Ezra and Joyce (oh my).

Next Wilson included *Harlot's Ghost* by Norman Mailer, a "docu-novel" about James Jesus Angleton, the head of the C.I.A. counter intelligence section for many years, which Wilson in *TSOG* calls "the best overview of TSOG/CIA operations in general." (TSOG stands for Tsarist Occupation Government.)

Then we have *Go Down, Moses*, a powerful volume of linked stories by William Faulkner, including "The Bear," which Wilson mentions in *TSOG* along with the films *The Edge* and *Legends of the Fall*, all three of which contain the Bear deity archetype. Next, Wilson includes *The Alphabet vs. the Goddess* by Leonard Slatkin, which give a history of humanity as an alternation between alphabet-oriented dominator thinking and goddess-oriented partnership living. The goddess theme fits in with *Finnegans Wake*'s Anna Livia Plurabella and *The Cantos'* Kupris Aphrodite, although I don't think Ezra would have liked the anti-Confucian sentiments of Slatkin's book. *Critical Path* by Bucky Fuller and *Saharasia* by James DeMeo later on the list provide two alternative histories of humanity. Reading all of the books on this list helped to open up my mind to seeing the human adventure (or obstacle course) in a variety of ways.

Coincidentally, Wilson said the Anthony Hopkins character in *The Edge* reminded him of Bucky Fuller. Of course, Hopkins also plays Hannibal Lecter in three films beloved by Wilson, as well as the title character in *Nixon*. E. Howard Hunt appears as a character in *Nixon* as well as *Harlot's Ghost*, and Wilson's *Everything Is Under Control* discusses a variety of folk who think Hunt may have taken a shot at JFK on November 22, 1963 C.E., the same day Aldous Huxley died.

Next we have *The Open Society and Its Enemies* by Karl Popper and *Confucius: The Great Digest, The Unwobbling Pivot and the Analects*, translated by Ezra Pound, portions of which have both the Chinese and Pound's English. In the essay "The Immediate Need of Confucius" in *Selected Prose,* Pound said of *The Great Digest (Ta Hio)*, "Christian theology is a jungle. To think it through, to reduce it to some semblance of order, there is no better axe than the *Ta Hio*." (Pound, *Selected Prose*, pg. 78) He also wrote, "We in the West *need* to begin with the *Ta Hio*." (Pound, *Selected Prose*, pg. 77)

Next we have *The Anti-Christ* by Nietzsche in H.L. Menken's translation, and *Chaos and Cyberculture* by Timothy Leary, the last collection of his essays published before his death. It includes interviews with William Gibson, William S. Burroughs and actress Winona Rider, and lots of wonderful writing. Next we have *Critical Path* by R. Buckminster Fuller, which Wilson frequently cites, along with Bucky's *Grunch of Giants*, for understanding the economics of our world.

Wilson next included *Instead of a Book* by Benjamin Tucker and *Digital McLuhan*. Both of these books have helped me better understand our current space-time situation, especially the Tucker. Wilson includes links to a few Tucker essays on his website. Then we have *Saharasia* by James DeMeo, *Science and Sanity* by Count Alfred Korzybski and *Progress and Poverty* by Henry George. I found the synergetic experience of reading the neo-Reichian vision of humanity's inhumanities by DeMeo alongside the other books on this list revelatory. One can see Wilson's books and the books on these lists as tools for awakening from the nightmares of history.

Lastly we have *The Natural Economic Order* by Silvio Gesell, who influenced both Pound and Wilson. After reading Fuller, Pound, Gesell, Tucker and George, as well as Wilson's writings on money, I feel like I have a better understanding of the central role of "money" in the lives of domesticated primates. I do feel a little out of touch with the folks who talk about money and politics on TV, though.

APPENDIX SHIN

Alternative Names for the
Eight Systems of the Mind-Body Meta-System

On the wonderful set of six tapes, *Robert Anton Wilson Explains Everything* (2001), Wilson says he has begun calling these aspects of the mind-body meta-system systems instead of circuits. He and Timothy Leary have labeled them in different ways over the years. Tim, in *Flashbacks*, wrote:

> This listing of possible future levels of human intelligence is necessarily tentative, suggestive, semantically fragile, and intellectually risky. (Earlier speculation on the subjects were published in my books *Neurologic, Exo-Psychology*, and *The Game of Life*.) However theoretical, these probes are of the utmost importance for our species. We cannot activate the future circuits of our CNS/RNA-DNA systems until we start developing a new language for it.
>
> — *Flashbacks*, pg. 386

From *Prometheus Rising* by Robert Anton Wilson, 1983 C.E., Second Revised Edition 1997 C.E.:

    I. The Oral Bio-Survival Circuit
    II. The Anal Emotional Territorial Circuit
    III. The Time-Binding Semantic Circuit
    IV. The "Moral" Socio-Sexual Circuit
    V. The Holistic Neurosemantic Circuit
    VI. The Collective Neurogenetic Circuit
    VII. The Meta-Programming Circuit
    VIII. The Non-Local Quantum Circuit

One can see the influence of Korzybski in his naming of the third system. Korzybski saw the difference between humanity and the other critters in humans' capacity to "time-bind," to send signals from one generation to the next, making progress possible. Each generation of bees, chimpanzees and dolphins lives pretty much the same way their ancestors did. However, humanity can learn from previous generations, even those long dead. The computer I use to write this text results from generation after generation of time-binding.

Wilson read *Science and Sanity* by Korzybski "perhaps two dozen times in the first ten years after discovering it," and Wilson wrote, "Everything I have written, however improved or disimproved by my own wisdom or idiocy, begins from the shock of taking a book off a library shelf and encountering the world of Alfred Korzybski." (*Chaos and Beyond*, pg. 1)

From *Quantum Psychology* by Robert Anton Wilson, 1990 C.E.

I. The oral bio-survival system.
II. The anal territorial system.
III. The semantic time-binding system.
IV. The socio-sexual system.
V. The neurosomatic system.
VI. The metaprogramming system.
VII. The morphogenetic system.
VIII. The non-local quantum system.

Here Wilson has reversed the order of the sixth and seventh systems, using the order favored by Leary. As quoted above, Leary suggested that discussing the higher systems seemed "necessarily tentative, suggestive, semantically fragile, and intellectually risky," so this reshuffling and non-dogmatic reassessment of the eight system model seems appropriate.

Wilson also renames the seventh system the morphogenetic system.

The first scientific model of this system appeared in Dr. Rupert Sheldrake's *A New Science of Life*. Where Leary and Grof, like Jung and Freud, assumed the non-ego information, not known to the brain, must come from the genes, Sheldrake, a biologist, knew that genes cannot carry such information. He therefore posited a non-local field, like those in quantum theory, which he named the morphogenetic field. This field communicates between genes but cannot be found "in" genes—just as Johnny Carson "travels" between TV sets but cannot be found "in" any of the TV sets that receive him.

— *Quantum Psychology,* pg. 191

(I remember in 1988 C.E. encountering Bob Wilson's use of the Johnny Carson metaphor for non-locality, and then later that evening watching "The Tonight Show," and, during Johnny's monologue, learning George Bush's middle names Herbert and Walker for the first time. This amused me, since it made me think about two physicists, Nick Herbert and Evan Walker, both of whom have written about non-locality.)

From *The Game of Life* by Timothy Leary, with Historical and Scholarly Scripts by Robert Anton Wilson, 1979 C.E.

VIII. Metaphysiology Circuit
VII. Neurogenetic Circuit
VI. Neurophysical Circuit
V. Neurosomatic Circuit
IV. Domestication Circuit
III. Mental Symbolic Circuit
II. Emotion-Locomotion Circuit
I. Bio-Survival Circuit

Leary tended to present the systems/circuits in the bottom-up fashion in this book to suggest upward and outward evolution to the stars. Note also that Leary divides each of the systems into three stages, for a total of twenty-four.

From *Info-Psychology [A Revision of Exo-Psychology]* by Timothy Leary, 1987 C.E.

I. Bio-Survival (Marine) Stages
II. The Terrestrial Mammalian Stages
III. The Symbolic Tool Stage

IV. Industrial
V. Cyber-Somatic Piloting Sensory Info
VI. Cyber-Electronic Piloting Quantum Electronic Info
VII. Cyber-Genetic Piloting DNA/RNA Data
VIII. Cyber-Nano-Tech Piloting Atomic Info

Leary wrote of this version, "The current update of these ideas emphasizes the Info-society. The quantum world is comprised of Cyber-persons piloting their way through the post-collective realities of the futures. (*Info-Psychology*, pg. 137)

From *Design for Dying*, 1997 C.E., published after Leary's death.

I. Biosurvival
II. Emotional
III. Laryngeal/Manipulative
IV. Sexual Domestication
V. Neurosomatic
VI. Neuroelectric
VII. Neurogenetic
VIII. Neuroatomic

Leary writes of the eight circuit model in the essay "Mutation:"

> You should know that SF writer and philosopher Robert Anton Wilson has done a much more lucid job than I of delineating, describing, and defending the model. I suggest you rush out and buy every book the man has ever written, but especially *Cosmic Trigger: The Final Secret of the Illuminati*, *The Illuminati Papers*, and *Prometheus Rising*.

I second Dr. Leary's suggestion.

APPENDIX NO LETTER

Illuminated Manuscript

Looking at Vatican Square from the Vatican,
1985 C.E.

The headquarters of
the Society of Jesus (the Jesuits),
1985 C.E.

Track 23, Train 3230 to Ingolstadt, Bavaria,
from Munich,
7/23/1985 C.E.

An apartment building in Ingolstadt
with an eye in the pyramid,
7/23/85 C.E.

The River Donau in Ingolstadt.
It reminded me of *Finnegans Wake*'s
"riverrun, past Eve and Adams,"
making me think of Eve and Adam Weishaupt,
7/23/85 C.E.

An ad for Ingolstadt's Medical Museum exhibit on ancient
Egyptian medicine.
Note the Eye of Horus,
7/23/85 C.E.

A gate at the Dachau Concentration Camp which says "Arbeit
Macht Frei." ("Work will set you free")
7/24/85 C.E.
The train from Munich to Ingolstadt passes Dachau.

The author at Dealy Plaza in Dallas, TX.
I did not see the Dealy Lama,
8/1987 C.E.

Rev. Ivan Stang of the Church of the SubGenius,
attending a Robert Anton Wilson
Finnegans Wake seminar,
8/1987 C.E.

The house in Providence, RI,
which H.P. Lovecraft used as the basis for
the home of Charles Dexter Ward,
12/1987 C.E.

The river Liffey in Dublin,
7/18/1989 C.E.

Gate to Dublin Castle,
7/18/89 C.E.
Justice looks into the castle, so she has her back to Ireland.
Some Dubliners see this a metaphor for the English
attitude towards Ireland.

The door to 7 Eccles St., home of Leopold Bloom,
preserved inside the Bailey pub since the fifties.
Poet Patrick Kavenaugh said,
"I now declare this door closed!"
when the Bailey first displayed this famous portal.
Picture taken 7/18/89 C.E.

Davy Byrne's pub, made famous by *Ulysses*,
7/19/1989 C.E.

The home of the late Paddy Dingham from *Ulysses*,
7/19/89 C.E.

Sweny's Druggist from *Ulysses*,
7/19/89 C.E.

A statue of Anna Livia on O'Connell St.,
7/19/89 C.E.

Howth Castle and Environs,
7/89 C.E.

The Confectioners Hall from *Ulysses*,
7/23/89 C.E.

Finn's Hotel in Dublin,
7/23/89 C.E.

Dublin's Freemason's Lodge,
7/23/89 C.E.

Shakespeare's mother's garden in
Stratford-Upon-Avon,
7/28/89 C.E.

Bryan Boru harp and statue of James Joyce at Joyce's grave in
Zürich, Switzerland.

Statue of Joyce at his grave in Zürich.

Statue of Joyce at his grave in Zürich.

Great picture of my Dad at the James Joyce pub in Zürich.

Amsterdam. Wilson refers to this city as "Paradisio" and/or a
"Temporary Autonomous Zone" in
TSOG: The Thing That Ate the Constitution,
5/1991 C.E.

The Alice Shop at Oxford, England.
Lewis Carroll based the sheep's shop in
Alice's Adventures in Wonderland on this building, 5/1991
C.E.

I 'n the pyramids, Giza, Egypt,
11/1994 C.E.

APPENDIX TAV

Illuminatus! Timeline

These dates seem pretty accurate to me. In 1988 C.E. I asked Wilson if the main action in *Illuminatus!* took place in 1976 C.E. He said no. In 1999 C.E. I asked him what year the main action in *Illuminatus!* did take place. He said 1976. Beware of tricksters and think for yourself.

Circa 28,100 B.C.E. Gruad born in Atlantis, according to the film *When Atlantis Ruled the Earth*.

Circa 28,000 B.C.E. Gruad invents good and evil, according to *When Atlantis Ruled the Earth*.

October 23, 4004 B.C.E. The world begins, according to Bishop Usher.

2500 B.C.E. The inscription of *The Seven Tablets of Creation* at the time of Sargon, and the formation of the Justified Ancients of Mummu. The J.A.M.'s wanted to get rid of usury and monopoly.

416 B.C.E. Massacre of the male inhabitants of Melos by the Athenians, where Malaclypse the Elder received transcendental illumination.

1307 C.E. The Knights Templar take the Shroud of Turin from Constantinople to Paris. A special thanks to the director of the Shroud Foundation who discussed this with me.

February 18, 1600 C.E. Giordano Bruno "terribly burned" at the stake for teaching that the Earth goes around the sun.

1723 C.E. Adam Weishaupt and Adam Smith born.

1734 C.E. The death of the "real Frankenstein" (*The Earth Will Shake*, pg. 203).

1750 C.E. Death of Johann Sebastian Bach.

January 12, 1762 C.E. In a letter to Malsherbes, Jean Jacques Rousseau wrote:

> All at once I felt myself dazzled by a thousand sparkling lights... [I realized] that man is by nature good, and that only our institutions have made him bad.
> — *The Earth Will Shake*, pg. 195

This reminds me of a poem I wrote when I learned of the popularity of writing theories of education a few hundred years ago.

Theories of Education

Montaigne did it.
Rabalais did it.
Even Jean Jacques Rousseau did it.
Let's do it.

February 2, 1776 C.E. Adam Weishaupt achieves illumination, discovering the law of fives.

May 1, 1776 C.E. Adam Weishaupt founds the Ancient Illuminated Seers of Bavaria in Ingolstadt. Adam Smith publishes *The Wealth of Nations* this year as well.

July 4, 1776 C.E. Comysimps in Philadelphia sign a revolutionary hedonistic document.

1785 C.E. The Bavarian government cracks down on the Illuminati. Perhaps the Illuminati reforms as the Reading Society which later commissions Beethoven's *Emperor Joseph Cantata*.

June 25, 1788 C.E. In a speech against the U.S. Constitution, Patrick Henry says:

The great and direct end of government is liberty. Secure our liberties and privileges, and the end of government is answered. If this be not effectively done, government is an evil.
— *The Earth Will Shake*, pg. 195

July 14, 1789 C.E. The storming of the Bastille, the beginning of the French Revolution.

Q: Who led the android revolution of 1789?
A: Robotspierre.

(I think I read that joke in an issue of *Science Fiction Review* twenty years ago.)

A tisket, a tasket, a head in a basket.
It will not reply to questions you ask it.
— Robert Anson Heinlein

1801 C.E. *Proofs of a Conspiracy* by John Robison published.

July 4, 1826 C.E. Both Thomas Jefferson and John Adams die of old age, fifty years to the day after the Declaration of Independence.

1843 C.E. Sir Charles Napier meets the first Aga Khan, a direct descendant of Hassan i Sabbah.

1880 C.E. The Illuminati refounded in Dresden according to Nesta Webster's *World Revolution*.

February 2, 1882 C.E. James Augusta Joyce born in Dublin. James Stephens later chose this day to celebrate as his birthday as well.

October 30, 1885 C.E. Birth of Ezra Loomis Pound in Hailey, Idaho.

1888 C.E. Chicago's Haymarket riot. The Cecil Rhodes faction kicks the J.A.M.'s out of the Illuminati, and Rhodes takes command of the Illuminati, or at least of one of the Illuminatis.

July 1889 C.E. The International Socialist Congress chooses May 1 for an International Labour demonstration. (*Illuminatus!*, pg. 105)

September 17, 1899 C.E. Invasion of earth by the Nova Mob in William S. Burroughs' *Nova Express*.

June 15, 1904 C.E. The shipwreck of the *General Slocum*, mentioned by Mama Sutra to Danny Pricefixer. It also plays a role in Joyce's *Ulysses*. James Cash Cartwright will later tell Joe Malik the Illuminati sank the *General Slocum*.

June 16, 1904 C.E. An ordinary day in which everything and nothing happens, according to Edna O'Brien. James Joyce and Nora Barnacle first go out walking together by the Pigeon House (electrical plant) in Dublin. "With the eyes of a saint" she gives him a hand-job, his first sexual experience with a woman for which he had not paid money. Joyce later immortalizes this day as the setting for his novel *Ulysses*.

Early June 17, 1904 C.E. Stephen Dedalus leaves the Bloom residence in the middle of the night, headed we know not where.

August 6, 1904 C.E. Arthur Flegenheimer (Dutch Schultz) and Robert Putney Drake born.

April 23, 1913 C.E. Date of newspaper article at the beginning of *Masks of the Illuminati*. That same year Ambrose Bierce disappears, and Phil Silverberg teases young Arthur Flegenheimer outside Flegenheimer's livery stable in the Bronx, "Do you really think you're big enough to knock over a house on your own?" (*Illuminatus!*, pg. 353)

1918 C.E. In France during World War I Robert Putney Drake wets his pants when he realizes all of his companions have died and he hears the Germans approaching.

1919 C.E. H.P. Lovecraft publishes "Dagon."

1921 C.E. Saul Goodman play-acts the role of the great detective after reading Arthur Conan Doyle.

February 2, 1922 C.E. Joyce's *Ulysses* published. Eliot's "The Waste Land" and Schönberg's 12-tone system published the same year. Mussolini comes to power in Italy as well that year. Also the year *The Great Gatsby* takes place.

1923 C.E. Adolph Hitler's initiation into the Illuminated Lodge in Munich beneath a pyramidal altar. He repeats the words of goat-headed man: "*Der Zweck heiligte die Mitte.*" (*Illuminatus!*, pg. 181), James Joyce works on *Finnegans Wake*, H.P. Lovecraft attends a party also attended by Hart Crane, and in Boston Robert Putney Drake tries therapy with Dr. Besetzung.

1924 C.E. John Dillinger first arrested by the Moorsville, Indiana, Police Force, which included James V. Riley.

August 23, 1928 C.E. Rancid, the Drake butler, reports to Robert Putney Drake's father that he has found glass and nails in RPD's shoes.

August, 1929 C.E. Robert Putney Drake experiments with sadism with a prostitute. His father pays her $500 to keep quiet.

October 29, 1929 C.E. Stock market crash.

October 30, 1929 C.E. Robert Putney Drake's father finds him begging on the street. His father insists he begin therapy again.

1930's C.E. Hagbard Celine takes a walking tour of Europe.

February 7, 1932 C.E. Dutch Schultz kills Vincent "Mad Dog" Coll, the same year as the kidnapping of the Lindberg baby. Dutch Schultz's high school principal, Jafsie Condon, serves as a go-between in the delivery of the Lindberg ransom money. Lindberg's father, a Congresscritter, had outspokenly criticized the formation of the Federal Reserve monopoly.

December 6, 1933 C.E. Hon. Judge Woolsey's decision lifts the ban on *Ulysses* in the U.S. That same month alcohol prohibition ends in the U.S. That same year Robert Putney Drake takes Psychology 101 from Professor Tochus at Harvard. His "psychic twin" Arthur Flegenheimer, a.k.a. Dutch Schultz, undergoes an initiation in New York, standing "before seventeen robed figures, one wearing a goat's head mask." (*Illuminatus!*, pg. 137) Hagbard Celine also had a run-in with Harvard's Tochus, perhaps in a different year. (*Illuminatus!*, pg. 142)

July 22, 1934 C.E. John Dillinger supposedly shot outside the Biograph Theater in Chicago after seeing "Manhattan Melo-

drama" starring Clark Gable and Myrna Loy. The attendant pub-
licity makes Loy a star. She always felt guilt that her fame came
at the cost of a man's death. Clark Gable served as the model for
Bugs Bunny (a scene of him eating carrot from *It Happened One
Night*) according to the film *Bugs Bunny Superstar*. Cynthia
Heimel wrote a wonderful article "When in Doubt, Act Like
Myrna Loy," which appears in her book *But Enough About You*.

October 23, 1935. Dutch Schultz killed by Charlie the Bug,
Mendy Weiss and Jimmy the Shrew per the instructions of
Banana Nose Maldonado. The Dutchman's last words play an
important part in *Illuminatus!* as well as in William Burroughs'
Last Words of Dutch Schultz.

That same year Robert Putney Drake talks with Carl Jung,
novelist Hermann Hesse and painter Paul Klee in Zurich.

April 1, 1936 C.E. Robert Putney Drake calls Federico Maldonado and quotes Dutch Schultz's dying words.

April 2, 1936 C.E. Drake calls Banana Nose Maldonado again,
Maldonado orders his son, a priest, to say one hundred masses
for the salvation of Dutch Schultz's soul. That night Drake takes
a young woman from the Morgan family to see *Tobacco Road*
and later has sex with her.

April 3, 1936 C.E. Both Louis Lepke and Robert Putney Drake
call Federico Maldonado Lepke to confront him about the soldiers Maldonado had following him, and Drake to quote the
Dutchman once again. (Wilson's *TSOG* mentions Wagner's
"Flying Dutchman Overture.") This time Drake issues Maldonado further instructions. Then Drake mails five copies of his
analysis of the Dutchman's dying words to the vaults of five different banks for insurance, all in keeping with the law of fives.
Next, Drake called Lepke and again quotes the Dutchman.

1937 C.E. H.P. Lovecraft dies at the age of 47.

January 30, 1939 C.E. Adolph Hitler, in a speech discussing the
"Jewish problem," uses the word *Vernichtung*, annihilation, for
the first time.

February 2, 1939 C.E. *Finnegans Wake* published. That same year sees the release of the film *The Wizard of Oz*, as well as the invasion of Poland by Germany. I find it interesting that the two most influential dream visions of the Roaring Twentieth Century came out the same year World War II went into full gear.

1940 C.E. Abe Reles blows the whistle on the entire Murder Inc. organization, naming Charley Workman as the chief gun in the Dutch Schultz massacre.

April 16, 1943 C.E. Albert Hoffman discovers LSD-25. That same year the Final Solution moves into high gear, and Louis Lepke announces he wants to talk before his execution. However, Lepke decides not to reveal anything of import when a fellow named Winifred from the State Department shows up. John Edgar Dillinger has a heart attack.

May 8, 1945 C.E. V-E Day (Victory in Europe). Also Thomas Pynchon's seventh birthday. He later wrote the novels *V*, *Vineland* and *Gravity's Rainbow*, which dealt with the end of World War II and its aftermath in Europe. Timothy Leary greatly valued *Gravity's Rainbow*.

August 6, 1945 C.E. Atomic bomb detonated over Hiroshima. Fission Chips, who later became Agent 00005, born.

March, 1946 C.E. Karl Haushofer, who introduced Hitler to the Illuminated Lodge in Munich, kills his wife and performs the Japanese suicide-rite *seppuku*.

1947 C.E. National Security Act passes.

November 10, 1948 C.E. The *Chicago Tribune* "announced the election to the Presidency of Thomas Dewey, a man who not only didn't get elected, but would not even have remained alive if Banana Nose Maldonado had not given such specific instructions concerning the Dutchman to Charlie the Bug, Mendy Weiss and Jimmy the Shrew." (*Illuminatus!*, pg. 76)

1952 C.E. Hagbard Celine gives away all of his money and "signs on as A.B.S. aboard a merchant ship to Norway." (*Illuminatus!*, pg. 496) He then "tramped across Europe," and began making notes for *Never Whistle While You're Pissing.* He settled in Rome for the autumn and winter.

1953 C.E. Hagbard Celine becomes an outlaw.

1954 C.E. Albert Bender shuts down the International Flying Saucer Bureau after a visit from three Men in Black.

Spring, 1955 C.E. Charles Mocenigo registers for his first semester at M.I.T. and marks his religion "in careful block capital letters, ATHEIST."

1957 C.E. Transition records releases *Jazz by Sun Ra.* Sun Ra says he comes from the planet Saturn, the planet of discipline.

Autumn, 1959 C.E. Malignowski's study "Retroactive Reality" printed in *Wieczny Kwiat Wtadza*, the journal of the Polish Orthopsychiatric Psociety. In it Malignowski concludes, "Reality is retroactive, retrospective and illusory." (*Illuminatus!*, pg. 281)

1962 C.E. Markoff Chaney learns about Markoff Chains at Antioch and begins his one man war against the Illuminati and the concepts of "average," "the above average" and "the below average."

November 22, 1963 C.E. Aldous Huxley dies. Harold Canvera shoots JFK in Dallas, TX (at least according to Hagbard Celine in *Illuminatus!*). Canvera had owned stock in Blue Sky, Inc., which made devices for landing on low gravity planets. Canvera sold his stock before Kennedy's announcement that the U.S. would put a man on the moon, which drove the price of the stock sky high. This drove Canvera crazy. (The rise in the price of the stock also provided Markoff Chaney with a lifetime income.) On November 22, 1963 C.E. John Dillinger had hoped to prevent the assassination by shooting Harry Coin before he could shoot JFK, but a number of other assassins showed up at Dealy Plaza. Later Mao Tsu-Hsi picks up "Frank Sullivan" at Los Angeles International Airport. That same day James Cash Cartwright flies from Dallas towards England to visit the tombs of his ancestors.

November 23, 1963 C.E. Ben Volpe meets Banana Nose Maldonado in Central Park and admits he didn't shoot JFK. Sometime in the early 1960's after JFK's assassination, Hagbard Celine contacted the Five leaders of Weishaupt's Illuminati. The Five resigned and appointed Celine and the Saure's as their successors.

November 24, 1963 C.E. Jack Ruby shoots Lee Harvey Oswald on national TV.

1965 C.E. Hagbard Celine read Dr. Faustus Unbewusst's notes on Robert Putney Drake in Agharti.

August 23, 1966 C.E. Simon Moon sees one of Markoff Chaney's signs in Chicago.

1967 C.E. Death of James V. Riley's wife. March on the Pentagon where Tobias Knight walks behind Norman Mailer and begins to become "half addicted" to marijuana.

August 25, 1968 C.E. In Lincoln Park in Chicago, Joe Malik protests the Democratic convention, along with William S. Burroughs, Allen Ginsberg and Simon Moon. Also in 1968 the Yippies run Pigasus the pig for President, and Billie Freschette, beloved of John Dillinger, returns to the Menominee Reservation in Wisconsin, where she will live until her death that same year. That year John Thomas Dillinger and Fission Chips got teargassed in Chicago.

September 15, 1968 C.E. Date set for Simon Moon's trial in Chicago.

June 11, 1969 C.E. Chart appears in the *East Village Other* revealing the current structure of the Illuminati. (*Illuminatus!*, pp. 96–97)

June 22, 1969 C.E. Joe Malik returns to Chicago to attend the last convention held by the Students for a Democratic Society.

June 25, 1969 C.E. "James Mallison" (Joe Malik) interviews James V. Riley about the death of John Dillinger. Rosemary gives birth to her infamous Baby on June 25 because that date stands at the extreme opposite of the calendar from Christmas, just as Walpurgisnacht (April 30) does from Halloween.

June 26, 1969 C.E. Joe Malik spends the whole day pouring over John Dee's translation of the *Necronomicon* at Miskatonic University in Arkham, MA.

June 29, 1969 C.E. Joe flies from Madison, WI, to Mexico City.

July 20, 1969 C.E. Neil Armstrong walks on the moon. ("Space is the place, next step Mars." — Sun Ra.) Early that same year John Thomas Dillinger died.

September 23, 1970 C.E. Timothy Leary, fugitive, passes five federal agents at O'Hare Airport in Chicago.

October 23, 1970 C.E. Simon Moon attends a meeting of the Knights of Christianity United in Faith (K.C.U.F.), along with Joe Malik, where they distribute some funky tomato juice. That same year Santesson publishes *Understanding Mu*.

November 23, 1970 C.E. Stanislaus Oedipuski's dead body found floating in the Chicago River. A former member of God's Lightning, his life had changed due to the funky tomato juice. (*The Trick Top Hat* has a Stan Oedipuski who has a much happier fate, although he got cut from the one volume *Schrödinger's Cat*.)

1971 C.E. Simon Moon and Padre Pederastia return to Chicago to "work on the heads of the local Heads, etc." (*Illuminatus!*, pg. 221)

Fall of 1972 C.E. Hagbard Celine takes Joe Malik to Atlantis. That same year sees the publication of *Sexuality, Magic and Perversion* by Francis King.

July 23, 1973 C.E. Monica Lewinsky born. That same year Saul Goodman and Rebecca meet; Hagbard Celine gives an explanation of the law of fives to Joe Malik, who sees the fnords and meets Mao Tsu-hsi that same year; and Captain Tequila y Mota reads Luttwak on the *coup d'etat*.

July 23, 1973 C.E. Robert Anton Wilson awakes with an intuition about the importance of Sirius.

1974 C.E. At *Confrontation* magazine, Joe Malik receives "Vampirism, the Heliocentric Theory and the Gold Standard" by Jorge Lobengula, a Fernando Poo national, the night after seeing the Atlantis movie.

February 2, 1976 C.E. (Joyce's birthday) The first dream comes to Dr. Charles Mocenigo, which leads to the invention of Anthrax-Leprosy-Mu.

March 13, 1976 C.E. Hagbard's computer FUCK-UP throws *I-Ching* Hexagram 23, "Breaking Apart".

March 14, 1976 C.E. Coup in Fernando Poo.

March 15, 1976 C.E. "The very name of Fernando Poo was unknown to every member of the House of Representatives, every senator, every officer of the Cabinet, and all but one of the Joint Chiefs of Staff." (*Illuminatus!*, pg. 19)

March 17, 1976 C.E. 00005 and W discuss Fernando Poo.

March 24, 1976 C.E. Generalissimo Tequila y Mota "found the book he was looking for, the one that was as precise and pragmatic about running a country as Luttwak's *Coup d'Etat* had been about seizing one" (*Illuminatus!*, pg. 69), *The Prince* by Machiavelli. (Ezra Pound uses Machiavelli's history of Florence in Canto XXI.) That same day Atlanta Hope gives a speech in Cincinnati about defending Fernando Poo. Students from Antioch College began to chant, "I don't want to die for Fernando Poo." "Seven ambulances and thirty police cars were soon racing to the scene." (*Illuminatus!*, pg. 70)

March 27, 1976 C.E. The Director of the C.I.A. shows the President aerial photographs of Fernando Poo.

March 29, 1976 C.E. The President asks the Joint Chiefs of Staff what they have that will terrify the Soviets even more than nuclear war. They tell him about Anthrax-Leprosy-Mu.

March 31, 1976 C.E. The President goes on television and says, "America will not shirk its responsibility to the freedom-loving people of Fernando Poo!" Conception Galore tells Fission Chips about the lloigor, "a very bad god," in the Hotel Durrutti in Santa Isobel.

April 1, 1976 C.E. 00005 walks into St. Toad's. Chaircritter of the Chinese Communist party discusses Fernando Poo with an aide. (The term chaircritter avoids the human chauvinism of the term chairperson.) John Dillinger visits Alligator Control under the UN building in New York. God's Lightning parades around UN Plaza, and Captain Tequila Y Moto walks before a firing squad.

April 2, 1976 C.E. In Las Vegas, Sherri Brandi tells her pimp Carmel about her client the scientist (Dr. Charles Mocenigo).

April 3, 1976 C.E. Carmel meets with Banana-Nose Maldonado, seeking a communist spy to whom he could sell secret information about germ warfare.

April 10, 1976 C.E. Tlaloc grins in Mexico. Tobias Knight broadcasts from his hotel room on Fernando Poo to an American submarine, "The Russkies and Chinks have completed their withdrawal, and Generalissimo Puta is definitely friendly to our side, besides being popular with both the Bubi and the Fang." (*Illuminatus!*, pg. 601)

April 10 or 11, 1976 C.E. Howard the dolphin swimming through Atlantis discovers no Dragon Star had ever fallen.

April 23, 1976 C.E. Joe Malik and Tobias Knight set the bomb in *Confrontation's* office. The Dealy Lama sends a telepathic message to Hagbard Celine *It's not too late to turn back.* Simon and Mary Lou listen to Clark Kent and His Supermen, George Dorn writes in his journal in Mad Dog, Texas, about the sound of one eye opening, and the Fillet of Soul drives into Ingolstadt, Bavaria.

April 24, 1976 C.E. Saul Goodman gets awoken in the early morning with news of the Confrontation bombing. George Dorn, rescued from Mad Dog Jail, boards the Leif Erikson and meets Hagbard Celine. Jim Cartwright calls Atlanta Hope from Mad Dog to tell her, "We let Celine's crowd take Dorn." (*Illuminatus!*, pg. 87)

Later that day in Chicago, Otto Waterhouse tells State's Attorney Milo A. Flanagan, "The word has come through from Ingolstadt that Project Tethys was aborted." (*Illuminatus!*, pg. 260) That night George Dorn spends some time with Tarantella Serpentine. The Thing on the Doorstep and other bands arrive in Ingolstadt.

April 25, 1976 C.E. The ad "In thanks to Saint Jude for favors granted. A.W." appears in 23 newspapers. John Dillinger notices more fnords than usual in *The New York Times*. Yog Sothoth drops by Robert Putney Drake's mansion on Long Island, and three miles down the road nine-year-old Patty Cohen goes mad. Carmel loots Maldonado's safe, and buries Sherri Brandi's body. He then drives over to Dr. Charles Mocenigo's house, hears a shot, and, driving away, sees flames. General Lawrence Stewart Talbot had shot Dr. Mocenigo, set the doctor's home on fire, and then shot himself.

Bucky Fuller flies to Nairobi to give a lecture which Nkrumah Fubar plans to attend. Senator Edward Coke Bacon gets shot in bed in Washington, D.C. George Dorn calls Rebecca Goodman looking for her husband Saul. The Signifying Monkey and other bands arrive in Ingolstadt. Saul and Rebecca consummate the Sixth Trip, and George passes a Gateless Gate, reimprinting the first circuit, and then knocks out Harry Coin.

April 26, 1976 C.E. The Magnificent Ambersons and other bands arrive in Ingolstadt. Markoff Chaney begins to feel the ill effects of Anthrax-Leprosy-Mu. He seeks medical attention, and the C.I.A. questions him. He escapes C.I.A. captivity in a coffee urn. (A proto-Javacrucian.) Later Saul and Barney run into Markoff Chaney and try to reason with him while he struggles to escape.

April 27, 1976 C.E. The FBI interviews every prostitute in Las Vegas, trying to find anyone exposed to Anthrax-Leprosy-Mu. The Seven Types of Ambiguity and many other bands arrive in Ingolstadt.

April 28, 1976 C.E. Hagbard abdicates spiritual leadership to Miss Portinari. Seated together at dinner, Hagbard explains a little about his abdication to George. The kachinas of Orabi begin their drum-beating, and Dillinger loads his gun. The 23rd Appendix and many other bands arrive in Ingolstadt for the rock festival. In Chicago, Otto Waterhouse shoots Milo A. Flanagan, and then drives to Minneapolis, flies to Montreal, back to Chicago, and then to Ingolstadt, Bavaria.

April 29, 1976 C.E. Danny Pricefixer listens to Mama Sutra. The Nine Unknown Men (before I joined the band), the Pisan Cantos, the Horse of Another Color, and many, many other bands arrive in Ingolstadt for the festival. Joe Malik pulls the Hierophant from the tarot deck. The Leif Erikson passes through a salt water lock roughly under Lyon, France, and later arrives in Lake Totenkopf near Ingolstadt.

April 30, 1976 C.E. Walpurgisnacht. Civil liberties suspended and a state of national emergency declared in the U.S.A., due to suggestions of Gracchus Gruad. Four Illuminati Primi (minus the fifth, Hagbard Celine) meet. Barney Muldoon and Saul Goodman lead Markoff Chaney into the mouth of Lehman Cavern. Rhoda Chief spikes the Kool-Aid at the Ingolstadt Festival, and the Closed Corporation sacrifice a rooster. An explosion damages the Pentagon, eerily forecasting September 11, 2001. An earthquake rocks California. The Nazi soldiers rise from the dead and emerge from Lake Totenkamf. They had taken cyanide *en masse* at the end of World War II, eerily forecasting the Jim Jones mass suicide.

May 1, 1976 C.E. In the early morning Hagbard takes the stage in Ingolstadt. Eris manifests to saves the day. (Earlier around 8 p.m., April 30, an unscheduled group, the Cargo Cult, sang, "We'll kill the old red rooster when she comes.") In Athens a classical scholar quotes Sappho in a small jail cell. Nkrumah Fubar learns that American Express has corrected their error on his statement. The Orabi drums stop. Saul, Barney and Markoff race towards Las Vegas while John Dillinger drives back to Los Angeles. Inspector Goodman does a T.V. interview revealing that the threat of Anthrax-Leprosy-Mu has ended. Hagbard and friends encounter Leviathan, and Joe concludes they all exist inside a book.

December, 1976 C.E. Before Chanukah, Patty Cohen sees a replica of the statue of the giant Tlaloc in Mexico City in the office of an elegant shrink on Park Avenue, and her recovery begins.

1984. Hagbard encounters Markoff Chaney in the U.S. Government Printing Office.

1999: Hagbard takes off for the stars.

APPENDIX

The Sun Never Sets on Your Horizon

To Debbie

Phil Dick read Dante all night through a toothache
abandoning hope and rediscovering it
    & then had a character do the same in a book.
I circle around
the softness of your eyes & lips and hair
    revolutions, convolutions, stillness with a lime.
Tart visions fill my dreams
since I met you & read your tarot cards.
    Since then, they read me & I
circle around, with glowing eyes and this silly grin which
remains when
    I disappear to study for years with secret masters in Tibet
who teach me how to
    love you & hear you & hold you & squeeze you
all night long.
We travel to Egypt and dance with the Sphinx, who
    relaxes her back & purrs at our
irresistible optimism,
and we begin
    our final migration
to the centre of this galaxy
or wherever we want in this
    ever-changing decentered Universe.
Debbie, you teach me
as California dreaming becomes a reality
    there's no place like home

ABOUT THE AUTHOR

Born in 1962 C.E. in Washington, D.C., to two former NSA computer programmers, Eric Wagner and his family moved to the San Francisco Bay Area in November, 1967 C.E. (Hephestus, 47 p.s.U.[5]) In 1982 C.E. he began reading Robert Anton Wilson's books, and 1986 C.E. the two began corresponding. In the years since Eric began reading Wilson, he has traveled from Ingolstadt, Bavaria, to Aswan, Egypt, from Country Kerry, Ireland, to Honolulu, Hawaii, attempting to understand the ideas behind Wilson's works. Eric has worked as a computer programmer, operator and microcoder, a musician, a poet, a technical writer, a dancer, a film historian and a teacher, etc.

---

[5] Ezra Pound created this calendar, suggesting modern civilization had begun with the completion of Joyce's *Ulysses*. He renamed the months after the twelve principal deities of ancient Greece.

SELECTED BIBLIOGRAPHY

BBC. http://news.bbc.co.uk/1/hi/world/south_asia/ 2282617.stm, 9/26/2002.

Carroll, Lewis, introduction and notes by Martin Gardner. *The Annotated Alice*. NY: Bramhall House, 1960.

Crowley, Aleister. *777*. Boston: Weiser, 1977.

—. *Magick in Theory and Practice*. NY: Dover, 1976. Originally published in 1929.

Dante Alighieri. *The Portable Dante*. NY: Penguin, 1947.

Eliot, Thomas Sterns (not Technical Sergeant or Terribly Sexy). *On Poetry and Poets*. NY: Farrar, Straus and Cudahy, 1957

Farmer, Philip Jose. *Tarzan Alive*. NY: Popular Lib, 1972.

Joyce, James. *The Critical Writings*. Ithaca, NY: Cornell UP, 1959.

—. *Finnegans Wake*. NY: Penguin, 1939.

—. *The Portable James Joyce*. New York: Penguin, 1946.

—. *Ulysses*. 1922. New York: Vintage, 1961.

Kenner, Hugh. Introduction. *James Joyce and the Making of Ulysses*. By Frank Budgen. Bloomington: Indiana U. Pr., 1960.

—. *Ulysses* Revised Edition. Baltimore: Johns Hopkins U. Pr., 1987.

Leary, Timothy. *Design for Dying*. San Francisco: HarperEdge, 1997.

—. *The Game of Life*. Culver City, CA: Peace Press, 1979; Tempe, AZ: New Falcon Publications, 1993.

—. *The Intelligence Agents*. Culver City, CA: Peace Press, 1979; Tempe, AZ: New Falcon Publications, 1996.

——. *Exo-Psychology.* Los Angeles: Peace Press, 1977; now *Info-Psychology*; Tempe, AZ: New Falcon Publications, 1987.

——. *Neuropolitics* (with Robert Anton Wilson and George Koopman); now *Neuropolitique.* Tempe, AZ: New Falcon Publications, 1987.

——. *Politics of Self-Determination.* Berkeley, CA: Ronin Press, 2000.

McNally, Dennis. *A Long Strange Trip: The Inside History of the Grateful Dead.* NY: Broadway Books, 2002.

Malaclypse the Younger, et al. *Principia Discordia.* Port Townsend, WA.: Loompanics Unlimited, no date. The fourth edition from Rip-Off Press came out in 1970.

Pound, Ezra. *Selected Prose 1909–1965.* NY: New Directions, 1973.

Rosen, Charles. *The Classical Style.* NY: New York, 1971, 1997.

——. *Critical Entertainments.* Cambridge, MA: Harvard UP, 2000.

——. *The Romantic Generation.* Cambridge, MA: Harvard UP, 1995.

Scholem, Gershom. *Kabbalah.* NY: Meridian, 1974.

Schönberg, Arnold. *Style and Idea.* Berkeley: U of C Press, 1975.

Wang, Robert. *Qabalistic Tarot.* York Beach, ME: Weiser, 1987.

Wilson, Robert Anton. *The Book of the Breast.* Chicago: Playboy Press, 1974. Now *Ishtar Rising,* Tempe, AZ: New Falcon Publications, 1989.

——. "Brain Books," *Trajectories* 16/17, San Jose: Permanent Press, 1996.

——. et al. *Chaos and Beyond.* San Jose, Permanent Press, 1994.

——. *Coincidance.* Tempe, AZ: New Falcon Publications, 1988.

——. *Cosmic Trigger I: Final Secret of the Illuminati.* Tempe, AZ: New Falcon Publications, 1977, 1986.

——. *Cosmic Trigger II: Down to Earth.* Tempe, AZ: New Falcon Publications, 1990.

——. *Cosmic Trigger III: My Life After Death.* Tempe, AZ: New Falcon Publications, 1995.

——. *The Earth Will Shake.* NY: Lynx, 1984; Tempe, AZ: New Falcon Publications, 2003.

——. *Everything Is Under Control.* NY: HarperCollins, 1998.

——. *The Homing Pigeons.* NY: Pocket Books, 1981.

——. *The Illuminati Papers.* Berkeley: And/Or Press, 1980.

——. *The Illuminatus! Trilogy.* NY: Dell, 1975.

——. *Ishtar Rising.* Tempe, AZ: New Falcon Publications, 1989. A revision of *The Book of the Breast.*

——. *Masks of the Illuminati.* New York: Dell, 1981.

——. *Natural Law.* Port Townsend, WA: Loompanics Unlimited, 1986.

——. *Nature's God* Port Townsend, WA: Loompanics Unlimited, 1986. Tempe, AZ: New Falcon Publications, 2004.

——. *New Inquisition.* Tempe, AZ: New Falcon Publications, 1987.

——. *Playboy's Book of Forbidden Words.* Chicago: Playboy Press, 1972. I found a copy in the reference section of the Scottsdale, AZ, library and read it over the course of many lunch hours while working at Hunter's Books. Wilson had begun working on a revision; hopefully that will come out soon.

——. *Prometheus Rising.* Tempe, AZ: New Falcon Publications, 1983, 1997.

——. *Quantum Psychology.* Tempe, AZ: New Falcon Publications, 1990.

——. *Reality Is What You Can Get Away With.*

——. "Re: Masks of the Illiffinati." E-mail to the author. 20 Oct. 2001.

——. *Right Where You Are Sitting Now.* Berkeley, CA.: And/Or Press, 1982.

——. *Robert Anton Wilson Explains Everything* (audiocassette). Boulder, CO: Sounds True, 2002.

——. *Schrödinger's Cat.* NY: Dell, 1979.

——. *Sex, Drugs & Magick.* Tempe, AZ: New Falcon Publications, 1973, 2000.

——. *The Trick Top Hat.* NY: Pocket Books, 1981. What a book. If you find a copy, do yourself a favor and snag it.

——. *TSOG: The Thing That Ate the Constitution.* Tempe, AZ: New Falcon Publications, 2002. Great stuff. Check it out.

—. *The Walls Came Tumbling Down.* Tempe, AZ: New Falcon Publications, 1997.

—. *The Widow's Son.* NY: Bluejay, 1985; Tempe, AZ: New Falcon Publications, 2004. On the tape set *Robert Anton Wilson Explains Everything* Wilson calls this his favorite of his books. Great, great stuff.

—. *Wilhelm Reich in Hell.* Tempe, AZ: New Falcon Publications, 1987.

—. www.rawilson.com. Check it out.

www.rawilsonfans.com/ A great collection of Wilson's writings, interviews, etc.

Elvis seems to have left the building

FROM ROBERT ANTON WILSON

COSMIC TRIGGER I
Final Secret of the Illuminati
The book that made it all happen! Explores Sirius, Synchronicities, and Secret Societies. Wilson has been called "One of the leading thinkers of the Modern Age."

"A 21st Century Renaissance Man. ...funny, optimistic and wise..."
— *The Denver Post*

ISBN 1-56184-003-3

COSMIC TRIGGER II
Down to Earth
In this, the second book of the *Cosmic Trigger* trilogy, Wilson explores the incredible Illuminati-based synchronicities that have taken place since his ground-breaking masterpiece was first published.
Second Revised Edition!

"Hilarious... multi-dimensional... a laugh a paragraph." — *The Los Angeles Times*

ISBN 1-56184-011-4

COSMIC TRIGGER III
My Life After Death
Wilson's observations about the premature announcement of his death, plus religious fanatics, secret societies, quantum physics, black magic, pompous scientists, Orson Welles, Madonna and the Vagina of Nuit.
"A SUPER-GENIUS... He has written everything I was afraid to write."
— Dr. John Lilly, psychologist

ISBN 1-56184-112-9